Maximizing .NET Performance

NICK WIENHOLT

Maximizing .NET Performance
Copyright ©2004 by Nick Wienholt

ISBN (pbk): 1-59059-141-0

Printed and bound in the United States of America 10987654321

Technical Reviewer: Simon Robinson

Editorial Board: Dan Appleman, Craig Berry, Gary Cornell, Tony Davis, Steven Rycroft, Julian Skinner, Martin Streicher, Jim Sumser, Karen Watterson, Gavin Wray, John Zukowski

Assistant Publisher: Grace Wong

Copy Editor: Ami Knox

Production Manager: Kari Brooks

Proofreader: Linda Seifert

Compositor: Gina Rexrode

Indexer: Michael Brinkman

Cover Designer: Kurt Krames

Manufacturing Manager: Tom Debolski

Distributed to the book trade in the United States by Springer-Verlag New York, Inc., 175 Fifth Avenue, New York, NY 10010 and outside the United States by Springer-Verlag GmbH & Co. KG, Tiergartenstr. 17, 69112 Heidelberg, Germany.

In the United States: phone 1-800-SPRINGER, email orders@springer-ny.com, or visit http://www.springer-ny.com. Outside the United States: fax +49 6221 345229, email orders@springer.de, or visit http://www.springer.de.

For information on translations, please contact Apress directly at 2560 Ninth Street, Suite 219, Berkeley, CA 94710. Phone 510-549-5930, fax 510-549-5939, email info@apress.com, or visit http://www.apress.com.

The source code for this book is available to readers at http://www.apress.com in the Downloads section.

To my wonderful wife, child, and family—
thank you for your love and support

Contents at a Glance

Contents

Foreword

"Managed code is too slow. We've got to do this in C++."

—Anonymous

BACK IN 1999, the ACM published a study[1] that presented a comparison of 40 independent implementations of a computationally intensive problem, created by different programmers in either Java—the then-current managed runtime environment—or C/C++. It concluded with the finding that interpersonal differences between the developers "are much larger than the average difference between Java and C/C++" and that "performance ratios of a factor of 30 or more are not uncommon between the median programs from the upper half versus the lower half."

This should teach you something: If you are not a guru-level C++ programmer, then the chance is quite high that a managed code implementation performs as well as the average C++ solution—especially given the fact that most .NET languages simply allow you fewer possibilities to introduce subtle memory-related or performance-related issues. And keep in mind that this study was conducted several years ago, and that Just-In-Time Compilation (JIT) as well as memory management and garbage collection (GC) technologies have been improved in the meantime!

This however doesn't mean that you can't create horribly slow, memory eating applications with .NET. That's why you should be really concerned about the other part of the study's conclusion, namely that "interpersonal differences . . . are much larger." In essence, this means that you have to know about how to optimize your applications so that they run with the expected performance in a managed environment. Even though .NET frees you from a lot of tasks that in C++ would have been your responsibility as a developer, these tasks still exist; these "little puppets" have only cleared the main stage and now live in some little corner behind the scenes. If you want your application to run in the top performance range, you will still need to find the right strings to pull to move these hidden figures and to basically keep them out of the way of negatively affecting your application's performance.

---

1. Lutz Prechtelt, "Comparing Java vs. C/C++ Efficiency Differences to Interpersonal Differences," *Communications of the ACM* 42, no. 10 (October 1999): 109–112

But knowing about the common language runtime's internals is still not enough, as lots of performance issues actually turn up during application design and not just during the coding stage. Collections, remoting, interoperability with unmanaged code, and COM components are not the only things that come to my mind in this regard.

It is the aim of Nick's book to enable you to understand the design issues as well as the underlying CLR mechanisms in order to create the programs that run on the better side of the 30-times performance difference quoted in the ACM study. Nick really managed to create a book that addresses these issues, which will otherwise turn up when carelessly coding to a managed environment. This book will allow you to get into the details without being overwhelmed by the underlying complexity of the common language runtime.

The only thing you have to resist after reading the book is the urge to overoptimize your code. I was delighted to see that Nick begins with a discussion of identifying an application's performance-critical sections and only later turns towards isolating and resolving these *real* performance bottlenecks. This is, in my opinion, one of the most important tasks—and also one of the most complex ones—when working with large-scale applications.

And now read on and enjoy the ride to the better side of a 30-fold performance difference.

Ingo Rammer, author of *Advanced .NET Remoting*
Vienna, Austria
http://www.ingorammer.com

About the Author

Nick Wienholt is a Windows and .NET consultant based in Sydney. Nick has worked on a variety of IT projects over the last decade, ranging from numerical modeling of beach erosion to financial and payroll systems, with the highly successful Passenger Information Display System (PIDS) project that he worked on as a consultant for Rail Services Australia being a career highlight. PIDS was developed and installed prior to the Sydney 2000 Olympics and was a key component in State Rail's success in moving hundreds of thousands of spectators during the period the Olympic games were held.

Nick is a keen and active participant in the .NET community. He is the cofounder of the Sydney Deep .NET User group; writes technical articles for Pinnacle Publishing, *Australian Developer Journal,* and the Microsoft Developer Network; is a keen participant in .NET-related newsgroups; and is a regular presenter at technical conferences. An archive of Nick's SDNUG presentations and articles is available at http://www.dotnetperformance.com. In recognition of his work in the .NET area, he was awarded the Microsoft Most Valued Professional Award in 2002.

Nick can be contacted at nick@dotnetperformance.com.

About the
Technical Reviewer

Simon Robinson is a well-known author specializing in .NET programming, and is editor of ASP Today, the leading ASP and ASP.NET-related Web site.

Simon's first experience with commercial computer programming was in the early 1980s when a computer project he was working on at college became the college's student timetabling program, running on the BBC Micro. Later on he studied for a Ph.D. in physics, and subsequently spent a couple of years working as a university physics researcher—a large part of this time was spent writing programs to do mathematical modeling of certain properties of super-conductors. Somewhere around this time, he realized there was more money to be had in straight computer programming, and ended up at Lucent Technologies doing mostly Windows COM programming before finally becoming self-employed, combining writing and freelance software development.

He has extremely broad experience in programming on Windows. These days his core specialism is .NET programming, and he is comfortable coding in C++, C#, VB, and IL; his skills range from graphics and Windows Forms to ASP.NET, to directories and data access, to Windows services and the native Windows API.

Simon lives in Lancaster, U.K. His outside interests include theatre, dance, performing arts, and politics.

You can visit Simon's personal Web site at http://www.SimonRobinson.com, or the ASP Today site at http://www.asptoday.com.

Acknowledgments

WRITING A BOOK CAN BE a long and lonely task, and without the constant support of my wife, this book would never have made it out the door. I am eternally indebted to her.

To my friends and colleagues in Sydney—Derek, Dan, Sam, Kristie, Troy, Adam, Helen, and Chuck—many thanks for the conversation, criticisms, and suggestions. The real-world sounding board that you provided was invaluable.

And finally, to the crew at Apress—Grace, Ami, and Kari on the production side, Simon on technical review, and Dan and Gary on the management side. Your assistance and support has made this book an immeasurably better product.

Introduction

LIKE OTHER AREAS OF nonfunctional software production, performance is often an afterthought to the construction process, and needs to be tacked onto an existing code base. With a new platform like .NET, the negative consequences of this production practice is more pronounced, as developers and architects do not have the same depth of experience that they did in the unmanaged world. In the Internet age, producing software with adequate performance characteristics is more important than ever, and in a climate of shrinking IT budgets, throwing hardware at poorly performing systems is no longer an option.

This book aims to arm developers and architects with the knowledge they need to design and implement software solutions that have great performance characteristics on the .NET platform. A familiarity with the .NET Framework is assumed, and if a reader is new to .NET, there are many wonderful titles from Apress that can provide a great introduction to the platform. For readers who know .NET and are seeking more advanced material on the best way to build performant software, this book has been written for you.

The book can be read cover-to-cover, or a reader may choose to consume a particular chapter in isolation. When consuming chapters in isolation, the reader is encouraged to read Chapters 1 and 2, which introduce the materials covered and lay the groundwork that the following chapters build upon. Chapters 3 through 14 focus on performance issues specific to a particular area of the .NET Framework, and the material in these chapters that relies on information in other chapters is deliberately highlighted for the reader who chooses to approach the material nonlinearly.

Chapter 15 presents a troubleshooting guide that aims to provide a systematic roadmap for diagnosing and solving performance problems in .NET applications. The chapter covers the tools and techniques that can be used to reliably work out why a program is running slowly or consuming too much memory, and how the problem can be solved.

The Appendix covers the benchmark test harness that was used to conduct the benchmarks discussed throughout the book. For those with an interest in extending and adding to the benchmarks presented, this material will prove of great interest.

The source code for this book is available from the Apress Web site (http://www.apress.com), and the reader is encouraged to download and analyze this material. The benchmark test harness has been written to allow easy reproduction of the benchmarks referenced in the book, and experimenting with these benchmarks is a valuable learning aid. Curiosity is an essential prerequisite for understanding performance, and the source code will hopefully provide the starting point for many new performance investigations for the reader.

CHAPTER 1

Introduction

SOFTWARE PERFORMANCE IS A topic rife with paradoxes, confusion, and mystery. To provide a few examples:

- Processor speed doubles every 18 months, but performance concerns never disappear.

- Two competing software platforms both show order-of-magnitude speed advantages over the other in benchmarks produced by their respective vendors.

- Languages and technologies are shunned due to their perceived lack of performance, but a precise measurement of the slowness is rarely produced, and the criticism of perceived slowness is discussed even if performance is not a project priority.

This book attempts to peel back some of the mystery surrounding the performance of code that targets the .NET Framework. The book has two main goals—to present a detailed discussion on the performance of various .NET Framework technologies, and to illustrate practices for conducting reliable performance assessment on techniques and methodologies that are not covered in the book. To address both these goals, every benchmark discussed in this book is available for download from the publisher's Web site (http://www.apress.com), and each test is clearly numbered for quick location in the code samples. This allows for an easy reproduction of the test runs on the reader's own systems, and also for analysis of the code that makes up the test. Chapter 2 contains a detailed discussion on conducting performance assessments, and the benchmark harness used to conduct the benchmark results presented is fully documented in the appendix.

The reader is encouraged to critically analyze the results presented. Service packs and new versions of the .NET Framework and operating system will mean that some of the results presented in this book may differ from those the reader obtains. In other cases, small changes in a test case can significantly change the performance of a method, and a test case on a particular technology may not be relevant to other uses of the same technology. Subtle changes can bring significant performance improvements, and a keen eye for detail is critical.

Material Covered

The focus of this book is .NET Framework performance. The book concentrates on Framework performance from the ground up, and does not include discussions of higher-level technologies like Windows Forms, ASP.NET, and ADO.NET. These technologies are important, and future volumes may well be written that focus on them, but it is critical to appreciate that all .NET code is built on a common base, which is the focus of this book. System-level developers will get the most out of this book, but every attempt has been made to ensure that the material is accessible and relevant to application developers who use higher-level technologies. By developing a strong understanding of Framework performance, application developers are in a much better position to identify and avoid performance mistakes in both their own code and high-level application libraries.

Key areas of coverage include the following:

- Analyzing the performance of software systems using black-box and white-box assessment techniques

- Designing types (classes and structures) so they have optimum performance characteristics, and interact efficiently with Framework design patterns

- Using remoting to build high-performance distributed systems

- Interacting efficiently with unmanaged code using COM Interop, P/Invoke, and C++

- Understanding the interaction between performance and language selection

- Working with the .NET garbage collector to achieve high-performance object allocations and collections

- Selecting the correct collection class for maximum performance

- Locating and fixing performance problems

Comparison between .NET and competing platforms like J2EE is not covered. While this information may be of interest to some, cross-technology performance comparisons are prone to much controversy and conflicting results, as the recent Pet Shop war between Java vendors and Microsoft demonstrated. At the end of the day, most cross-technology comparisons are motivated by commercial considerations, and do not assist developers in writing faster and more efficient code on either platform. This book is focused on giving developers the information and tools they need to write high-performance code using the .NET Framework, and cross-platform sniping would only detract from that goal.

For readers interested in independently verified benchmark comparisons between the offerings of various vendors, the Transaction Processing Performance Council results, available at `http://www.tpc.org`, are an excellent resource.

Solving Specific Performance Problems

If this book has been purchased to assist with optimization of a section of code that is taking a long time to complete its task, Chapter 15 is the optimal starting point. This chapter explores the tools and techniques available for determining the cause of poorly performing .NET applications, and will assist the reader in investigating and rectifying a performance problem, even if the specific answer to the problem is not contained in this book. The remaining chapters cover specific topics related to the .NET Framework and performance, and attempt to highlight relevant performance trade-offs, pitfalls, and optimizations for the particular technology.

Performance and the Development Process

A structured development process is crucial in producing software with adequate performance characteristics. Regardless of the particular development methodology that an organization follows, it is critical that the development priorities of the project or product reach the people who actually architect and develop the software system. In the absence of development priorities, a system will revert to a particular developer or architect's "natural state," and the emphasis may be on code readability and maintainability, development speed, performance, testability, or simply on technology familiarity. Whatever the case, in the absence of clear communication, it will only be through chance that developer and project priorities coincide, and such coincidental goal convergence is not likely to happen all that often.

Achieving the correct performance characteristics for a software application starts during the design phase of a project. If architects and business analysts fail to provide any guidance regarding performance targets, they should surrender their right to criticize the result of the development process as slow. Failing to define or communicate the priorities of a system to the developers and testers responsible for building the system invariably leads to some degree of disappointment with the finished result. If this book is being read with a view to correcting perceived performance problems that are the result of an inadequate software development process, the reader is encouraged to also gain access to material on software development methodologies. Compensating for poor planning with post-development tune-ups is a losing battle, and the problem is more effectively combated further upstream.

Performance Priorities

It is important that some general performance goals are communicated to the development team before development begins. A development task can fall into three broad categories of performance priority.

Performance Insensitive

In this mode, performance really does not matter at all. The software can end up quite slow with no real adverse consequences, and even naive performance mistakes are acceptable. Software that fits into this category is typically single- or special-use, such as a program that will perform a once-off data migration task. If the software ends up slow, the task can be run on a weekend or on a spare machine; in this case development time and quality issues are much more important than speed.

There is nothing inherently wrong with this development mode—in a number of project types, it is much better for a client or manager when the software comes in twice as cheap but ten times as slow. It is important that developers can swallow their pride in this mode, and appreciate the pressures and priorities under which the software is being developed.

Performance Sensitive

This is the normal development mode for most applications. In this mode, producing software that is "not too slow" is the goal, though other development priorities may be more important than performance. Producing detailed metrics that describe how fast "not too slow" is can be hard to achieve, but a few simple goals can be defined to allow a common understanding of the performance targets for the application. For end-user applications, response time and memory usage are two criteria that are easy for all stakeholders to understand, and can be defined as they relate to a target hardware environment. There will usually be application actions that fall outside the response time goals, and the remedies required in terms of both the product (for example, adding a progress bar) and the project (for example, noting the issue in a project manual) should be defined.

Server-side application performance is usually defined in terms of client load, average response time, and, optionally, the response time at some statistical distance from the mean. The expected client load can be difficult for nontechnical stakeholders to appreciate, and there is often a tendency to propose an exaggerated figure. The cost of scalable software design and implementation, particularly on the .NET platform, is not greatly more than a nonscalable design, which leaves hardware, server licenses, and other operational costs as the price delta in supporting an increased load. These costs are easy to quantify, and nontechnical stakeholders generally have no problem in making cost-based decisions.

With some effort, a realistic understanding of hardware requirements and response time can be established with the client, and easily measurable performance goals can be established for the development and testing teams.

Performance Critical/Real Time

This is a rare development mode for Windows applications, and even rarer for .NET applications. The Windows NT family of operating systems can be considered a soft real-time operating system, where a timely response can be expected most of the time, and the average response time is dependable. Venturcom (http://www.vci.com) has released a series of real-time extensions for Windows XP that can support hard real-time operation, in which the timeliness of a response is guaranteed 100 percent of the time.

For .NET applications, the common language runtime (CLR) adds a layer of indeterminacy that results in the real-time functionality of the OS being diminished below the soft real-time barrier. During a garbage collection, there is a point at which all managed code is suspended, which has a significant impact on the ability of managed code to guarantee any type of response time. Other factors also affect the runtime's ability to guarantee response times, including Just-In-Time (JIT) compilation and module loading, though these events can have determinant performance characteristics in a closed system. Given these factors, even soft real-time systems are not advisable on the .NET platform. As was seen with Java, it is likely that future Common Language Infrastructure (CLI) implementations will be developed that guarantee some real-time capabilities, and that performance-critical development will be feasible using .NET.

Regardless of platform capabilities, real-time development is a complex and difficult topic, and beyond the scope of this book. For readers interested in real-time software development, *Doing Hard Time: Developing Real-Time Systems with UML, Objects, Frameworks, and Patterns* by Bruce Powel Douglass (Addison-Wesley, 1999) is an excellent reference. Although real-time development is not feasible in the short term, high-performance development is possible with the .NET platform, and CLR and Framework enhancements are likely to deliver performance characteristics that rival native code as .NET matures.

Wrap-Up

By spending a brief amount of time during the design phase of a project in identifying the priority of performance, the specifications of the hardware environment, and some basic performance criteria, the probability of project success is greatly enhanced. Not only do all parties gain a consistent expectation about how the software should perform, but performance risk areas are also more likely to be identified, which allows them to be dealt with early during the design and development phases.

Test Environment and Practices

When developing software where performance is a high priority, performance testing is a critical activity. There are three rules for performance testing:

- Secure access to the target hardware environment early.

- Test early.

- Test often.

For applications where performance is not a high priority, performance testing during a development iteration is not necessary, particularly if the application uses standard architectural patterns and contains no major risk areas. Overeager optimization can lead to complexity and development delays, and should generally be avoided.

For applications where performance is a priority, access to test hardware is an important element of project success. The all-too-common occurrence of the test machine arriving a week after the system is deployed is a recipe for performance headaches. Development machines are usually high-end boxes with plenty of RAM and fast CPUs, and it is impossible to accurately extrapolate performance results of code running on a high-end machine to the results that may be expected on the target hardware environment. If an application is memory intensive, memory paging may destroy the performance when the code is run on the target platform, and this performance problem will not be apparent during unit testing on a high-end development machine. If an exact replication of the target environment is not available, scrounging up a machine of the approximately correct configuration should be possible in most circumstances. If a low-end test machine is not available, removing RAM and disabling performance-oriented hardware features via the BIOS or motherboard jumpers will allow some indication of application performance on low-end machines to be achieved. If hardware modifications are being attempted, ensure that the appropriate safety practices are followed, and take care not to damage either the hardware or the software engineer—both can be expensive to replace.

In addition to processor and memory similarities, peripheral hardware relevant to the particular application, such as video adapters for video-intensive applications and hard disks for high-IO applications, should resemble the target environment. If the application is to be deployed on legacy operating systems such as Windows 98 or Windows ME, it is critical that the application is also tested on these platforms, as the CLR implementation has many subtle differences that can result in performance issues that do not exist on Windows 2000/XP.

Once a reasonable hardware environment has been established for performance testing, it is important to develop adequate test scenarios, with representative system inputs, and preferably automated test cases. Many automated test tools exist, and a number of excellent free tools are available.[1] It is important to establish the test environment early on in the project, and test the product periodically. The early versions of an application that contain skeleton components with stubbed-out methods will run much quicker than the full release, and if performance is poor in the early releases, architectural problems exist, and it is critical to address these problems early.

Unit testing tools, which are typically used for testing the logical correctness of code, can also be used to test the performance correctness of code. The correctness of a method is generally determined by a Boolean expression at the end of a test case, and timing tests can be used instead of the usual logic tests to ensure that code has the correct performance characteristics.

In addition to preventing unpleasant surprises late in the development cycle, regular performance testing makes identifying performance bugs much easier, and reduces the need for many of the tools covered in the following chapters. A marked decrease in performance between two test runs indicates that code that has been added to the system between tests has introduced or triggered the problem, and this makes tracking down the culprit code much easier than starting from scratch.

Developer Responsibilities

The individual responsibilities of developers in achieving the correct performance characteristics of a software system are often not properly considered. In a naive process-engineering view of software development, developers are often classed as generic resources that need to be added to a task in a cookbook-style approach. This is profoundly incorrect, and the skills and knowledge that developers

---

1. One of the most popular test tools is NUnit, which is a free unit testing tool available from http://www.nunit.org.

possess are reflected in the code they produce. It is the developer's *individual* responsibility to be sufficiently knowledgeable regarding the Framework and software principles to allow for the production of code that has reasonable performance characteristics. The developer does not need to possess a profound knowledge of the internals of the CLR, but should be familiar enough with the product to select the appropriate tools to correctly code a system component. For example, the developer should know that `System.Text.StringBuilder` is better than `System.String` for performing multiple string manipulations, that objects that encapsulate unmanaged resources need explicit cleanup, and that different collection classes have different performance characteristics for insertion, deletion, and searching.

In addition to the numerous books on .NET, the MSDN Library is an excellent resource for learning about the various features of the .NET Framework. The .NET Framework SDK documentation (`http://msdn.microsoft.com/library/en-us/cpguide/html/cpcongettingstartedwithnetframework.asp`) provides detailed coverage of a wide range of topics, and also includes many samples that demonstrate the use of .NET technologies in various languages.

Conclusion

The .NET Framework has a clean and consistent design and implementation that reduces the possibility of producing poorly performing software. Like any new technology, the Framework is not a silver bullet for performance headaches, and having clear development priorities, and supporting these priorities with ongoing testing and monitoring, is an important component in avoiding costly project or product delays caused by slow systems.

CHAPTER 2

Investigating
Performance

INVESTIGATING THE PERFORMANCE OF a particular method, technique, or technology is an interesting challenge. The first step in the investigation is determining what performance aspect is actually being investigated within a particular scenario. The specific performance issue can involve the comparative performance assessment of two or more technologies, system capacity analysis, or the cause of sluggish reaction time within a particular section of an application.

By explicitly defining the precise performance questions that are being investigated, a plan of attack becomes easier to formulate. For example, if the maximum throughput of a particular system needs to be determined, running the system on representative hardware using load generation tools will be the most effective path of investigation. In contrast, an investigation to determine why a particular piece of software is running slow is best conducted by gaining an understanding of what activities the software is completing, determining the elements that are performing the slowest, and finding opportunities to eliminate, speed up, or substitute these elements.

This chapter discusses tools and techniques for conducting detailed performance assessments. The material is most applicable when conducting such an assessment of a technology *before* it is actually used with a software system. The tools and techniques that are discussed were used when researching the material presented in subsequent chapters, and represent some of the more advanced and esoteric performance investigation techniques.

The end result of conducting a performance investigation using the techniques described in this chapter is a comprehensive understanding of how to achieve the highest performance with a technology or third-party product. Conducting a detailed performance investigation will not be warranted in most situations, but when performance is an important project objective, and understanding the performance implications of using a technology in a particular way is critical to project success, this chapter will provide the reader with a toolkit to meet this goal.

For readers interested in solving a specific performance problem, Chapter 15 is the recommended starting point. Troubleshooting a specific performance issue is a very different activity from conducting an overall performance assessment, and while there is some overlap in tools used and tests undertaken, the techniques used in the two exercises are quite different.

Performance Investigation Patterns

Performance can be investigated using two distinct techniques—white box investigation and black box investigation. *White box investigation* involves looking at the implementation of a particular piece of functionality, and deriving performance characteristics based on the complexity and perceived cost of completing a particular unit of work. In contrast, *black box investigation* ignores implementation, and instead relies on execution timing data to access performance. The techniques are not mutually exclusive, and it is possible to quickly switch between the two techniques to analyze performance issues.

The two different investigation techniques have certain strengths and weaknesses. The greatest strength of white box testing is that it promotes a better understanding of the technology, and allows optimizations and performance pitfalls to be identified and targeted. White box investigation also gives a reasonable indication about the future validity of the investigation result. Some performance issues are caused by a particular implementation problem, which may be removed or optimized in the next service pack or release of a product. Other performance problems are more structural in nature, and while the current implementation is efficient, getting the task completed involves finishing a number of computationally expensive tasks, and the performance characteristics are unlikely to improve markedly without major structural changes.

The main weakness of white box investigation is the lack of quantitative results that the technique produces. White box investigation can, at best, provide an order of magnitude estimate of the relative performance of various technologies, and it is quite easy to actually arrive at a totally incorrect result when using white box investigation in isolation. The main obstacle that prevents production of a definitive result is complexity. Even for simple sections of code that may contain only a few dozen lines, calls to methods in other classes and loop statements, which cause the same instructions to be executed multiple times, can result in millions of machine instructions being executed by the processor. Code that may appear complex and slow to execute may actually run quite fast due to caching, optimizing compilers, runtime library optimizations, and hardware support, while seemingly efficient code can run slowly due to problems in supporting system elements.

The relative strengths and weaknesses of black box testing are the converse of the qualities of white box testing. Black box testing delivers a set of hard and unambiguous performance metrics, and allows precise determination of the maximum capacity of a particular test case. However, the results achieved are specific to the precise test case run using the particular version of the software and operating system involved, and are only directly relevant to the hardware that the tests were run on. The large number of software and hardware configurations available results in the so-called combinatorial explosion, in which the range of possible combinations for various components of a system is so large that the number of distinct systems that can be created is impossibly large. While it is unusual for changes in hardware and supporting software systems to cause the results of a comparative benchmark to be reversed, significant changes in the relationships between results are possible.

Small changes in a test case can result in very large changes in a test's performance. When defining a test case, it is critical that factors unrelated to the test case are minimized so that they do not interfere with the execution of the test case. A full discussion on creating a benchmark is presented later in the chapter.

Which Technique Is Best?

The optimum technique depends on the type of performance assessment being conducted, and the scale of the system being examined. For very large systems, the sheer quantity of code means that a white box analysis will not be practical as the sole means of analyzing the performance of the system. Lack of source code availability, which can occur in applications that make use of third-party components, limits the applicability of white box investigations, but unless the system of interest is hosted on remote servers and only accessible via network protocols, inspection of the disassembled instructions that define the system is a feasible, though somewhat tedious, form of implementation inspection.

For the performance investigations carried out to support the material presented in this book, a combination of white and black box investigations were undertaken. A benchmark was created and executed to quantify the performance results, and the reason for the numbers achieved in the benchmark was investigated and documented. The process is an iterative cycle, with white box investigation required to correctly construct the benchmark code, and the results of benchmarks motivating further investigations into the inner workings of the Framework, which were then tested with modifications to the benchmark code. A similar approach is recommended for achieving the best insight into system-level performance.

White Box Investigation

Defining an explicit goal is critical when using white box investigation techniques. It is easy to be overwhelmed with the complexity and magnitude of the information available during a white box investigation, and without explicit goals defining information that is being sought, ineffective meandering through thousands of lines of source code or machine instructions is possible.

The type of information that can be feasibly derived from white box investigations includes the algorithm being used to implement certain functionality, optimizations that will allow code with certain qualities to execute faster, the general quality of the system, and the underlying technologies that a method or type employs.

The tool descriptions that follow are presented in order of complexity and difficulty of use. The recommended approach is to start with the first tools listed, and only move on to the next tool when it is not possible to progress any further with the current tool. The tools and techniques discussed toward the end of the section require a certain amount of experience to use effectively, and can be quite time consuming to master.

Disassemblers and Decompilers

Disassemblers and decompilers allow the binary executable image of an assembly to be reverse engineered into a format that is human readable. Disassemblers use a direct mapping to convert from the binary file format used by the .NET runtime to a text format, whereas a decompiler will perform a conversion of the low-level, instruction-based format of Microsoft Intermediate Language (MSIL) into a high-level language like C#, which is easier to read and comprehend. A decompiler will not be able to convert every method into a high-level language equivalent, as a number of the instructions available in MSIL have no high-level language equivalent, so resorting to a disassembler may be the only available option in some cases. When considering the use of disassemblers and decompilers, be sure to consult the licensing agreement of the software to check limitations on reverse engineering.

MSIL disassemblers and decompilers will be ineffective for performance investigation in some circumstances. A small number of methods in the Framework Library are marked as internalcall; this means that the method is a stub for an unmanaged code implementation, which is provided at runtime by a hard-coded lookup map contained in the CLR. While internalcall methods are limited to a very small portion of the Framework Libraries, and are unlikely to be the direct cause of performance problems because they represent an optimization technique for providing high-performance implementations of commonly used methods, any managed method can call out to unmanaged code through P/Invoke or COM Interop to complete various tasks. When this occurs, investigating the implementation can become difficult, and MSIL disassembly will not be effective.

The final case in which disassembly can prove to be ineffective is for assemblies that have been obfuscated, which is a process whereby the MSIL and metadata within an assembly are scrambled for intellectual property protection. In this case, the software vendor is actively making efforts to keep implementation details confidential, and these wishes should be respected.

More important, an obfuscated assembly is likely to ship with a licensing agreement that prohibits reverse engineering, which means that disassembling or decompiling is explicitly forbidden. If a component is needed for a performance-critical task, and knowledge of the internal workings of the component is required, ensure that the component is not obfuscated, or choose a vendor that is likely to provide support to address performance issues. The Framework Library code is not obfuscated.

When examining .NET assembly code in disassemblers or decompilers, there are two analysis paths to follow. If the assembly contains a significant amount of logic expressed in managed code, an effective analysis technique is to determine which data structures and algorithms are being used, and from that, determine what the most efficient means of employing the method or type would be. On the other hand, if the assembly is a thin wrapper over an underlying native API, determining the exact native methods called and searching for performance literature of these functions is the best way forward.

MSIL Disassembler (Ildasm.exe)

The MSIL Disassembler (Ildasm.exe) utility that ships with the .NET Framework SDK is one of the simplest and most effective tools for conducting investigations into the performance of .NET assemblies for which the source code is not available. Executable images that use the .NET runtime contain MSIL instructions stored in a binary format, and the MSIL Disassembler can convert this binary format into a text form.

MSIL is a relatively high-level language compared to the x86 machine instructions that are generated by unmanaged compilers, and is quite readable with a little practice. The IL instruction set reference is part of the ECMA specification (Partition III), and is installed in the Tool Developers Guide folder when the Framework SDK or Visual Studio .NET is installed. The most recent version of all the ECMA specifications can be downloaded from http://msdn.microsoft.com/net/ecma. In addition, *CIL Programming: Under the Hood of .NET* by Jason Bock (Apress, 2002) and *Advanced .NET Programming* by Simon Robinson (Wrox, 2002) provide comprehensive coverage of MSIL.

The MSIL Disassembler can operate in two modes—as a command-line utility to dump output to a text file, and as a Windows GUI application to view type and method information in various windows. The range of command-line options supported by Ildasm is documented in the MSDN Library, with the exception of the advanced options, which can be viewed with the /adv /? command-line switch. The documentation for the advanced options is contained in the Word document entitled IldasmAdvancedOptions.doc that is part of the Framework SDK, and installed in the Tool Developers Guide\docs folder.

For performance investigation, using Ildasm as a GUI application is usually the most convenient option. The namespaces contained with an assembly are displayed using a tree view control that allows a given type to be easily located, and the methods of the type are displayed as child nodes. Double-clicking a method brings up a new window with the MSIL implementation of the method. Figure 2-1 shows the Ildasm view of the code sample that follows the figure. The code represents one of the test cases for analyzing language performance issues contained in Chapter 14.

Figure 2-1. Ildasm view of a method's implementation

```
public void TypeOfAndCast(Int32 numberIterations){
  for (int i = 0;i < numberIterations;++i) {
    if (_base.GetType() == typeof(Derived)){
      Derived d = (Derived)_base;
      _add += d.G();
    }
  }
}
```

When using Ildasm to investigate performance, the first step is to determine the method or methods of interest. Methods that fall into this category will typically be those that are most frequently called, or those methods that implement the core functionality of a type. Many methods contained within a type will simply be property get/set implementations or overloads that provide default parameters and forward the call on to another method that contains the actual implementation.

Once the "workhorse" method has been located, a brief inspection of all the method's instructions should be conducted to look for obvious performance issues like the need to make remote calls, security demands, and the use of reflection to invoke methods. After the initial inspection, it is often necessary to conduct a more thorough analysis of the implementation by breaking down the method into smaller instruction units, and analyzing these units in an attempt to work out the motivation for their presence. By determining why various instruction groups are present in a method, insights into performance issues that may otherwise go unnoticed can be uncovered, and the precise techniques for using the method in the most optimum manner can be determined. This technique is very time consuming, and is only practical for methods and types that are frequently employed within a technology. For many methods, a brief scan for obvious performance pitfalls will suffice.

Decompilers

If Ildasm seems too complex, a number of tools are available that can decompile IL to a high-level language, which makes implementation analysis extremely easy (license agreement permitting). Anakrino is a free decompiler that can be downloaded from http://www.saurik.com/net/exemplar/. Anakrino offers output in C# and Managed C++, and presents a similar UI to Ildasm. The high-level code produced by a decompiler will not be identical to the original source code, but will be logically equivalent.

When using decompilers, the analysis pattern is identical to that used with Ildasm—determine the method of interest, and analyze the implementation. The actual tool being used to conduct the assessment is of secondary concern, and concentrating on developing effective investigation techniques will produce much better results than focusing on a particular tool.

Rotor

If browsing through the Framework Libraries using Ildasm does not produce sufficient insight into a performance issue related to .NET, the next step is to grab the Shared Source Common Language Infrastructure (SSCLI) implementation, which is also know by the codename Rotor (available for free download from `http://msdn.microsoft.com/net/sscli`), and look at the underlying CLR implementation. The *MSDN Magazine* article "Shared Source CLI Provides Source Code for a FreeBSD Implementation of .NET" by Jason Whittington (July 2002) is a great introduction to what is and isn't included in the SSCLI, but, at a very high level, the SSCLI can be seen as the CLR and Framework Library source code with some of the trade-secret and Windows-only material removed. Much of the SSCLI code is identical to that which runs as part of the CLR, and it offers a powerful tool in tracking down strange performance behavior. A strong knowledge of C++ is required to get the most out of the SSCLI.

x86 Disassembly

If all else fails, the disassembled x86 instructions are always available for analysis and debugging. In a sense, there is no greater authority than the generated machine instructions that make up the operating system and the CLR, though the vast number of instructions required to perform most tasks makes tracing through x86 a time-consuming activity. The lack of type information and variable names also contributes greatly to the complexity of x86 analysis, and it is often necessary to annotate groups of instructions with their intent or effect to allow a coherent picture of execution patterns to emerge. *Microsoft System Journal* published two articles on using "just enough assembly language to get by." (*Under The Hood* column, February and June 1998), which are a good primer for understanding assembly language. For the keen and adventurous, the complete x86 Instruction Set Reference can be freely downloaded from the Intel Web site in PDF format (`http://www.intel.com/design/Pentium4/manuals/245471.htm`).

The Visual Studio .NET debugger is an excellent tool for inspecting the x86 instructions that the JIT compiler produces. When an application is in break mode, Ctrl-Alt-D will bring up the disassembled x86 for the method, and the instructions can be stepped through just like any other code. Figure 2-2 shows the disassembly for a method call made through an interface reference.

When CLR debugging is active, the x86 instructions displayed may be inaccurate, and it can be impossible to step into various methods. To overcome this problem, CLR debugging needs to be disabled. This can't be accomplished through a standard debug session launch in Visual Studio .NET, but by starting the process outside the debugger, it is then possible to attach the debugger with CLR debugging disabled. If the code needs to be broken at a specific point, a call to the Win32 `DebugBreak` function can be used, which allows the debugger to be attached with the code paused at a known point. Disabling managed debugging removes the ability to interact with source code, so it is not an easy technique to master.

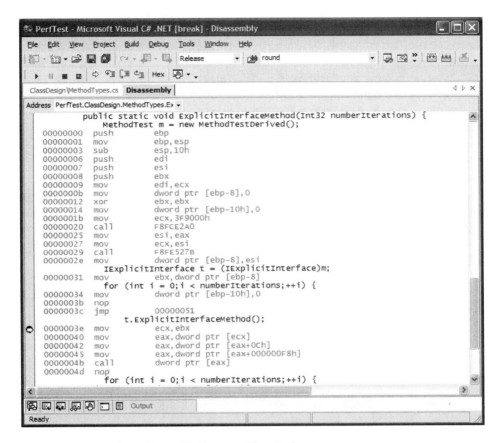

Figure 2-2. Visual Studio .NET disassembly window

Profilers and System Utilities: Grey Box Investigation

For some forms of performance investigation, the sheer quantity of source code and disassembled instructions that define a system make classical white box inspection unfeasible. For situations like this, an aggregate view of the implementation of a system is required to allow performance investigations to be carried out. Instead of analyzing a system on a line-by-line basis, summary statistics are collected to allow a complex system to be simplified to the point of comprehension. In this type of analysis, significant events in the system's execution are identified and monitored, and the results of this monitoring are used to build a picture of what the system is doing internally.

One of the most effective and simple tools for generating summary statistics about a particular assembly or application is a profiler. The main use for profilers is to allow the percentage of time for each line of code to be accessed, but most profilers will also generate summary statistics at the completion of a profiling run that shows the full range of methods that were called from the profiled code, the number of times the methods were called, and the percentage of execution time spent inside these methods. This allows the external assemblies and DLLs that an assembly uses to be identified, and provides some insight regarding how these external components are being used. Compuware offers an excellent entry-level profiler for .NET for free at http://www.compuware.com/products/devpartner/profiler/default.asp.

System monitoring utilities can also provide insight into the inner working of complex systems. Sysinternals.com has a wide range of system utilities that can monitor many aspects of the operating system, including disk access, registry access, network access, and process information. By observing application behavior with these tools, significant insights into performance can be gained.

Black Box Investigation Using the Benchmark Test Harness

Black box investigation in the form of benchmarking plays a crucial role in performance analysis. By measuring how code performs when executed as part of a benchmark, performance insights that are not possible through code inspection are available. However, constructing an accurate benchmark is a deceptively complex task. Simply surrounding blocks of code that exercise a particular technology or technique with timing statements can produce spectacularly inaccurate results, and careful design and result analysis is required to arrive at an accurate result.

A number of tools for conducting black box assessments of complete systems are available, such as Microsoft's Application Center Test (ACT), which ships with Enterprise editions of Visual Studio. These tools are designed to run end-to-end tests on a production solution, and are not effective at running benchmark tests that exercise a particular technology or component. For informal testing of method and assembly-level performance, it is possible to insert timing statements between method calls that exercise the element in question, but this technique suffers from a number of practical and accuracy problems, and is only suitable for casual benchmarking exercises. A full discussion of the problems of using simple timing statements mixed with benchmark code is presented in the appendix.

To fill the void between full-scale system test applications and timing statements inserted in methods, a benchmark test harness was developed to support the performance assessments conducted for this book. The implementation and architecture of the benchmark test harness is fully discussed in the appendix, and this section will concentrate on the motivation for the

development of the harness, and the techniques for using the harness to conduct black box investigation.

The benchmark test harness uses delegates to define test methods, and
these delegates are executed for a certain number of test runs in a random order.
Timing data for each test run is collected and presented to the user after all the
test runs. The benchmark harness has the following features:

- Benchmark code is clearly separated from timing functionality.

- Test cases are run on threads of a user-defined priority.

- Feedback of benchmark progress is displayed to the user.

- Cancellation of a benchmark suite execution is supported.

- Multiple runs of the same test case can be conducted in a single test-suite
  execution to eliminate once-off performance hits, such as module loading
  and JIT compilation, from benchmark results.

- User-defined pre- and post-benchmark setup and teardown methods can
  be run for each test case.

- Simple statistical analysis of benchmark results is provided.

- A custom attribute to allow benchmarks to be annotated with a name and
  benchmark motivation description is included.

- A standard interface for result presentation is used to allow user-defined
  result output.

- Timing of test runs is conducted using the high-resolution
  `QueryPerformanceCounter` and `QueryPerformanceFrequency` Windows API
  functions.

- Predefined output for charts, XML files, and message boxes is included.

To provide a realistic example of the steps needed for a benchmark assessment, conducting an assessment of the performance of string emptiness checks
will be presented. Constructing a suite of test cases begins by defining the various techniques that can be used to satisfy the benchmark motivation, which is
testing a string for emptiness in this case. Three techniques can be used for this
particular test—an equality check of a string against `String.Empty`, an equality
check of a string against the empty string literal (`""`), and an equality check of
the `String.Length` property with zero. Each of these methods needs to be defined
in a separate method, as shown in the following code block:

```csharp
static string s = "";
public static void StringEmpty(Int32 numberIterations) {
 for (int i = 0;i < numberIterations;++i) {
  bool b = (s == String.Empty);
 }
}
public static void EmptyString(Int32 numberIterations) {
 for (int i = 0;i < numberIterations;++i) {
  bool b = (s == "");
 }
}
public static void Length(Int32 numberIterations) {
 for (int i = 0;i < numberIterations;++i) {
  bool b = (s.Length == 0);
 }
}
```

The method signatures need to conform to the delegate definition provided
with the benchmark harness, which takes a single Int32 parameter and has no
return type. After the methods have been defined, they need to be grouped
together, and various metadata for the test executions, such as the number of
iterations for each loop, needs to be defined. Once this is done, the grouped test
delegates can be passed to the TestRunner.RunTests method, which is provided
by the benchmark harness. The RunTests method returns an object of type
TestResultGrp, which is another type defined by the benchmark harness, and
is used to group timing data. A custom attribute can be used to record a name
and motivation for the benchmark, though the use of this attribute is not
compulsory. The following code sample demonstrates the delegate grouping
and execution:

```csharp
public class EmptyTest {
 [Benchmark("Compares speed of emptiness checks on a string")]
 public static TestResultGrp RunTest() {
  const int numberIterations = 100000000;
  const int numberTestRuns = 5;
  TestRunner tr = new TestRunner(numberIterations, numberTestRuns);
  TestRunner.TestCase testCases = null;
  testCases += new TestRunner.TestCase(EmptyTest.StringEmpty);
  testCases += new TestRunner.TestCase(EmptyTest.EmptyString);
  testCases += new TestRunner.TestCase(EmptyTest.Length);

  return tr.RunTests(testCases);
 }
 //delegate methods go here
}
```

The `TestResultGrp` object can be consumed as is, or passed onto the various result formatter types defined by the benchmark harness. The output of the XML formatter provided by the benchmark harness is shown in the following code block, with the results for the string emptiness check contained. Various metadata related to the test cases, the timing results for each delegate execution, and statistical data relevant to each `TestCase` is included in the file.

```
<testresults
 Name="EmptyTest"
 Motivation="Compares speed of emptiness checks on a string"
 TestTime="Tue, 29 Apr 2003 08:06:50 GMT"
 MachineName="NICK_W2"
 CLR_Version="1.1.4322.573"
 OS="Microsoft Windows NT 5.1.2600.0"
 NoProcessors="1"
 ProcName="   Mobile Intel(R) Pentium(R) 4 - M CPU 2.00GHz">

  <testresult Name="StringEmpty" Min="509.504" Median="517.008"
  Max="523.384" NormalizedTestDuration="3.278531">
    <testrun>523.384</testrun>
    <testrun>509.504</testrun>
    <testrun>515.886</testrun>
    <testrun>517.008</testrun>
    <testrun>519.335</testrun>
  </testresult>

  <testresult Name="EmptyString" Min="509.278" Median="513.023"
   Max="516.587" NormalizedTestDuration="3.253261">
    <testrun>509.343</testrun>
    <testrun>509.278</testrun>
    <testrun>513.023</testrun>
    <testrun>516.587</testrun>
    <testrun>515.263</testrun>
  </testresult>

  <testresult Name="Length" Min="155.466" Median="157.695"
   Max="269.549" NormalizedTestDuration="1">
    <testrun>269.549</testrun>
    <testrun>155.466</testrun>
    <testrun>155.921</testrun>
    <testrun>160.927</testrun>
    <testrun>157.695</testrun>
  </testresult>

</testresults>
```

The most important figure contained within the results is the NormalizedTestDuration attribute of the testrun element. This figure is calculated by dividing the median test run length with the minimum median time for all test cases. The median, which is defined as the middle value in a sorted range, is used in preference to the mean to prevent the results being distorted by outliers that may be due to external events interfering with a particular test run. The NormalizedTestDuration for the fastest test case will always be one, and the higher numbers indicate the test cases that took the longest to execute.

For the string emptiness checks, comparing String's Length property to zero was about three times quicker than comparing a string to either "" or String.Empty. The results also show that all test cases were very cheap to execute, and 100 million comparisons can be conducted on the test hardware in around half a second, meaning that the choice of equality check is only relevant for extremely large data samples.

Designing Benchmarks and Common Pitfalls

The first step in designing an effective benchmark is to explicitly decide what is being benchmarked. Although this step appears obvious, a poorly defined or vague benchmark motivation will make implementing test cases time consuming and difficult. Once the motivation is fully defined, the next step is to list all the different techniques that can be employed to satisfy the benchmark's motivation, and then implement these techniques in code. Once the code has been written, the tests can be run using the benchmark test harness, as shown in the preceding section.

A number of common pitfalls can result in benchmarks delivering inaccurate indications of the performance of a particular technology:

- *Optimized-away test cases:* If a test case has a very simple implementation, the language and JIT compilers can collapse and even remove the test case implementation, which obviously produces incorrect results. To avoid this, ensure that the logic expressed in the test case code is not resolvable at compile time. This may be achieved by including a call out to a method in another assembly, or the storage of data in a class-level variable that can be accessed after the test run completes.

- *"Unrelated equalizer" test suite:* When benchmarking at a low level, a few x86 instructions may be all that separates the performance of a number of test cases. A seemingly trivial call to a method like DateTime.Now, which takes hundreds of instructions to execute, can totally obscure the results of a test.

- *Overly short test runs:* A small but not insignificant cost is involved in setting up and running a test case. For test runs below, say, 50ms, the overhead in executing a test case can result in performance between cases appearing closer than it actually is. In this case, increasing the number of iterations will allow more accurate results to be achieved.

- *Unfair comparisons:* Each benchmark test case should achieve a result that is logically similar, even if there are some physical differences between the results achieved. The logical similarity of the result is dependent on the test case, but by explicitly defining a motivation for the benchmark in the form of "compares various methods for completing task X," a test case will only be valid if task X is completed as part of the test case.

- *Unrelated interferences:* The operating system and hardware on which test cases run are busy places. Many other threads will be competing for processor time, and the managed nature of .NET means that executing code can be suspended for activities like garbage collection, JIT compilation, and security checks. Unless these external activities are part of the test, it is important to minimize their impact on test case execution. The primary way this is achieved in the benchmark harness is to default to running all test cases on a thread with the highest thread priority supported by the Framework Libraries. Running at this priority starves other threads of processor time and makes the system appear unresponsive, but goes some way to minimizing the impact of other activities on test results. The benchmark test harness also supports the nomination of a delegate method that can be used to inform the harness if an event has occurred that would render the test case result invalid. In this case, the test run is repeated a certain number of times in an attempt to produce a valid run.

Conclusion

Up-front planning has been deliberately emphasized numerous times in this chapter as critical in achieving satisfactory results when conducting performance investigations. Preparing focus points before wading into code or benchmarks can prevent many fruitless hours spent nibbling at the edges of a problem.

An important element of up-front investigation is determining whether the investigation will be conducted using a white box, black box, a combined investigation technique. The decision will be influenced by the desired outcome of the investigation, availability and accessibility of source code, and the skill set of the investigator. A combined approach, if feasible, will generally deliver the best outcome.

Always maintain a degree of skepticism over the results obtained from benchmarking. The high precision of timing data can give a false sense of validity to benchmark results, and it is often tempting to mistakenly interpret the results as immutable laws. Results that indicate unbelievably bad or good performance should be treated with great skepticism, and the code should be profiled if necessary to discount any unexpected delays. For unbelievably good results, Anakrino, Ildasm, or x86 instruction inspection can be used to ensure that compilers have not optimized a test case away.

CHAPTER 3

Type Design and Implementation

DESIGNING TYPES SO THAT they interact well with the CLR and Framework Library requires some effort. When designing the interface of a type, and defining the type's interaction with other types, modeling the problem domain is usually the highest priority. This is quite reasonable, and is one of the main benefits object-oriented programming offers. Taking a type whose semantics were developed from an analysis of the problem domain and getting it to work efficiently with the CLR is the subject of this chapter. Any type that can pass the tests of a compiler and be converted into intermediate language will enjoy a reasonable existence with other CLR types, but when efficiency and elegance are important design goals, conforming to CLR design patterns is an important consideration.

A number of the optimizations presented in this chapter are quite specialized, and will not deliver significant performance benefits for many types. The techniques that are presented allow performance improvements in specific situations. It is not necessary or advisable to apply all the techniques presented to every type, but rather the developer should store them in a mental toolkit, and apply them in situations where high performance is an important goal.

Reference and Value Types

The most fundamental design decision relating to type design is the category of type to use. The CLR supports two basic categories of types: value types and reference types. Value types have the characteristics of language primitives, and are usually composed of a small group of existing primitives. They have limited support for object-oriented concepts—they cannot be derived from; they cannot contain an explicit default constructor when expressed in many languages, including C# and VB .NET; and they have limited support for finalization. In contrast, reference types provide the ability to model more complex entities, and typically exhibit more complex behavior.

The two type categories have different allocation behavior. Reference types are always allocated on the managed heap, whereas value types are allocated on the call stack when declared as local variables, and are allocated inline with the containing type when used as member variables. This allocation model means that stack-allocated value types are much quicker to use in an application, and in a simple test case of allocating instances of value and reference types that both contain three 32-bit integer member variables, value types could be allocated an order of magnitude faster (see Test 3.01). The lower allocation rate of reference types is partially caused by the need to periodically pause allocation and perform a garbage collection, which is not the case for stack-allocated value types.

NOTE   The code used to conduct all the tests referenced in the book can be downloaded from the Apress Web site at http://www.apress.com.

The faster allocation speed of value types is partially offset by their copy-by-value semantics when used as parameters in method calls. When a value type is passed as a parameter, a copy is made and placed on the call stack. In contrast, reference types are passed to functions by reference, which only requires that the address of the object be placed on the call stack. This performance offset has led to some suggestions to restrict the size of value types to fewer than 16 bytes. Benchmarks indicate that 16 bytes is not always an optimum value, and that a value type of 64 bytes is still twice as quick as an equivalent class when allocation and a single method call is used. It is not until the ratio of allocation to method calls was moved to 1:8 that 64-byte reference types became more efficient than 64-byte values types (see Tests 3.02, 3.03).

The performance of value types as parameters can be improved by passing the value types to methods using references. This technique is trivial to employ, as demonstrated by the following code snippet:

```
public void UseDateByRef(ref DateTime dt){}
public void UseDateByVal(DateTime dt){}
public void DateTimeUser(){
  DateTime now = DateTime.Now;
  UseDateByRef(ref now);
  UseDateByVal(now);
}
```

Using this technique, the fast allocation of value types and the fast parameter performance of reference types can both be achieved. Passing a value type by reference means that the method being called can modify the member variables of the value type if they are exposed through public variables or property accessors. This is the same behavior that a reference type exhibits, and there are a number of strategies to prevent or negate the changes an external function may make on a type passed by reference.

Object Allocation and Population

Achieving the correct performance characteristics for an object's creation, member variable population, usage, and destruction is important in the overall performance of a system. A typical production system will create millions of objects, which means that poor performance of objects in any phase of their physical lifetime can have a significant impact on the overall performance of an application.

Class Constructors

The CLR guarantees that all types are initialized prior to first access. It does this by setting all allocated memory to zero, which means that reinitializing a variable to zero, false, or null is not required. Some developers will still feel the urge to initialize primitives to zero and references to null in the object constructor, but the practice is pure overhead. The cost of the extra initialization is very small (less than a 4 percent performance delta from the no-reinitialization case [see Test 3.04]), but signifies an arbitrary lack of trust in the CLR that is unjustified.

Member variables can be assigned values before or after the call to the base class constructor. In C#, variable initialization before calling the base class constructor is achieved by assigning a value to a variable on the same line in which the variable is declared, such as private int maxCount = 5. The decision has no performance implications as long as the variable is not then reinitialized in the constructor body. The following code demonstrates a double initialization case:

```
public class DoubleInit{
public string s = String.Empty;        //initialize once
public DoubleInit(string s){this.s = s;} //initialize twice
}
```

In the preceding case, the double initialization makes allocating this class about 16 percent slower than for the case where s is not set to an empty string first (see Test 3.05). Obviously this is not a huge performance hit, but it is nevertheless poor programming practice, and detracts from the cleanness of the code. The DoubleInit type can avoid this problem by providing a parameter-less constructor that sets the string member variable to String.Empty.

```
public class SingleInit{
   public SingleInit (){this.s = String.Empty;}
   public SingleInit (string s){this.s = s;}
}
```

There is no requirement to populate all the member variables of a type when the type is first created. If a class contains a member variable that is expensive to create and not always used, delaying the population until the member variable is required makes sense. This technique, know as *lazy initialization*, is discussed later in this chapter.

If a class exposes only static variables and only has static member variables, it is worth preventing object creation, which is achieved by declaring a protected or private constructor. Hiding the constructor prevents client code from mistakenly creating the object prior to using a static method. System.Math is an example of a Framework Library type that displays the use of this design pattern.

Static Constructors

CLR types can contain a static constructor, which is typically used for initializing static member variables. The CLR guarantees that the static constructor will be called only once per type per application domain, and will be called before the first access to any static variables.

Static constructors can be used with great effect to populate data variables that need to be accessed at various places throughout an application. The data will not be populated until it is first accessed, and will only be populated once per application domain, which can prevent the expensive repopulation on each access that is likely with nonstatic data stores. For example, an application that needs to call a Web service to retrieve various application parameters can expose the Web service data to the application through static member variables that are populated by a static constructor. Be aware that this technique can cause an unexpected pause in an application when an expensive static constructor is invoked, which may be an unsatisfactory user experience if no feedback is given. In this case, it is feasible to raise an event in the constructor that can be consumed by user interface code, informing the user of the reason for the delay.

Static Construction Timing

The timing of the call to the static constructor can be influenced by the use of the BeforeFieldInit type attribute. By specifying this attribute, the CLR is not required to invoke the static constructor until the first access of a static variable, even if instance methods and variables are accessed. For types with expensive static constructors, delaying or even avoiding the constructor can be a significant performance benefit, and the BeforeFieldInit attribute results in the latest possible execution.

Most high-level languages use some type of heuristics to determine whether BeforeFieldInit should be applied to a type. C# and Visual Basic will both add

`BeforeFieldInit` if no explicit static constructor is present, even if static member variables have initialization code declared inline with the member declaration, which results in the generation of a static constructor when the code is compiled. In Visual Basic .NET, the following class will have the `BeforeFieldInit` attribute applied:

```
Class BFI
  Shared i As Integer = 1
  Shared j As Integer = 1
End Class
```

whereas the following code will not have the attribute applied:

```
Class No_BFI
  Shared i As Integer = 1
  Shared j As Integer
  Shared Sub New()
   j = 1
  End Sub
End Class
```

Regardless of the high-level language that code is originally developed in, round-tripping the code through Ildasm and Ilasm allows attributes like `BeforeFieldInit` to be tweaked to the desired setting. To accomplish this, simply use Ildasm with the `/OUT` command-line switch to disassemble the assembly's content to MSIL, find the required type, apply `BeforeFieldInit`, and use Ilasm to reassemble the MSIL into an assembly.

 NOTE   Round-tripping an assembly suffers from two potential pitfalls. If the assembly contains embedded native code, which can be the case if the assembly is produced with the Visual C++ compiler, Ildasm will be unable to disassemble the native code, leaving the generated MSIL in an invalid state. The second problem with round-tripping is that subsequent compilation will overwrite any changes made during the round-tripping process. This problem can be addressed by adding Visual Studio .NET post-build steps that automate the round-tripping. A command-line regular expression tool can make the IL modification task simple and robust in an automated post-build solution.

Canonical Instances

A *canonical instance* of an object is a special instance that is needed so frequently that it makes sense to have it available all the time. The concept is best illustrated by an example—the empty string. While comparing a string reference to an empty string is logically equivalent to comparing the Length property to zero, the empty string comparison is often used for its syntactic neatness or out of habit. Constructing an empty string just for comparison purposes is wasteful, and recognizing this, the designers of String provided a static Empty property to compare strings against. This allows the following more efficient code to be written:

```
if (nameTextBox.Text == String.Empty) {}
// if(nameTextBox.Text == new String()){}  - wasted heap allocation
```

To implement a canonical instance, a static constructor is used to create the canonical instance, perform any initialization required, and assign the instance to a static member variable that is exposed through a static read-only property. Whether the class constructor is publicly exposed in addition to the canonical instance depends on whether all possible states of the object can be easily represented by canonical instances. For a class like System.String, this is clearly not the case, but for a type that can only exist in a limited number of states, the constructor should be hidden, and all type access made through canonical instances. The following sample demonstrates how to provide a canonical ChristmasDay instance for a hypothetical type used to represent public holidays that fall on the same date each year:

```
public class PublicHoliday {
  public PublicHoliday(string name, int month, int dayOfMonth) {
    _name = name;
    _month = month;
    _dayOfMonth = dayOfMonth;
  }

  static PublicHoliday(){
    _christmasDay = new PublicHoliday("Christmas", 12, 25);
  }
  private static PublicHoliday _christmasDay;
  public static PublicHoliday ChristmasDay{get {return _christmasDay;}}

  private int _month;
  public int Month{ get{return _month;}}

  private int _dayOfMonth;
```

```
public int DayOfMonth{ get{return _dayOfMonth;}}

private string _name;
public string Name{ get{return _name;}}
```

}

    C# and VB .NET allow a static constructor to be implicitly defined by initializing a static member variable in the same statement as the declaration, so the ChristmasDay canonical instance could be declared and initialized with the following statement:

```
private static PublicHoliday _christmasDay =
  new PublicHoliday("Christmas", 12, 25);
```

Destructors

CLR-based types cannot have traditional destructors, and languages that provide destructor-like semantics will produce Finalize methods once compiled to MSIL. Finalize methods are covered in depth in Chapter 7.

Class Encapsulation

Encapsulation is one of the fundamental principles of object-oriented programming. Encapsulation provides the ability to migrate a type's implementation behind a stable interface, which is critically important in types used in widely distributed systems. Maintenance of data consistency is another prime benefit of encapsulation, and prevents client code from prying into a type's implementation details.

    Properties provide a syntactically elegant way to achieve encapsulation. The type's member variables remain hidden, while client code can access the logical data fields of a type using the familiar type.member syntax. Accessing member variables through properties is no slower than accessing a public member variable if the property's get and set methods simply return a private or protected variable, as the JIT compiler will simply generate inline calls to the property accessors. Virtual properties do carry an overhead—they are significantly slower than a public field access due to the extra lookups required to determine the correct property accessor to invoke, and the inability of the JIT compiler to generate inline method access. Test 3.06, which assesses the effect of retrieving 32-bit integer member variables through virtual and nonvirtual properties, indicates that virtual properties are about eight times slower for this scenario.

Hiding implementation details with property accessors can lead to large performance improvements by allowing type initialization to be implemented using two performance-oriented design patterns. The simpler design pattern is to delay population of an object's fields until they are actually required. This pattern, known as lazy initialization, works well when the fields are expensive to populate, and the data contained in the fields is rarely accessed. Consider a type that represents information on a persistent file stored on a hard disk. It is reasonable to assume that simple properties such as size and creation data will be accessed more frequently than more obscure properties like the access control entries (ACEs) that define permission of various Windows uses and groups. A prudent design decision would be to populate the common properties on creation, and use a Boolean or bit flag to track which properties have been populated. When using this pattern, it is advisable to access the value of member variables using property accessors inside class methods as well, as this allows the management of the lazy initialization to be centralized in a few key places. The following code shows a lazy initialization sample:

```
[Flags]
enum PopulatedFields{
   MemberVariable1    = 0x0001,
   MemberVariable2    = 0x0002
}

public class LazyInitialization {
  //keeps track of populated fields
  private PopulatedFields _populationTracker;

  //actual field
  private int _populatedOnDemand;
  //method to populate field
  private int FillVariable1(){return 1;}
  //property accessor
  public int PopulatedOnDemand{
    get{
      if ((_populationTracker & PopulatedFields.MemberVariable1) == 0){
        _populatedOnDemand = FillVariable1();
        _populationTracker |= PopulatedFields.MemberVariable1;
      }
      return _populatedOnDemand;
    }
    set{
      _populationTracker |= PopulatedFields.MemberVariable1;
      _populatedOnDemand = value;
    }
```

```
  }

  private string _alsoPopulatedOnDemand;
  //read-only property
  private string FillVariable2(){return "Populated";}
  public string AlsoPopulatedOnDemand{
    get{
      if ((_populationTracker & PopulatedFields.MemberVariable2) == 0){
        _alsoPopulatedOnDemand = FillVariable2();
        _populationTracker |= PopulatedFields.MemberVariable2;
      }
      return _alsoPopulatedOnDemand;
    }
  }

}
```

A more complex approach to improve performance is to use background population of field data on worker threads. In situations where member variables take a significant amount of time to populate, but are likely to be accessed at some stage after the object is created, it is possible to offload the initialization to a background thread. If the member variables are likely to be accessed as soon as the object is created, delayed or background population will not deliver a performance advantage. The CLR thread pool, discussed in Chapter 10, allows the background population to be achieved without the expense of constantly creating threads for every background population task, and also ensures that the number of threads created with a process is maintained at an appropriate level. The following code sample shows a class that uses background initialization to populate a member variable:

```
using System;
using System;
using System.Threading;

public class BackgroundInitialization {
  private bool _backgroundPopulationDone;
  private ManualResetEvent _populationDoneEvent;

  public BackgroundInitialization(){
    _populationDoneEvent = new ManualResetEvent(false);
    ThreadPool.QueueUserWorkItem(new WaitCallback(BackgroundPopulator));
  }

  //actual field
```

```
private int _populatedInBackground;
//method to populate field
private void BackgroundPopulator(object state){PopulatedInBackground = 1;}
//property accessor
public int PopulatedInBackground{
  get{
    if (!_backgroundPopulationDone)
      _populationDoneEvent.WaitOne();
    return _populatedInBackground;
  }
  set{
    lock (this){
      _backgroundPopulationDone = true;
      _populatedInBackground = value;
      _populationDoneEvent.Set();
    }
  }
 }
}
```

 NOTE   Properties are generally used for data that can be retrieved without significant computational cost on the part of the callee. For the case where data population is expensive, the type designer may prefer to use methods rather than properties as a hint to the type's consumers about the performance cost of the operation.

Implementing Interfaces

In unmanaged C++, interfaces were not a formal concept, and needed to be simulated by using a base class containing only abstract methods. This meant that implementing an interface had the same effect as inheriting for any other class—a virtual function table (vtable) pointer for each inherited interface was added to the memory footprint of every object based on the interface implementing type. In COM, where the number of interfaces a class could be expected to implement could run into the dozens, particularly for ActiveX controls, the cost of all these vtable pointers was significant. In response to this cost, a tear-off interface design pattern was developed, in which the main COM object did not implement rarely used interfaces; if these interfaces were required, a secondary object that implemented the requested interface was created, and a reference to this new object was returned.

Within the CLR, interfaces are a first-class concept, and the vtable pointer per implemented interface problem does not occur. Each instance of a type has a single pointer that allows the type's member functions to be located, and implementing an interface has no intrinsic per-instance cost.

Implementing an interface can become expensive in terms of memory if the number of member variables that a type contains is increased. This can occur for a number of reasons—caching various results that are expensive to calculate, or storing variables that are needed between invocations of the interface methods. If the amount of data added to the type is large, say 20 bytes or greater, and it is expected that the interface will not be used frequently, it is possible to employ a Just-In-Time (JIT) interface implementation pattern, where the implementation of the interface methods is delegated to a derived class, and an instance of the derived class is created on demand to satisfy interface method calls. The UML diagram in Figure 3-1 and the code that follows show an example of this pattern.

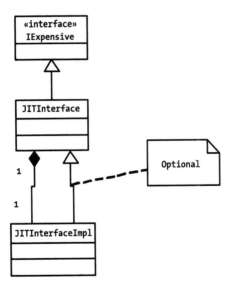

Figure 3-1. Just-In-Time interface implementation

```
interface IExpensive{int MethodA(); int MethodB();}

class JITInterface: IExpensive{
  //normal class stuff
  public int i;
  public virtual int UnrelatedMethod(){return i;}
  //other unrelated methods
```

```
//JIT interface implementation
private JITInterfaceImpl impl;
private void CheckImpl(){if (impl == null) impl = new JITInterfaceImpl ();}
public virtual int MethodA(){CheckImpl(); return impl.MethodA();}
public virtual int MethodB(){CheckImpl(); return impl.MethodB();}
}

class JITInterfaceImpl: JITInterface {
private int a, b, c, d, e, f; //used for IExpensive
public JITInterfaceImpl (){
  ; //initialize member variables
}
public override int MethodA() {} //some calculation involving member variables
public override int MethodB() {} //some calculation involving member variables
}
```

The decision of whether the interface-implementing type is derived from the main type depends on whether the implementing type requires access to protected methods and variables. If access is not required, no inheritance is required. Alternatively, it is possible to use a nested type to implement the interface, as a nested type has access to the containing type's private and protected member variables, which means that no inheritance is required.

For the case where the interface methods are called in only 10 percent of the instances, and the bloat in object size caused by the interface is 24 bytes, a 13 percent performance increase is achieved by using this pattern (see Test 3.07).

User-Defined Type Conversion

User-defined type conversions provide the ability for a type to masquerade as other types if required. Although inheritance implies an "is-a" relationship, user-defined conversions imply a "can-act-as" relationship. Classes that wrap and enhance the functionality of basic numeric types provide the prototypical example of types that benefit from implementing user-defined conversions. User-defined conversions come in two flavors—explicit and implicit. Explicit conversions require cast syntax, whereas the high-level language compiler will silently invoke implicit conversions as required. There are no performance implications for the implicit versus explicit choice (see Test 3.08)—use the conversion syntax that makes sense for the type.

User-defined conversion allows primitive type wrappers to be used seamlessly in low-level numeric routines in a syntactically neat function, but be aware of the performance cost that this neatness brings. For the test case of wrapping a 32-bit integer inside a reference type, using a wrapper with a user-defined conversion is about nine times slower than using the actual underlying type. This cost is not significant in most areas of an application, and the test case demonstrates a worst-case scenario, but is obviously important for lengthy numerical calculations (see Test 3.09). The cost of wrappers is highly dependent on the conversion implementation, and it is worth assessing the cost of the conversion in situations where performance is a development priority.

Method Modifiers

The performance delta for the different type of method modifiers (static, virtual, and instance) is small, and it is generally not worth considering performance when deciding on the use of method modifiers. Methods that are frequently used will benefit from being static, as static methods generally reduce the number of object allocations required; however, breaking encapsulation by making a class state-estranged so that it can expose static methods will rarely result in noticeable performance increases.

 NOTE *State-estranged methods* are methods that require state to perform their functions, but rely on client code to manage their state for them. A method that takes a database ID as a parameter and pulls data out of a database to perform some function could be considered state-estranged. These methods are often referred to as stateless, but this is not technically correct.

The performance difference between the various method modifiers is the result of the levels of indirection that exists in making the method call. For static functions, there is no indirection, and the only instruction generated is a simple x86 CALL instruction. For nonvirtual instance methods, a single MOV instruction is required to invoke the method in addition to the CALL instruction; for virtual methods, two MOV instructions are required; and for interface methods called through the interface, four MOV instructions are required. Unless a program is being optimized down to the level of accounting for every machine instruction generated, which will almost never be the case for applications running on the CLR, method modifiers on nontrivial methods are an irrelevant performance consideration in most situations.

Properties and other very short functions that can be inlined are one area that the virtual modifier can have a significant impact on performance. Test 3.10, which assesses the performance of methods that simply return a constant 32-bit integer, shows virtual methods do have a performance impact for very short methods; for longer methods that cannot be inlined, the performance effect will not be significant. Nonvirtual methods are much easier for the JIT compiler to inline, and while it is technically possible for a virtual method to be inlined during JIT compilation if it is detected that polymorphic calling behavior is not required, the chance of inlining is significantly reduced.

Overriding the Equals Method

Every CLR type is guaranteed to expose an Equals method. Reference types will inherit the implementation in System.Object if no type in their inheritance hierarchy overrides the Equals method, whereas for value types, System.ValueType provides an implementation if Equals is not overridden. The System.Object implementation returns true if both objects refer to the same underlying object on the heap—a form of equality known as *reference equality*. The ValueType implementation is more complex, and returns true only if both objects are of the same type, and all the member variables of the type are equal. This form of equality is known as *value equality*.

The implementation of the Equals method in System.ValueType is surprisingly complex. For value types that do not have an explicit layout attribute specified and do not contain reference types, the Equals method will do a bitwise equality check if the Object parameter passed into the Equals method is of the same type as the method callee. A bitwise comparison is insufficient for some value types, particularly those that contain reference types—two value types could contain references to different reference type instances, but these reference types may have overridden their Equals method to test for value equality. In this case, the value types will contain different bits (the pointers to the heap allocated reference typed will be different), but the value types will still be Equal. In this situation, the ValueType implementation will use reflection to iterate through each member variable and invoke the Equals method.

From a performance perspective, the ValueType.Equals implementation is problematic for a number of reasons. One of the most obvious performance hits is the boxing that must occur to invoke the Equals method. When overriding ValueType.Equals, it is simple to provide a strongly typed method that overloads the default Equals method, which avoids the boxing hit. The second problem with the ValueType implementation is the check to determine whether a bitwise equality comparison is sufficient—this check occurs every time the method is invoked, and imparts some cost every time Equals is called. The final problem is the use of reflection to iterate through the member variables of the object. In addition to the performance degradation caused by the reflection, all Equals calls are made using object references, which results in a boxing cycle for each value type member variable. For types where bitwise equality is sufficient, these performance hits mean that the ValueType implementation is 38 times slower than a strongly typed overload for an 8-byte value type, and for types that cannot use a bitwise comparison, the ValueType.Equals call is *180* times slower than a strongly typed overload (see Test 3.11). These performance deltas are very large, and make it worthwhile exposing a strongly typed `Equals` and equality operator for all value types publicly exposed from an assembly.

 NOTE The precise rules that `ValueType` uses to determine whether bitwise equality is possible are not documented. One case where `ValueType` cannot use bitwise equality is when a `ValueType` contains reference-type member variables. In this case, two `ValueTypes` could contain references to two different reference types, but these reference types may have overridden their `Equals` implementation to provide value-based equality. The two `ValueTypes` will be physically (bitwise) different, but logically `Equal`. Do not rely on bitwise equality being used by `ValueType`, and always override `Equals` for widely used value types.

The code that follows shows a prototypical implementation for equality checks on a value type:

```
struct S{
 //member variables
 private int _i;
 private long _j;

 //properties
 public int I{get{return _i;} set {_i = value;}}
 public long J{get{return _j;} set {_j = value;}}

 //overridden version of Equals
 public override bool Equals(object o){
  return o is S && this == (S)o;
 }

 //strongly types Equals overload
 public bool Equals (S s){
  return this == s;
 }

 //equality operator - all equality checks eventually defer here
 public static bool operator ==(S a, S b) {
  return a._i == b._i && a._j == b._j;
 }

 //inequality operator
 public static bool operator !=(S a, S b) {
  return !(a==b);
```

```
    }

    //GetHashCode implementation - types overriding Equals must override
    GetHashCode
    public override int GetHashCode (){
      return i.GetHashCode() ^ j.GetHashCode();
    }
}
```

There are a number of points worth noting about the preceding code:

- The type exposes a static equality operator and a strongly typed Equals overload for significantly enhanced performance.

- The GetHashCode method of System.ValueType is overridden. The ValueType implementation uses reflection to iterate over each member variable in the type, calling GetHashCode on each variable. Like the ValueType.Equals method, this method has very poor performance. Hash codes and equality checks have a strong relationship, which is discussed further in the "GetHashCode Implementation" section.

- The Equals(Object) method uses the is operator. Using the is operator is feasible for value types because there is no possibility that a derived type can be passed into the function. For reference types, the caller or callee may be on a derived type, and the GetType method should be used instead. Performing type checks before a cast prevents an InvalidCastException being raised in the case of a type mismatch, which would significantly decrease performance.

- The actual logic to determine equality is only contained in the type once. All other equality checks perform any necessary casts and checks that need to occur before calling the static equality operator, which conducts the actual check.

The implementation of Equals inherited from System.Object is adequate for most reference types. The check performed by Object.Equals is a simple pointer comparison, so there is no performance motivation to override Equals. If value equality makes sense for a reference type, overriding the Equals method is not overly complex. For types that derive directly from System.Object, the Equals method has the following form:

```
public class Base{
  private int _i;
  public int I{
```

```
  get{return _i;}
}
private float _j;
public float J{
  get{return _j;}
}

//extra methods removed for brevity

public override bool Equals(object o){
  return (o != null && o.GetType() == this.GetType ()
   && this == (Base)o);
  }
public override int GetHashCode(){
  return i.GetHashCode() ^ j.GetHashCode();
 }
}
```

The only significant difference between the reference type and value type implementations is the use of the GetType method to check that the object passed in to the Equals method is of the same type as the instance that method was called on.

For types lower in the inheritance hierarchy, implementing the Equals method is even easier—call the Equals method of the base class, and check for equality on any member variables added in the derived class.

```
public class Derived: Base{
 //extra methods removed for brevity
 private long _extraData;
 public long ExtraData{
  get{return _extraData;}
 }
 public override bool Equals(object o){
  return base.Equals(o) && _extraData ==  ((Derived)o)._extraData;
 }
}
```

GetHashCode Implementation

The contract for GetHashCode states, in part, that the value returned by the function must be constant for a given instance of a type. It is common practice to calculate the hash code for an object based on the values of member variables, and this can be problematic for fulfilling the GetHashCode contract. Member variables can and do change, but if a hash code changes, the object it refers to can be lost in collections that rely on a constant hash code to locate objects.

Fulfilling this contract when calculating a hash code for a value type is easy—boxing means that value types that have been moved from the stack onto the runtime heap are constant. The process of unboxing the value type, modifying the member variables, and boxing the type back to a heap-based object creates a new instance on the heap. The hash code for the original object will still be valid, as will the new hash code for the modified object. For the uncommon case where the value type implements an interface that can modify its member variables, the situation is the same as for reference types, which is discussed next.

For reference types, the situation is more complex. A reference type is always allocated on the runtime heap, and modification of its member variable does not necessitate any object reallocation. Because of this, the implementation of Object.GetHashCode returns a value that is not dependent on the values of the instance's member variables. In contrast, the ValueType.GetHashCode implementation uses reflection to return the hash code of the first nonnull member variable.

The naive solution to this problem with reference types would be to not base the hash code calculation on the member variables of the type. This solution conflicts with the second half of the GetHashCode contract, which states that two Equal objects must have the same hash code. In other words, the hash code must be based on at least one member variable used to determine equality. Returning the same hash code for two objects that are not equal does not violate the GetHashCode contract, but leads to bunching in a hash table, which decreases lookup speed.

This leaves two options for implementing hash code:

- Base the value returned by GetHashCode on constant or read-only member variables.

- Make the object immutable.

Many classes have no member variables with which constant or read-only modifiers make sense. In this case, making the object immutable is the other viable option. Immutability gives the reference type the assignment semantics of a value type, where each modifying operation returns a new instance of the object. These semantics make sense for many reference types, with System.String being the prototypical case.

If either option for implementing a constant hash code is not feasible, the type must be documented as being unsuitable for use as a key in any collection that uses hash codes for storing and locating objects.

GetHashCode Normalization

A hash code that is evenly distributed yields the best performance for Hashtables. However, the data that a hash code is calculated from will often be bunched around a small range of its possible values. For example, a System.Char variable can have integral values that range from 0x0000 to 0xFFFF, but in the English release of a program, the values will be clustered around the first 128 ASCII characters, which occupy a tiny portion of the full range. If the GetHashCode implementation of System.Char simply returns the integral value of the character, significant clustering of the returned values would occur. To avoid this problem, the Char.GetHashCode method bitshifts the integral value of Char left 16 bits, and performs a bitwise OR on this value with the original integral value. Although this technique does not increase the number of possible values, a more even distribution is achieved, which reduces bunching in collections that use internal groupings based on hash code ranges.

The following guidelines can help avoid bunching in GetHashCode implementations:

- Analyze the typical data that the type will contain, and identify natural bunching. Consider using logging in a debug version to record typical data that the type will contain if implementing a well-distributed GetHashCode method is important.

- Use left bitshifts and bitwise ORs to fill the full 32 bits of the hash code for types that have less than 32 bits of data.

- Use right bitshifts and bitwise XORs for types that have more than 32 bits of data.

- Incorporate the hash code of the base type (if the type is not directly derived from System.Object or System.ValueType) and the hash code of immutable member variables to generate a hash code. Use XOR to combine the results.

The preceding section on implementing equality checks contains samples that demonstrate using these techniques to calculate hash codes, and these samples are included with the code downloads available from the publisher's Web site (http://www.apress.com).

 NOTE   The implementation of types within the Framework Library is not documented, and may change in future versions of the Framework. Discussion of the current implementation is intended to demonstrate best practices for implementing various functionality, and software should not be written that relies upon the implementation remaining constant.

Boxing and Unboxing

Value types are heap allocated when declared as local variables, a quality that gives them great performance characteristics, but they can also be passed as arguments to functions that require a reference type. To achieve these conflicting behaviors, value types undergo a process know as *boxing* when they are required to take on the behavior of a reference type. Boxing creates a heap-allocated object that is equivalent to the stack-allocated value type. The boxed value type is physically a reference type, but can be converted back to a value type with an appropriate cast. Casting back to a value type is known as *unboxing*.

A number of characteristics of boxing are noteworthy from a performance perspective:

- The boxing process offsets the performance benefits of value types by requiring a heap allocation.

- It is possible for a large number of temporary objects to be allocated in methods that require boxing.

- Boxing cannot be avoided in some circumstances—for example, collection classes need reference types to function correctly.

- Generics would alleviate the need for boxing in a number of scenarios, but generics are not included in version 1 of the CLR.

Type designers can eliminate the need for boxing by providing method over-loads that take common value types as parameters. Providing overloads for all primitive types is a significant undertaking, and is only worthwhile for types that are likely to be employed on critical pathways. System.Convert is a good example of a class that meets these criteria, and a number of its methods have many overloads that allow conversion without the need for boxing. In a contrived test case, calling Convert.ToInt64 with an Int32 value is an order of magnitude faster than calling the ToInt64 method with the identical value boxed as an object (see Test 3.12).

Conclusion

For widely used types, performance is an important consideration in type design. The techniques described in this chapter will not only help with designing and implementing types with optimum performance characteristics, but also ensure that a type conforms with many of the design patterns established in the Framework Library.

The decision of whether to implement a type as a reference or value type is the most fundamental type design decision, and has consequences for most aspects of the type's behavior. Value types are much quicker to allocate, but boxing, which occurs when a value type needs to take on the characteristics of a reference type, can cause the performance of value types to become significantly worse than reference types. Value types make the most sense for types that exist simply to collect related pieces of data, whereas reference types are the best choice when modeling real-world entities.

It is important for types to have an efficient and correct `Equals` and `GetHashCode` implementation, especially if a type's instances are likely to be stored in specialized collections like `Hashtable` that make heavy use of equality and hash code data. The default implementation of the `Equals` method that value types inherit has poor performance characteristics, and it is worthwhile over-loading and overriding the `Equals` method to provide an efficient implemen-tation.

Method modifiers, like static and virtual, have a very small impact on appli-cation performance, and it is rarely worthwhile assessing the performance aspect of modifiers when considering their use. It is only within very tight numerical loops that the effect of the different method invocation techniques is noticeable.

CHAPTER 4

Strings, Text, and Regular Expressions

THE UNIFICATION OF ALL STRING types into a single, coherent entity is a simple yet profound improvement from the multitude of strings that have evolved under Win32 and COM. `System.String` represents an immutable Unicode string that is fully supported by all languages that target the CLR. Strings are a fundamental language construct, and a number of languages targeting the CLR use aliases for `System.String`, such as the C# `string` alias, which makes strings appear to be a language primitive rather than a member of the Framework Library. The alias is resolved at compile time to `System.String`, and hence the choice of `System.String` or the language alias is entirely cosmetic.

The `String` type exposes a reasonably comprehensive set of manipulation and extraction methods and properties, and implements the `IEnumerable` interface so that functions can operate on the characters of a string in a generic manner. The `System.Text` namespace contains a group of types designed for more specialized string processing, such as encoding and regular expressions.

From a performance viewpoint, immutability is one of the most interesting qualities of `String`. This characteristic means that those methods of `String` that perform modifications to the string yield new objects, which increase the likelihood of creating numerous anonymous objects as part of a string operation. Anonymous objects are objects that are never assigned to a variable, and hence can only be used for a single call, after which they become available for collection. For the statement `string1.ToUpper().Equals(string2.ToUpper())`, the two `String` objects created by the calls to the `ToUpper` method are both anonymous. Three factors balance this potential performance problem—the CLR garbage collector has optimizations to deal with the frequent allocation of small, short-lived objects, string immutability eliminates the need for the use of expensive synchronization primitives, and no reference counting is needed for copying of strings.

String immutability gives rise to the `System.Text.StringBuilder` type, whose purpose is to allow string modification operations on a mutable string. `StringBuilder` offers no additional functionality over the `String` type, and simply exists to support high-performance string modification operations. Once the desired string is built using `StringBuilder`, the `ToString` method can be used to extract a `String` object. `StringBuilder` is discussed in the "System.Text.StringBuilder" section.

The String type is sealed, which means that it cannot be derived from to form new types. In addition to the security issues that sealing String prevents,[1] the CLR can safely rely on implementation details of String to perform optimizations, knowing that the implementation details will not be modified by a derived type. A significant amount of String's functionality is implemented in unmanaged code, and accessed via the unmanaged functions annotated with the internalcall method attribute, which is an attribute that allows method implementations to be provided internally by the CLR, and is quicker than a standard unmanaged code transition.

NOTE   Testing the performance of a string operation involves defining test cases that contain strings of certain lengths. Changing the length of these strings can impact test results, and readers should be aware that a test result may not be directly relevant to strings of other lengths.

Comparing Strings

String comparison is a topic that appears simple at first glance, but can rapidly decompose into complexity in many situations. The simplest definition of string equality is that two strings are identical when both strings have the same length, and the character at each position in the string is identical. This definition, referred to as *binary equality,* is sufficient for most situations, but falls short in some scenarios where case sensitivity and locale-specific formatting need to be taken into account. The definition of strings as being equivalent despite binary differences is known as *logical equality.*

System.String supports binary equality with the three Equals methods it exposes. Two instance methods exist—one is strongly typed to take a String parameter, and the other is an override of the Equals method inherited from Object. String also exposes a static Equals method that employs a performance-oriented design pattern used in many places in the Framework Library. The static method first performs a reference equality check to determine if the parameters refer to the same object, followed by a check to see if either of the parameters is null. If these checks do not produce a result, the virtual instance method is then called. These optimizations make the static method about twice as fast for the case where half the equality determinations can be made using the static method alone (see Test 4.01). The static Object.Equals uses the same short-circuit checks as the static String.Equals, but is less performant due to the need to perform type checks.

---

1. Strings are a frequently used type in most kinds of applications, and often contain sensitive data like passwords. Injecting a derived String type into an application could result in the capture of sensitive user data.

The op_Equality method of String, which is the MSIL representation of the C# operator ==, simply forwards the call to the static Equals method, and is hence nearly as fast as this method. Programmers from a C++ background are often more comfortable with the syntax of the operator == method, and there is no performance reason to shy away from it in C#. It is worth noting that this is not the case in VB .NET; the equality operator is handled by a VB helper function to preserve backwards compatibility with the Option Compare functionality in VB 6, and is over twice as slow as the C# statement for the comparison of a six-character string (see Test 4.01). Option Compare is a source file–level switch that controls the forms of equality check used in VB .NET, and results in the compiler generating a call to the Microsoft.VisualBasic.Strings.StrComp method regardless of the forms of equality check nominated by Option Compare. The following code sample demonstrates the various equality check options commonly in use in C# and VB .NET:

```
'VB.NET — all calls logically identical
Dim s1 As String = "a"
Dim s2 As String = "b"

'Call to Microsoft.VisualBasic.Strings.StrComp generated
Dim b1 As Boolean = s1 = s2

'No language-level calls made
Dim b2 As Boolean = String.Equals(s1, s2)

'No language-level calls made, but call can be slightly
' slower than shared Equals
Dim b3 As Boolean = s1.Equals(s2)

//C# — all calls logically identical
string s1 = "a";
string s2 = "b";

//direct call to String.op_Equality
bool b1 = s1 == s2;

//direct call
bool b2 = String.Equals(s1, s2);

//direct call, but call can be slightly slower than static Equals
bool b3 = s1.Equals(s2);
```

Compare Methods

String augments the limited functionality of the Equals methods with the more powerful Compare methods. The Compare family of methods has parameters that allow for case-insensitive comparisons, and also allow for the provision of System.Globalization.CultureInfo information to be supplied for use in the comparison. CultureInfo is used to store information that allows output data to be formatted in a cultural-specific manner, and can be approximately thought of as the store for the information that a user would nominate in the Regional and Language Options applet in the Windows Control Panel. For methods with no CultureInfo parameter, the CultureInfo object associated with the current thread is used. Unlike the Equals methods, which return a Boolean value, the Compare methods return an integer representing the lexical difference between the two strings, with zero indicating that the strings are lexicographically identical.

The added functionality of the Compare methods comes at a performance cost, which is largely dependent on the CompareInfo object associated with the function call. The rules for implementing comparisons vary across different cultures, and the complexity of the rules will generally determine the performance impact. For the test case of moving through each word in the English translation of *War and Peace* and calling the Compare method against the previous word, using a CultureInfo based on traditional Spanish (which has reasonably complex comparison rules) in a case-insensitive comparison is 56 percent slower than a U.S. English comparison (see Test 4.02). The code that follows shows the two test cases, which assume that a string array called _words has been initialized with *War and Peace:*

```
public void TraditonalSpanish(Int32 numberIterations) {
  int res = 0;
  CultureInfo tradSpain = new CultureInfo( 0x040A, false );
  for (int i = 0;i < _words.Length-1 ;++i) {
    res = String.Compare(_words[i], _words[i+1], false, tradSpain);
  }
}


public void USEnglish(Int32 numberIterations) {
  int res = 0;
  CultureInfo usEng = new CultureInfo( "en-US", false );
  for (int i = 0;i < _words.Length-1 ;++i) {
    res = String.Compare(_words[i], _words[i+1], false, usEng);
  }
}
```

NOTE *War and Peace* and many other classic pieces of literature that are no longer covered by copyright restrictions are available for download from the Project Gutenburg site (http://www. gutenberg.org/). In addition to being excellent reading material, they are a great source of real-world input for test cases.

The cost of the `Compare` method can be eliminated by two techniques—identifying string comparisons where string case and locale-specific rules can be ignored, and using `String.Equals` in addition to `String.Compare`. Ignoring case and locale specifics may sound less robust, but in some cases, a set of specifications will guarantee binary equality for identical strings, and the use of the `Compare` method is not required. String data that originates from fixed back-end systems and text collected from embedded systems are two common sources of data where this optimization is possible.

In the situation where case and locale-specific checks are required, but binary equality is more likely, calling `Equals` before `Compare` can result in a performance win. The following code demonstrates this technique:

```
System.String string1 = GetStringFromSomewhere();
System.String string2 = GetStringFromSomewhereElse();
if (string1 == s2 || String.Compare(s1, s2) == 0){
    //processing required for identical strings
}
```

If the strings exhibit binary and logical equivalence, the more expensive call to `String.Compare` is avoided. The exact performance win is proportional to the percentage of checks that can be completed without having to invoke the `Compare` method. If the percentage of strings that can be assessed with calls to the `Equals` method is small, using both tests will end up slower, as both `Equals` and `Compare` will be invoked to complete a comparison. For the test case where `Equals` is true 50 percent of the time, the use of both checks is twice as fast as just using `Compare` (see Test 4.01), but for the case where only 10 percent of the Equality checks succeed, a slowdown of 24 percent occurs for the `Equals` and `Compare` technique (see Test 4.03).

The case-insensitive comparisons that `String.Compare` offers are able to perform the comparison without creating new `Strings`, and for the test case of six-character strings, `String.Compare` was three times faster than a call to `String.Equals` using two new strings generated by calls to `String.ToUpper` (see Test 4.04). If a group of strings needs to take part in many comparisons, converting all the strings to a constant case and using these new strings to conduct equality checks will be faster. For the test case of a six-character string, using new strings of uniform case becomes faster than `Compare` if more than four equality checks are conducted (see Test 4.04).

String Formatting

Moving data into and out of strings is a common activity in most programs. In recognition of this fact, the CLR and Framework Libraries have a strong and comprehensive support for conversion between strings and other types. The most obvious string conversion support comes from the ToString method that, through inheritance from System.Object, is available on every object. The default behavior of ToString is to return the full name of the type, but this can be over-ridden to provide a more appropriate implementation. The typical ToString implementation will make use of the data in member variables to provide a partial representation of the object's state.

For advanced string output, the IFormattable interface can be implemented. The first parameter of the overloaded ToString method that IFormattable provides is a string argument containing formatting arguments, and the second parameter is an object implementing IFormatProvider. IFormatProvider is responsible for providing culturally specific data, such as the symbol used for the decimal place, that will be used by the IFormattable-implementing object when building the string output. Passing in a null reference for the IFormatProvider parameter will typically result in the use of the IFormatProvider associated with the thread's culture. The following code snippet illustrates the use of an IFormattable implementing type:

```
IFormattable  if1 = DateTime.Now;
Console.WriteLine(if1.ToString("G", null));
//Output: "10/07/2003 11:02:50 AM" on en-AU system
Console.WriteLine(if1.ToString("G",
   new System.Globalization.CultureInfo("en-US").DateTimeFormat));
//Output "7/10/2003 11:02:50 AM"
```

The Framework Libraries provide many ways to convert objects to strings, including String.Format and various formatting methods offered by StringBuilder. All these methods eventually defer to the object's ToString method, which makes providing an optimized ToString implementation essential for widely distributed types.

When using string conversion methods, the choice of which technique to use does have some performance implications. As noted previously, ToString will eventually be called to convert the object, but the error checking and allocations that occur for a successful call to the ToString method can become significant.

String.Format is the slowest of the general-purpose conversion techniques, as it lacks the strongly typed overloads of StringBuilder, which means that value types passed to String.Format will trigger a boxing operation. StringBuilder.Append and StringBuilder.AppendFormat can be used to keep parameter checks and boxing to a minimum, and will provide the fastest method for converting multiple objects to a single string. For the test case of a string built by appending a formatted `DateTime` object, an unformatted `Int32`, and another string object, `String.Format` is 62 percent slower than using a combination of `StringBuilder.Append` and `ToString` method calls (see Test 4.05).

Enumeration

Visiting each character in a string is typically accomplished using two distinct techniques. The classic enumeration pattern is to treat a string as a character array, and use a counter variable and indexer-based access to directly reference each character. The Framework Library offers a simpler enumeration pattern that uses the `IEnumerable` interface to allow generic navigation of a collection-like object. The following code sample illustrates the use of the two techniques:

```
private void Enum(){
   string s = "123";
   //classic enumeration
   for (int ix = 0; ix < s.Length; ++ix)
     Console.WriteLine(s[ix]);

   //IEnumerable enumeration through C# foreach statement
   foreach(char c in s)
     Console.WriteLine(c);

}
```

The use of the `IEnumerable` interface, either directly or through language-level wrappers like `foreach` (C#) and `For Each` (VB .NET), has no negative performance impacts compared to using the `String`'s indexer property inside a loop to navigate over all of the `String`'s characters (see Test 4.06). The `CharEnumerator` object returned by `String`'s `GetEnumerator` method has a strongly typed `Current` property, which prevents a boxing operation on the `Char` value type. This means that the underlying logic used to enumerate the string is close to identical for both cases, and hence results in similar performance.

String Emptiness

Testing for an empty string is most efficiently achieved by comparing the `String`'s `Length` property to zero. The static `op_Equality` method of `String`, which is exposed as the `==` operator in C#, is often favored over checks for zero length on the grounds of syntactical neatness. The canonical `String.Empty` instance can be used in the comparison, avoiding any object allocation, but the relative cost of the check is still greater than using the Length property, which only needs to examine the String's metadata.

Benchmarking indicates that the Length check is about three times quicker than testing against an empty string for the current .NET release (see Test 4.07).

Intern Pool

Every string literal declared in an assembly is maintained in an intern pool. This pool allows the interned copy of the string to be used throughout the program, saving memory usage. The String type provides an Intern method for adding strings to the pool, and another static method called IsInterned for checking whether a string is stored in the intern pool. In addition, interning can be performed by the compiler when a constant string is defined in an assembly, which means that a constant string defined in a number of places will reference the same underlying piece of memory. The following sample illustrates a compiler-generated interned string, a dynamically generated interned string, and a noninterned string:

```
public static void InternFun(){
    string constantString = "I never change";
    string addedToIntern = DateTime.Now.ToShortDateString();
    String.Intern(addedToIntern);
    string notInterned = DateTime.Now.ToLongDateString();

    Console.WriteLine("constantString is interned: {0}",
        String.IsInterned(constantString)!=null);
    Console.WriteLine("addedToIntern is interned: {0}",
        String.IsInterned(addedToIntern)!=null);
    Console.WriteLine("notInterned is interned: {0}",
        String.IsInterned(notInterned)!=null);
}
/* Output:
constantString is interned: True
addedToIntern is interned: True
notInterned is interned: False
*/
```

The ability to interact with the string intern pool at runtime provides the facility to keep dynamically generated strings, such as those that are read from a file or the user-interface, alive for the life of the application domain. Adding strings to the intern pool too frequently will mean that the memory consumption of the application domain will be increasing constantly, and, from an external perspective, appear as a memory leak. If different code segments are creating the same string (say, for example, they were all reading the same file), using interned strings would guarantee that the string data would only be held in memory once. Rather than relying on interning, it would usually be better practice to factor out the common string creation code, and simply provide the ability for other code to retrieve a reference to the string, as shown in the following sample:

```
public static string GetFooterForAllDocsProduced(){
  return "© DotNetPerformance.com 2003";
}
```

For situations where some of the code cannot be altered, interning would prove a viable option to direct reference sharing.

The intern pool means that identical interned strings will point to the same physical piece of memory, which can be used to optimize equality checks. The `Object.ReferenceEquals` method, which performs a simple pointer comparison, can be used instead of the more expensive `String.Equals` method, which performs a character-by-character comparison. Although this optimization is technically feasible, and over five times faster for a test case where inequality can be determined based on `ReferenceEquals` alone (see Test 4.08), the scope for applying this optimization is quite limited, and needs to be applied very carefully to avoid introducing bugs. Using the static `String.Equals` method, which performs a pointer comparison before forwarding the call to the instance `String.Equals` method, allows the intern pool comparison optimization to be applied with no additional code, and it is preferable to use this technique over the `Object.ReferenceEquals` method.

System.Text.StringBuilder

`StringBuilder` exists solely to support high-performance string operations. As discussed earlier, `String` objects are immutable, which means that any operation that modifies a `String` results in a new `String` object being created. Immutable strings work best when they are shared frequently and modified infrequently—sharing is cheap because no locking or reference counting is required, and the `String` object can be accessed directly, rather than relying on abstraction and copy-on-write sharing schemes. In some cases, the design scenario of frequently shared and infrequently modified stings breaks down, and a type that represents a mutable string is required.

`StringBuilder` represents a mutable Unicode character array that supports high-speed modification operations. When the modification operations are complete, the `ToString` method may be called to extract a standard `String` object. The default initial capacity of `StringBuilder`'s internal character array is 16 characters in .NET 1.x, but a number of constructors exist to allow this capacity to be set.

When an operation results in an increase in the number of elements required in the character array, a new array that is double the size of the previous array is created, and the contents of the old array are copied across. This internal reallocation is expensive, particularly as the amount of data that needs to be copied during the reallocation becomes larger. If information is available that can be used to estimate the number of characters that a StringBuilder object will be required to store, it is a worthwhile optimization to explicitly set the initial size, which can be accomplished with an overloaded version of the constructor, as shown in the following sample:

```
Dim sb as System.Text.StringBuilder = new System.Text.StringBuilder(100)
```

The exact point that StringBuilder becomes more efficient than String when performing modification is dependent on system parameters. For the test case of appending a single character to either a String or StringBuilder object, the StringBuilder object becomes slightly faster when the number of append operations reaches six (see Test 4.09). This figure will vary to some degree between different systems and different versions of the runtime, but a reasonable rule of thumb would be to switch to StringBuilder when the number of modifying operations heads towards ten. Above this number, the performance impact of using String for modifying operations will begin to become noticeable for performance-sensitive code sections.

In .NET 1.x, calling the ToString method returns a String object that references the internal character array of the StringBuilder object, which means that no copying needs to occur. The character array becomes immutable once a String object is referencing it, and subsequent operations on the StringBuilder will result in a copy operation occurring. If feasible, it is best to defer calls to ToString until all modifications are complete, and to use the ToString overloads that allow a substring of the StringBuilder character array to be accessed.

Reversing Strings

The lack of a built-in method to reverse strings is a noticeable omission from the String type. Although string reversal is not an everyday activity, on many occasions efficiently generating a reversed string is required. This section builds upon the material that has been presented earlier in the chapter, and explores the fastest method for performing a string reversal.

There are a number of different ways that a reversed string can be produced with the various types defined in the Framework Library. Four possible techniques are:

- The generation of a character array using String.ToCharArray, followed by a call to Array.Reverse, and the creation of a new string from the resulting character array.

```
string s = "1234567890";
char[] ca = s.ToCharArray();
Array.Reverse(ca);
string res = new string(ca);
```

- The Microsoft.VisualBasic.Strings.StrReverse method, which is used in Visual Basic .NET to implement the language's Reverse function.

```
string s = "1234567890";
string res = Microsoft.VisualBasic.Strings.StrReverse(s);
```

- The use of StringBuilder, with each string character appended to the StringBuilder object in reverse order, followed by a call to ToString.

```
string s = "1234567890";
StringBuilder sb = new StringBuilder(s.Length);
for (int ix = s.Length-1; ix != 0; –ix){
   sb.Append(s[ix]);}
string res = sb.ToString();
```

- The use of a character array, with each character from the original string appended to the character array in reverse order, followed by the construction of a new string from the character array.

```
string s = "1234567890";
char[] chars = new char[s.Length];
int ix = s.Length - 1, j = 0;
while(ix >= 0)
   chars[ix–] = s[j++];
string res = new string(chars);
```

Benchmarking for the reversal of a ten-character string indicates method 4 is the fastest; followed by method 3, which is 73 percent slower; method 1, which is 89 percent slower; and method 2, which is 155 percent slower (see Test 4.10).

Achieving the fastest reversal with the solution that makes the least use of Framework Library illustrates a noteworthy point on performance—the more general a method is, the more likely that the performance will not be optimal for a specific case. This is not an immutable law, but is rather a general trend, and for high-performance situations, developing a specialized solution can often result in performance wins. The cost of developing a specialized solution will not be warranted for the bulk of development tasks, and by using good software engineering practices such as modular design and loose coupling between types, developing a specialized solution for the performance-critical areas of an application during the optimization phases will be possible.

The full code for a character array-based reversal method is shown in the following code snippet:

```
string ReverseString(string inputString){
  if (inputString == null || inputString.Length == 0)
   return inputString;
  char[] chars = new char[inputString.Length];
  int ix = inputString.Length - 1, j = 0;
  while(ix >= 0)
   chars[ix-] = inputString[j++];
  return new string(chars);
}
```

Regular Expressions

The Framework Library provides a comprehensive regular expression toolkit in the System.Text.RegularExpressions namespace. Regular expressions are a powerful text manipulation tool, and allow verbose and suboptimal text manipulation routines based on string manipulation methods to be compressed into a few lines of efficient, regular expression-based manipulation. Regular expressions are essentially a specialized programming language, and like all programming languages, have certain usage patterns that provide the most efficient behavior. For introductory material on regular expressions, the MSDN Library is a good starting point, and for more in-depth material, *Mastering Regular Expressions, Second Edition* by Jeffrey E. F. Friedl (O'Reilly & Associates, 2002) is an invaluable aid.

A regular expression library can be built upon a number of different types of processing engines. The two main categories are nondeterministic finite automaton (NFA) and deterministic finite automaton (DFA). The difference between the two categories is based on the algorithm that is used to determine matches within a string. DFA-based algorithms check over a search string at most once, and identify matches as they go along. NFA-based algorithms use a different approach in which the elements that make up a regular expression are evaluated separately and then combined at the end, meaning that the different elements of the regular expression may end up visiting a section of the search string a number of times.

The consequence of the algorithm differences is that DFA-based engines are quicker, whereas NFA-based engines are more powerful. NFA are further divided into traditional and POSIX categories, which are differentiated along similar lines to the DFA-NFA divide. The .NET Framework Library uses a traditional NFA engine, which offers a good balance between performance and power, and is very similar to industry-standard regular expression toolkits like Perl.

The Regex Type

The Regex type is the cornerstone of the .NET regular expression library, and provides the ability to execute regular expressions against a nominated text string. When a regular expression is presented to a Regex object, it is converted to a high-level semicompiled representation, which is cached and reused if the same regular expression is executed during the application domain's lifetime. To increase the speed of the text processing, a particular regular expression can be compiled to MSIL, which will then be JIT compiled to native code before execution.

The compilation of regular expressions results in a dynamically-generated assembly, and like all assemblies loaded within an application domain, it will not be unloaded until the application domain is unloaded. This means that both the MSIL and JIT-compiled native code will be retained in memory, and will not be shared across other processes, even if the other processes compile the same regular expression statements. To partially alleviate this problem, it is possible to persist the compiled regular expression to a disk-based assembly using the Regex.CompileToAssembly method, which allows the MSIL code to be shared across all processes that load the module on NT-based operation systems. The CLR supports the creation of multiple application domains within a single process, and this technique can be used to allow a compiled regular expression to be unloaded after use without terminating a process. Assembly unloading with multiple application domains is further discussed in the Chapter 14.

The following sample shows a simple C# console application that produces an assembly containing a compiled regular expression. The name of the assembly, type information, regular expression options, and the regular expression pattern are all passed on the command line. The assembly produced will contain a type derived from the System.Text.RegularExpressions.Regex that initializes the regular expression pattern string in the constructor.

```
using System;
using System.Reflection;
using System.Text.RegularExpressions;

class RegExToAssm {
  static void Main(string[] args) {
```

```
            string name = args[0];
            string nameSpace = args[1];
            string assmNameStr = args[2];
            string regExString = args[3];
            RegexOptions options = (RegexOptions)Convert.ToInt32(args[4]);

            RegexCompilationInfo info = new
                RegexCompilationInfo(regExString, options, name, nameSpace, true);
            AssemblyName assmName = new AssemblyName();
            assmName.Name = assmNameStr;

            Regex.CompileToAssembly(new RegexCompilationInfo[]{info}, assmName);

        Console.WriteLine("Regular expression successfully compiled to "
            + assmNameStr);
        }
    }
```

The assembly containing the compiled regular expression can be used like any other .NET assembly. Types derived from System.Text.RegularExpressions.Regex can be instantiated and used in exactly the same way as Regex, and the only difference from normal Regex usage will be that the regular expression pattern does not need to be specified. The following code sample demonstrates the use of a precompiled regular expression produced with the RegExToAssm type that matches nonalphanumeric characters in an input string:

```
//RegExToAssm command line: RegExEng DotNetPerformance
//    RegExAssm [^a-zA-Z0-9] 0
using System;
using System.Text.RegularExpressions;

class UseRegExFromAssm {
    static void Main(string[] args) {
        string seachString = args[0];

        DotNetPerformance.RegExEng regExEng = new DotNetPerformance.RegExEng();
        foreach(Match m in regExEng.Matches(seachString))
            Console.Write(m.Value);
        Console.WriteLine("Press Enter to exit");
        Console.ReadLine();
    }
}
//input: ab*klmnc?-12!cd
//output: *?-!
```

The performance improvement that can be achieved by compiling a regular expression is dependent on the actual expression, but executing a regular expression that checks for repeating letters (like the tt in "letters") on sample text gives a rough indication. The interpreted version of the regular expression `(?<a>\w)\k<a>`, executed on Tolstoy's *War and Peace*, takes twice as long as the compiled version (see Test 4.11). For those unfamiliar with regular expressions, the expression used captures a word letter, which is similar to creating a reference, and then uses a back reference match on the next character, which has the effect of detecting repeating word characters.

By default, regular expressions are case sensitive. The `RegexOptions` enumeration, which is accepted by an overloaded version of the `Regex` constructor, allows for the specification of case-insensitive matching. Case-insensitive matching increases execution time by 22 percent when searching for repeating letters over *War and Peace*, which is slower than the 5 percent performance hit caused by converting the string to an all-uppercase version first, and then using case-sensitive matching (see Test 4.12). In situations where it is feasible, converting the search string to all upper- or lowercase and then using case-insensitive matching will deliver a performance win.

Like all languages, regular expressions allow the same piece of logic to be expressed in many different forms. When text-parsing speed is an important element of an application, it is worthwhile testing different combinations of regular expression elements against sample text, and observing how each regular expression performs. The performance benchmarking application that accompanies the book has a predefined test case that allows for the nomination of two regular expressions and a filename, and will compare the speed of the two expressions against each other (see Test 4.13).

When performance testing regular expressions, it is important to include malformed and unexpected strings in the test case, especially if the text being searched originates from untrusted sources. Consider the regular expression `([\w]* ?[\w])*\.`, which is a less-than-perfect attempt to match word characters and spaces followed by a period. For an expected input like "Give me what I want.", the execution time of the regular expression is trivial, but when an unexpected string like "I_was_not_expecting_a_string_like_this" is presented to the same regular expression, execution time increases massively, and, even when left running overnight, the regular expression fails to complete. This is an extreme example, but it is always worth throwing in corrupt or unexpected text during the performance testing phases to ensure that the application's performance is still satisfactory.

Chapter 4

Conclusion

The unification of all string types into a single, coherent entity is a big step forward. Having a single means of expressing string data eliminates the performance overhead of constantly replicating string data to match the binary format of software components written in different languages and using different libraries. A single string type also means that developers can become familiar with the performance characteristics of a particular type, and adopt patterns that promote optimum performance.

`StringBuilder` provides the ability to execute methods against a mutable string, in contrast to the `String` type, which is immutable and returns a new object for all modifying operations. As the number of mutating operations performed on a string heads towards double figures, `StringBuilder` will offer better performance.

The `System.Text.RegularExpressions` namespace offers a high-performance NFA regular expression engine capable of operating in both an interpreted and compiled form. While compilation offers faster execution speeds, attention needs to be given to the working set of the process, as compiled regular expressions cannot be unloaded from memory unless they are loaded as part of a separate application domain.

NFA regular expression engines are sensitive to small differences in the way regular expressions are constructed, and for performance-sensitive code, testing of the performance for well-formed and poorly formed input is critical. If the input for a regular expression originates from external sources, denial of service attacks that exploit bugs in a regular expression are possible, and defenses should be put in place to prevent this.

CHAPTER 5

Collections

COLLECTIONS OCCUR NATURALLY IN most problem domains—a company has a group of employees, an operating system has a collection of processes competing for processor time, and a graphics package has a number of shapes that exist on a drawing layer. For simple collections, System.Array can be effectively used to represent data groups; but for collections with more complex needs like data mapping, addition, and insertion, more advanced types are required, and the System.Collections and System.Collections.Specialized namespaces provide a number of types offering these abilities. Choosing the correct collection is important for achieving elegant and efficient code. The different collection types have varying abilities to perform certain tasks, and also have very different performance characteristics for certain activities.

The performance of various collection operations is characterized by the operation's complexity, which is expressed in "big-O" notation. An operation that is unaffected by the size of the collection, such as retrieving the collection's Length property, is a constant-time operation, and has a complexity of O(1). Operations whose performance is in proportion to the linear size of the collection are described as having O(n) complexity, and include such methods as ArrayList.ToArray and Array.IList.Contains. When choosing the appropriate collection, the complexity of the methods that will be called frequently is a major performance consideration, and the MSDN Library, which documents the complexity of most operations, should be consulted.

System.Array

The only collection implemented directly at a runtime level is System.Array, and all other collection types are implemented using Array. Arrays have a certain duality in their nature—they are both a built-in part of the runtime that can be manipulated directly by MSIL instructions such as ldlen (which retrieves the number of elements in an array), and are also a type in the Framework Library represented by Array. The duality is achieved by a runtime technique of simulating derivation from System.Array for array data types. This means that the MSIL instruction newarr System.Int32 constructs an object of type System.Int32[], which acts as if it is derived from System.Array if required to do so. The runtime and compiler vendors are the only parties permitted to derive from `Array` directly, and using a language's support for arrays is preferable to using `System.Array` directly, due to type safety and performance issues.

An array can have one or more dimensions, and can contain any managed type. The CLR supports hard-typed arrays, and this feature is made available by most high-level languages. Type safety has many advantages—errors can be detected at compile time rather than runtime, and value types avoid boxing and unboxing when moving in and out of collections. When using language-level arrays, array manipulation through the language features rather than through `System.Array` is a more direct and efficient means of manipulation. The following snippet demonstrates the two techniques for array element access:

```
Dim arr As Integer() = {1, 2, 3}
Dim i As Integer = CType(arr.GetValue(0), Integer) 'Bad - incurrs a boxing hit
Dim j As Integer = arr(0) 'Good - no performance problems
```

Rectangular vs. Jagged Arrays

The CLR has the ability to remove internal bounds checks for single-dimension arrays accessed within loops that are terminated by a check against the array's `Length` property. The following code sample demonstrates array iteration where this optimization will occur:

```
int [] arr = GetArray();
for (int ix = 0; ix < arr.Length; ++ix){
 //use arr[ix]
}
```

For multidimensional arrays, this optimization is currently not implemented as of .NET 1.x, and this makes iteration over multidimensional arrays much slower than iteration over the equivalent collection implemented using jagged arrays. Jagged arrays are simply single-dimension arrays that contain other arrays as elements. The code sample that follows illustrates the use of both jagged and rectangular creation and element access:

```
int[][] jagged = new int[][]{
 new int[] {0,1,2,3,4,5,6,7,8,9},
 new int[] {10,11,12,13,14,15,16,17,18,19}
};

int[,] rectangular = new int[,]{
 {0,1,2,3,4,5,6,7,8,9},
```

```
{10,11,12,13,14,15,16,17,18,19}
};

int jaggedElement = jagged[0][0];
int rectangularElement = rectangular [0,0];
```

The ability to avoid bounds checks when iterating over an array is a significant performance boost, particularly for numerical applications. For the test case of iterating over a three-dimensional array (10 by 10 by 2) of Int32 elements and calculating the total sum, jagged arrays are eight times faster than rectangular arrays (see Test 5.01), and similar results are obtained for arrays containing reference types (see Test 5.02).

Array Initialization

Value type array initialization in C# can be achieved in two distinct ways—inline with the array variable declaration, and through set operations on each individual array element, as shown in the following snippet:

```
//inline
int[] arrInline = new int[]{0,1,2};

//set operation per element
int[] arrPerElement = new int[3];
arrPerElement[0] = 0;
arrPerElement[1] = 1;
arrPerElement[2] = 2;
```

Both techniques result in an identical array, but are implemented differently in the compiled assembly. For a value type array that is initialized inline and has more than three elements, the C# compiler in both .NET 1.0 and .NET 1.1 generates a type named <PrivateImplementationDetails> that is added to the assembly at the root namespace level. This type contains nested value types that reference the binary data needed to initialize the array, which is stored in a .data section of the PE file. At runtime, the System.Runtime.CompilerServices.RuntimeHelpers:: InitializeArray method is called to perform a memory copy of the data referenced by the <PrivateImplementationDetails> nested structure into the array's memory location. The direct memory copy is roughly twice as fast for the initialization of a 20-by-20 element array of 64-bit integers (see Test 5.03), and array initialization syntax is generally cleaner for the inline initialization case.

VB .NET does not currently support optimized array initialization, and a VB .NET array declared inline will compile to MSIL instructions that populate each element individually.

Array Synchronization

System.Array is not thread-safe by default, which is beneficial from a performance viewpoint, as no thread locks are taken out during array access for the most common case of single-threaded access. The preferred method of implementing thread-safe operations on an Array is to lock the object reference returned by the SyncRoot property. The following snippet shows the use of the SyncRoot property for locking through the C# lock statement and explicitly through the Monitor type. The lock statement is simply a syntactic shortcut for using Monitor locking in a try-finally block, and either technique is equally valid.

```
int[] arr = new int[]{0,1,2,3};

lock(arr.SyncRoot){
    arr[0] = arr[1];
}

System.Threading.Monitor.Enter(arr.SyncRoot);
try{
    arr[2] = arr[1];
}
finally{
    System.Threading.Monitor.Exit(arr.SyncRoot);
}
```

Array does not provide a Synchronized method like the collection types in the System.Collections namespace, but ArrayList can be used instead of Array if this functionality is required. ArrayList uses an Object array internally, and for reference types, the performance difference between ArrayList and Array is not great. For value types, boxing occurs when using an ArrayList, which is a significant performance hit, and the use of an Array or a strongly typed ArrayList, which is discussed in the "System.Collections" section, is preferable.

Unsafe Array Access

The CLR supports direct access to data at arbitrary memory locations, and this can be used to directly manipulate the contents of arrays. Direct element access is quicker than the normal accessor functions, which perform bounds checking and guarantee type safety, but this direct access comes at the expense of code verification. Code that wishes to access direct memory addresses requires the

`SkipVerification` security permission, which is only granted to highly trusted code. This makes unsafe code unsuitable for assemblies that must operate in a limited trust environment, and also introduces the potential for serious software bugs. Reading and writing memory at incorrect locations can crash an application, and can also introduce security vulnerabilities that allow a malicious party to inject code into the running process.

Not all languages support unsafe array access, with VB .NET being the most prominent example. In C#, direct element access is supported through the `fixed` statement and pointers, as shown in the following snippet:

```
int[] arr = new int[]{1,2,3};
int sum = 0;
unsafe{
   fixed(int* pArr = &arr[0]){
     int* pElement = pArr;
     sum += *pElement;
     ++pElement;  //move to next element
     sum += *pElement;
     ++pElement;  //move to next element
     sum += *pElement;
   }
}
```

For primitive value types like `Int32`, which have direct MSIL accessor instructions that allow optimized manipulation, tests show that the speed of unsafe element access is very similar to normal element access methods (see Test 5.04). The real performance benefit of unsafe array access comes with non-primitive value types, which do not have the direct MSIL accessor instructions. For the test case of accessing a value type containing three `Int32` member variables, using unsafe code is almost four times quicker (see Test 5.05).

The MSDN Library ships with an unsafe code sample that uses the C# `fixed` and `unsafe` keywords to implement an "optimized" routine for copying the contents of byte arrays to other byte arrays. The "optimized" routine is twice as quick as a similar implementation using standard element access, but is 50 percent slower than simply using the built-in `Array.Copy` method (see Test 5.06). The performance problem with the unsafe copy sample is the need for multiple method calls to perform the copy, compared to the single call required with `Array.Copy`. `Array.Copy` is internally implemented in unmanaged code and accessed through the `internalcall` method attribute, allowing direct access to the array's memory. The results highlight that unsafe array access is not always the solution with the highest performance, and it is preferable to leverage existing methods in the Framework Libraries before resorting to direct memory access techniques.

The .NET memory management system is optimized for cases where memory occupied by objects is in a contiguous block. During a garbage collection, objects are moved to the beginning of the heap to fill the spaces left by objects that are no longer referenced, and this benefits performance (as discussed in Chapter 7). Pinning an object prevents it being moved during a garbage collection, and this leads to heap fragmentation, which can significantly slow allocation and collection efficiency. This means that long-term pinning of memory should generally be avoided.

The use of unsafe code has security implications, and can affect the distribution options available for an assembly. It may be necessary to provide two implementations of a particular method—one safe and one unsafe—and use conditional compilation to switch between implementations depending on the software distribution model in use. For distribution via installation programs, the assembly will be copied to the local disk, and have a high level of trust under the default security settings. For smart-client distributions, however, the permissions available to the assembly will be more restricted, and a verifiable assembly may be required, though various deployment strategies can allow assemblies to gain the required permissions to execute nonverifiable code.

System.Collections

The System.Array type exhibits the classic features of language arrays—a fixed-size, strongly typed container that supports fast lookups. A collection with these characteristics is adequate for many programming tasks, but is tedious and slow when more advanced collection characteristics are required. The System.Collections and System.Collections.Specialized namespaces contain a number of collections with more advanced and special-purpose characters that can be used in preference to Array. The most important performance consideration with using the Collections types is to choose a collection whose semantics best match the semantics of the real-world entity that they are being used to model. When programming for performance, syntactic niceties often need to be sacrificed to achieve the required speed, but in the case of collections, the opposite is true—the closer the collection comes to modeling the entity they represent, the more natural and compact the surrounding code becomes.

Table 5-1 shows the names and characteristics of the collection classes that are currently available in the Framework Library.

Table 5-1. Collection Class Characteristics

NAME	CHARACTERISTIC	TYPICAL USES	EXAMPLE
ArrayList	Similar to System.Array, but grows on demand, and supports insertion and deletion at arbitrary indexes	Used in place of Array when the final size of the collection is not known at the time the collection is declared	Storage of bytes read from a stream
BitArray	Holds a fixed-length array of bit values, and supports low-level bit operations at an array level, such as Xor	Used to store large collections of true/false values	Storage of the read-only status of all files on a disk
BitVector32	Same as BitArray, but optimized for the case where storage size is a maximum of 32 bits	Used to store a small collection of true/false values	Storage of the state of a number of Boolean or small integer member variables of a type
CollectionBase	Provides a base class for implementing a strongly typed ArrayList	Quick implementation of a reference type collection with strongly typed accessors	Employee collection with element access by index
ReadOnly CollectionBase	Same as CollectionBase, but read-only	Same as CollectionBase	Same as CollectionBase
StringCollection	An ArrayList of String objects	Same as ArrayList	Same as ArrayList
Hashtable	An associative collection class that allows keys to be mapped to values	Used when element access by an arbitrary key is more convenient than index-based access	Loosely typed Employee collection with element access by Social Security number
DictionaryBase	Provides base class for implementing a strongly typed Hashtable	Quick implementation of a reference type key-value collection with strongly typed accessors	Employee collection with element access by Social Security number

Table 5-1. Collection Class Characteristics (Continued)

NAME	CHARACTERISTIC	TYPICAL USES	EXAMPLE
NameObject-CollectionBase	Provides base class for implementing a strongly typed Hashtable keyed by String objects	Quick implementation of a reference type key-value collection with strongly typed accessors	Employee collection with element access by name
ListDictionary	Hashtable implementation optimized for small collections	Same as Hashtable	Same as Hashtable
HybridDictionary	Takes on the implementation of ListDictionary, and switches to Hashtable as collection size increases	Same as Hashtable	Same as Hashtable
StringDictionary	A Hashtable keyed by String objects	Same as Hashtable	Same as Hashtable
Queue	First-in, first-out collection	Used to store a collection of objects that are retrieved in the order that objects were placed in the collection	Storage of print jobs waiting to be sent to the printer
Stack	First-in, last-out collection	Used to store a collection of objects that are retrieved in the *reverse* order that objects were placed in the collection	Implementation of Undo functionality, where the commands of the user are stored in a stack
SortedList	Has characteristics of both Hashtables and ArrayLists, allowing by-index and by-key referencing of an element	Used to store a collection where element lookup flexibility is an important consideration, and where automatic sorting is required	Storage of a collection of words that are always alphabetically sorted

The collection classes share a number of common characteristics:

- All the collections, with the exception of BitVector32, implement the ICollection interface, which supports a Count property, synchronization information, and the ability to copy the collection to System.Array.

- All the collections, with the exception of BitVector32, implement the IEnumerable interface, which supports a consistent element enumeration pattern.

- The collections are inherently unsafe for multithreaded writes, but support multiple readers.

- Element accessor functions are loosely typed, with the exception of BitArray in the System.Collections namespace, and a number of types in the System.Collections.Specialized namespace.

- System.Array is used to implement all the collection classes, with the exception of BitVector32.

- The collections are implemented entirely in managed code.

The range of collections is limited, but provides a sufficient basis upon which to construct more specialized collection classes. For example, an STL-like multimap, which allows a single key to be mapped to multiple values, can be implemented using a Hashtable of ArrayLists. The lack of a linked list is a major omission, and future versions of the Framework Library are likely to include this. A free third-party linked list implementation can be downloaded from http://www.pixeldustindustries.com/samples.htm.

The loosely typed nature of most collection class interfaces and the use of Object arrays to store a collection's data leads to significant performance problems with value types. All insertion functions require a boxing operation, and all retrieval functions require an unboxing operation. This means that a new object is created for every insertion operation. In addition to the performance considerations, boxing can introduce some nonintuitive value type behavior, as demonstrated in the following snippet:

```
ArrayList al = new ArrayList();
int i = 0;
al.Add(i); //add i to collection
++i;   //increment i
Console.WriteLine(i);     //stack-based value
//outputs: 1
Console.WriteLine(al[0]); //heap-based value
//outputs: 0
```

Two techniques are available to combat the boxing problem: wrap the value type in a reference type, exposing the required mutator functions to allow the value type to be manipulated, or use a code generator to build a strongly typed collection class that provides the same features as the Framework Library collection types.

Wrapping value types is a simple yet tedious exercise, and is accomplished by declaring a reference type with the value types exposed as a member variable, either directly or through a property. The following code demonstrates a simple C# wrapper for Int32. In a test case, using this wrapper type is nearly four times faster than using a raw Int32 variable for ArrayList element access (see Test 5.07). The speed improvement is achieved by removing the object creation needed for every element insertion, which is what occurs in a boxing operation, and instead having a single object created for each element when the ArrayList is first populated.

```
public class IntWrapper{
  public int Int;
}
```

For maximum performance with value types in collection classes, strongly typed collections are required. To provide a strongly typed ArrayList, the base collection that the ArrayList is built upon needs to be changed from an array of objects to an array of the required value type, and strongly typed accessor methods need to be added. In addition to the performance benefits, strongly typed collections ensure that the objects stored in the collection are all of a particular type (or are objects of a type that inherits from the main type), which improves code robustness. Implementing a strongly typed ArrayList is discussed toward the end of this section.

Testing the performance of a strongly typed Int32 ArrayList against the standard ArrayList shows an order-of-magnitude increase in speed for element addition and access operations for the strongly typed version (see Test 5.08), and is about two-and-a-half times faster for element enumeration (see Test 5.09). For System.Double, a strongly typed ArrayList is six times faster than the standard ArrayList for basic element access (see Test 5.10), and about three times faster for enumeration (see Test 5.11). It is worth emphasizing that these large performance improvements are mostly due to the elimination of boxing that occurs with the standard ArrayList type, and reference type elements, which do not require boxing, will not experience the same dramatic improvements for strongly typed collections. For a strongly typed String ArrayList, the performance improvements are 17 percent for basic access (see Test 5.12), and enumeration is twice as fast (see Test 5.13).

The lack of generics in the CLR makes implementing a strongly typed collection tedious. There is no universal method for implementing a strongly typed collection class that can be handled entirely by language compilers, and third-party code generation tools or language-specific cut-and-paste operations are required. For C#, type aliases, available through the using directive, make the cut-and-paste operation relatively clean, as the entire collection can be written in terms of the type alias, which is then resolved at compile time. The only type-specific information that needs to be added to the file is the type name in a using statement, and the type-specific collection name. The following code example demonstrates this technique:

```
using T = System.Int32;

namespace StronglyTyped.Int32{
[Serializable]
public class Int32Collection : IList, ICollection, IEnumerable, ICloneable {
  //members
  private T[] _data;
  private int _size;
  internal int _version;
  private static int _defaultCapacity = 16;

  //constructors
  public Collection() {
    _data = new T[_defaultCapacity];
  }
  //rest of class implementation
```

For languages that lack type aliases, a code generation tool is the best option. Visual Studio .NET allows code generation tools to be integrated with the build event, which can be used to simulate generics. Building the tools that implement this technique with Visual Studio takes a lot of effort, but thankfully others have done the hard work, and tools like the freeware CodeSmith application (available at http://www.ericjsmith.net/codesmith/) allow the compile-time generation technique to be applied quite simply.

Enumeration

The IEnumerable interface indicates a type containing child elements that can be sequentially accessed. The IEnumerable.GetEnumerator method returns a type implementing the IEnumerator interface, which supports forward scrolling (MoveNext), moving to the beginning of the collection (Reset), and retrieving the value at the current location (Current).

Client code does not typically deal with the enumeration interfaces directly. Higher-level languages can expose keywords that compile to IEnumerable and IEnumerator calls at an MSIL level, such as the C# foreach statement and the

VB .NET For Each . . . Next statement. These statements retrieve an enumerator object, and call the GetNext method followed by the Current property during each loop cycle. These statements eliminate off-by-one iteration bugs that can occur when a collection is iterated over using a loop counter and indexers, but do have some runtime cost. In some cases, such as simple array enumeration, a language compiler can actually generate the equivalent of a for loop when a construct like foreach is used, though this happens entirely under the covers, and is an optimization that comes with no effort on the part of the developer.

There are three areas where the performance of enumerators can suffer compared to manually coded loops and indexer-based element access:

- The creation of the enumerator object

- The cost of maintaining synchronization with the underlying collection

- The indirection caused by the increment and retrieval functions

The cost of the enumerator's creation and synchronization with the collection is dependent upon how the enumerator is implemented. For small collections, it is most efficient to simply copy the contents of the collection to a new collection owned by the enumerator, and return values from this private collection. For large collections, the extra memory usage and time required to copy the full collection is prohibitive, and the enumerator simply maintains a reference to the original collection. To deal with the possibility that the collection will be modified while it is being enumerated, a member variable that tracks the collection's version number is maintained by both the collection and the enumerator. Mutating methods of the collection increment the version member number, which the enumerator compares against its copy of the version number on MoveNext calls. If the two numbers are different, an exception is thrown.

For copy-on-creation enumerators, creation will have some performance cost, while for enumerators that use collection references, maintaining version synchronization with the underlying collection will have a performance impact.

All System.Collections and System.Collections.Specialized enumerators keep a collection reference rather than keep an independent copy of the collection, making the enumerator cheap to create, but slower during iteration. Interestingly, this is also the case with System.Collections.Specialized. ListDictionary, which is optimized for small collections.

For the System.Array type, the compiler is free to ignore the enumeration classes altogether, and generate identical code to the explicit loop counter case. The reason that an Array can use this optimization is that it is guaranteed to be a fixed size. The Array enumerator does not maintain a version member variable because of the fixed-size guarantee.

To quantify the performance impact of using an enumerator, each element in a collection containing every word from Tolstoy's *War and Peace* is visited to determine the length of the string stored in that element, giving a count of the total number of nonwhitespace characters in the text. With an Array as the collection, using an enumerator is actually 5 percent quicker than a for loop (see Test 5.14), but for an ArrayList, the enumerator is 120 percent slower than the for loop (see Test 5.15), highlighting the cost of needing to check the underlying collection version number for every loop.

One area in which the performance of enumerators can have a strong performance impact is value type enumeration. The signature for the get_Current method of IEnumerator returns an Object reference, which means that value types have to be boxed to an Object, and then unboxed back to the original value type, causing a significant performance hit. The boxing hit can be eliminated by adding a new method to the IEnumerable-implementing type called GetEnumerator. The GetEnumerator method returns an object reference to a strongly typed enumerator. To accurately implement the IEnumerable interface, a method that returns an IEnumerator reference must be available, and this can be achieved through an explicit interface implementation, as shown here:

```
IEnumerator IEnumerable.GetEnumerator() {
 return new Enumerator(this);
}

public Enumerator GetEnumerator() {
 return new Enumerator(this);
}
```

On the IEnumerator-implementing type, a similar technique can be used for the Current property, with a strongly typed Current method and an explicit interface implementation of the IEnumerator.Current property. The following example shows part of a strongly typed integer enumerator:

```
public int Current {
 get {
  return curr;
  }
}

object IEnumerator.Current {
 get {
  return Current;
}
```

Exposing these additional methods allows language-level statements, like the C# `foreach` statement, to iterate over a value type collection without any boxing hits. As discussed in the "System.Collections" section, avoiding boxing is a significant performance advantage.

Loop Termination

Most access of collection elements outside unsafe code blocks is checked to ensure that the bounds of the collection are not exceeded. When an attempt is made to access an element beyond the range of the collection, an `IndexOutOfRangeException` is thrown. For large collections, the cost of checking the termination condition for each loop becomes greater than simply iterating until the internal bounds checks through an `IndexOutOfRangeException`. This is not the case for `Array`, where the internal bounds checks can be optimized away; but for other large collections, iteration until exception may deliver a minor performance win. In the test case of iterating over each element of a ten-million-member `ArrayList`, checking the termination condition on each loop is 23 percent slower than running until an exception occurs (see Test 5.16). Running until an exception occurs is a minor optimization, and more likely to hurt performance than benefit it. It should be avoided in most circumstances.

Loop Invariants

It has long been popular practice to remove the function call that retrieves the collection size from the loop termination check, and replace the function call with a variable that has been assigned the collection's size. The JIT compiler will do this automatically, and no performance gain results from doing it manually. The actual machine code executed will be essentially identical in both cases, and benchmarking confirms no performance difference (see Test 5.17).

Collection Synchronization

As with `Array`, collection classes in the `System.Collections` namespace implement the `System.Collections.ICollection` interface, which exposes the `SyncRoot` property. Client code that wishes to take out a synchronization lock on a collection should lock the object reference returned from `SyncRoot` property, rather than lock the higher-level collection object directly. The rationale behind the `SyncRoot` property is that many collections are composed of lower-level collections, and locking the higher-level object may be insufficient to guarantee thread safety if the collection class exposes functionality that makes it possible to retrieve a reference to the underlying collection data. For example, a `Company` type may implement the ICollection interface to allow its contained Employee objects to be manipulated by generic functions that operate on the ICollection interface. In the absence of SyncRoot, it would be unclear which object reference should be locked to prevent concurrent access to the Employees collection. If one thread locked the Employee collection reference, and another locked the Company reference, data corruption caused by simultaneous updates could occur. The SyncRoot property thus provides a single location for all clients attempting to lock an object.

The use of SyncRoot locking can become tedious to code for each operation on a collection. To support guaranteed thread-safe operations, all collection classes within the System.Collections namespace, with the exception of BitArray, provide a static Synchronized method that takes a reference to the collection class, and returns a new reference that is guaranteed to be thread-safe for all operations. The Synchronized wrapper is implemented by a private nested type that takes out a Monitor lock on the parent object's SyncRoot, and then forwards the call through to the parent, which is the original object that was passed into the Synchronized method. Once the parent method has returned, the Monitor lock is released.

Using the Synchronized wrapper makes thread-safe operations easy and robust, but does come at some cost. There is a trade-off between concurrency and raw speed in any multithreaded system. Taking out a lock has some expense, so the fewer locks that need to be taken out, the faster that system will run. Holding a lock too long can starve other threads of resources, and decrease the overall throughput of a system. In some situations, the lock granularity of the Synchronized wrapper will not be optimum, and manual lock management will deliver better performance. Consider the case where an ArrayList of integers requires each element to be incremented by one. The value of each element has to be retrieved, incremented, and returned to the ArrayList. The following snippet shows three test cases that demonstrate an explicit lock per loop, a single explicit lock for all data modification, and the use of the Synchronized wrapper, respectively:

```
public void ExplicitLockPerLoop(int numberIterations){
  for(int i = 0; i < numberIterations; ++i){
    System.Threading.Monitor.Enter(data.SyncRoot);
    try{
      data[i] = (int)data[i] + 1;
    }
    finally{
      System.Threading.Monitor.Exit(data.SyncRoot);
    }
  }
}
```

```
public void ExplicitLock(int numberIterations){
  System.Threading.Monitor.Enter(data.SyncRoot);
  try{
    for(int i = 0; i < numberIterations; ++i){
      data[i] = (int)data[i] + 1;
    }
  }
  finally{
    System.Threading.Monitor.Exit(data.SyncRoot);
  }
}

public void SynchronizedAL(int numberIterations){
  ArrayList synch = ArrayList.Synchronized(data);
  for(int i = 0; i < numberIterations; ++i){
    synch[i] = (int)synch[i] + 1;
  }
}
```

If the Synchronized wrapper is used, the exercise will involve two locks being taken out for each element. It is more efficient to lock the collection once per element, and also more correct, as another thread cannot modify the contents of the element between a read and a write operation, which is known as a *race condition*. The following code block breaks down the synchronized wrapper test case, and illustrates where the two separate locks are taken out:

```
//a lock is taken out and released here
synch[i] =
//the next statement also acquires and releases a lock
//another thread can read or write to the element between lock acquisitions
(int)synch[i] + 1;
```

For the test case of a one-million-element array, it is 16 percent quicker to use explicit array locking rather than relying on a Synchronized wrapper. If a lock is held for the entire operation, speed is increased 35 percent, but holding a lock this long could hurt the overall system performance (see Test 5.18). Chapter 10 presents a more detailed discussion on the locking granularity.

Hashcodes and IHashCodeProvider

A hash table is composed of buckets that hold the collection's elements, and the bucket that holds a particular element is located by using the hash code of the key object. When a hash table is constructed, it has a certain number of buckets, and each bucket is used to store values with a particular range of hash codes. To deal with multiple objects being assigned to the same hash table bucket, a hash table can use two techniques—linked lists or double hashing. For the *linked list implementation,* each bucket maintains a linked list of values, and locating a particular object is achieved by identifying the correct bucket based on the hash code, and then navigating the linked list until the object is located. The alternative implementation, known as *double hashing,* is to store a single value per bucket, and to use a secondary hashing function to relocate elements when a collision occurs. The simplest relocation method is to simply try the surrounding buckets until a vacant bucket is located, but this implementation leads to bunching. To prevent this bunching, most relocation techniques use a value determined by a secondary hashing function, which may involve bitshifts, modulus operations, and arithmetic operations on the initial hash, to move a certain distance away from the occupied bucket. If the second bucket is full, another step is taken in an attempt to find an empty bucket, and this process is repeated. Figure 5-1 illustrates the bucket location strategy used in double hashing. The current implementation of System.Collections.Hashtable uses a double hash.

In either implementation, a stage will come when the existing bucket array is too full to be effective. A new bucket array needs to be created, and all the values rehashed and placed in new buckets. This process is expensive, and can lead to severe performance problems if it occurs too often. Avoiding bucket reallocation can be achieved in two ways—nominating an appropriate initial capacity and choosing a load factor that prevents too frequent reallocation. The .NET 1.x implementation of Hashtable uses the load factor to determine when a reallocation is necessary, with a load factor of 0.5 meaning that a reallocation occurs when half the buckets are full. The default load factor of 1.0 means that all buckets will be filled before a reallocation occurs.

The initial load factor that Hashtable uses can be specified through one of the constructor overloads. The default value provides a reasonable trade-off between memory usage and element access speed, but if profiling of an application indicates that element access speed is overly slow, experimenting with different initial load factors can bring significant performance gains. Be aware that a lower load factor will cause more frequent allocations, and could actually hurt lookup speed if memory usage becomes excessive and page faults become frequent.

The evenness of a hash code distribution has a massive effect on the performance of hash tables. An even distribution of hash codes for key objects will ensure that the secondary hashing function is not used an excessive number of times during key location. To illustrate how dramatically the evenness of a hash code distribution can affect performance, each word from *War and Peace* is used as a key in a hash table. The first implementation uses the built-in hash code for System.String, the second implementation uses the modulus of 100 of the original hash code to simulate a bunched hash code implementation, and the third implementation uses a constant value of 1. The modulus 100 hash code is 180 times slower than the original hash code implementation, and the constant hash code is 4300 times slower (see Test 5.19). These figures dramatically illustrate how important a well-distributed hash code is to the performance of hash table.

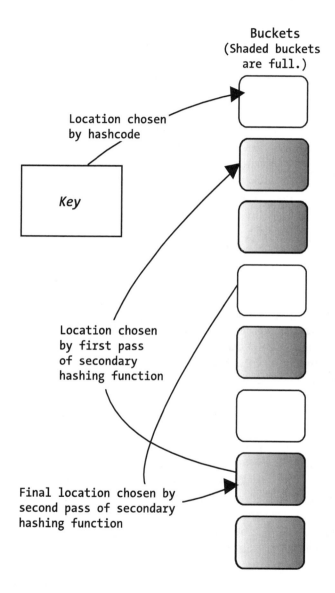

Figure 5-1. Hashtable bucket location using double hashing

To inspect the distribution produced by a type's GetHashCode method, an effective technique is to populate a collection of objects with representative data, dump the hash codes of each object to Trace.WriteLine, and plot the result in Excel. The chart in Figure 5-2 shows System.String's hash code distribution for the first 3000 unique words of *War and Peace*, with the hash code of words on the y-axis and the position of words in the text on the x-axis. It is evident that a reasonable distribution between System.Int32.MinValue and System.Int32.MaxValue has been achieved, though some bunching around 2 * 10^8 and 2 * 10^9 is evident.

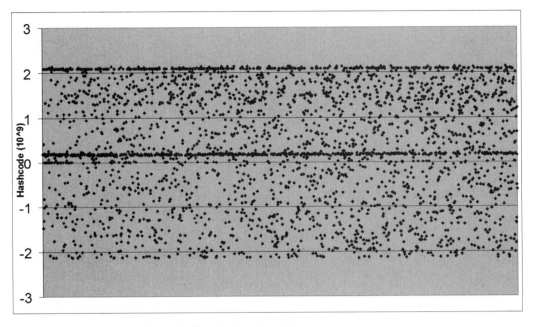

Figure 5-2. Example hash code distribution for String

If a particular type has a poor hash code distribution, there are three options for remedying the problem:

- Use a different type.

- Derive from the original types and override GetHashCode.

- Pass an object implementing IHashCodeProvider to the Hashtable constructor.

The second and third options are only slight variations on the same theme, and typically involve passing the member variables and properties of the key object through some mathematical formula to achieve a better hash code calculation than the original type. Techniques for achieving good hash code distributions are covered in Chapter 3. The following snippet shows the use of the second and third techniques:

```
'type with very poor hash code
Class PoorHashCode
```

```vbnet
        Public Sub New(ByVal i As Integer, ByVal j As Single)
            Me.I = i
            Me.J = j
        End Sub
        Public Overloads Overrides Function Equals(ByVal obj As Object) As Boolean
            Return True
        End Function
        Public Overrides Function GetHashCode() As Integer
            Return 1
        End Function
        Public ReadOnly I As Integer
        Public ReadOnly J As Single
    End Class


    'fix PoorHashCode by inheritance
    Class HashCodeFixByInheritance
        Inherits PoorHashCode
        Public Sub New(ByVal i As Integer, ByVal j As Single)
            MyBase.New(i, j)
        End Subs
        Public Overrides Function GetHashCode() As Integer
            Return I.GetHashCode() Xor J.GetHashCode()
        End Function
    End Class


    'fix PoorHashCode by interface
    Class HashCodeFixByInterface
        Implements IHashCodeProvider
        Public Function GetHashCode1(ByVal obj As Object) As Integer _
          Implements System.Collections.IHashCodeProvider.GetHashCode
            If obj.GetType() Is GetType(PoorHashCode) Then
                Dim phc As PoorHashCode = CType(obj, PoorHashCode)
                Return phc.I.GetHashCode() Xor phc.J.GetHashCode()
            End If
            Return obj.GetHashCode()
        End Function
    End Class


    'use IHashCodeProvider solution
    Module Mod1
        Dim hcp As New HashCodeFixByInterface
        Dim ht As System.Collections.Hashtable =
          New System.Collections.Hashtable(hcp, Nothing)
    End Module
```

Stack Allocation

Arrays and the other collection classes are the preferred method of storing large sets of data, but for small pieces of data, a collection class located on the run-time heap does not deliver the optimum performance. For small collections of data that only need to be used locally within a method, stack allocation offers better performance than heap allocation. The CLR provides the ability to allocate memory on the call stack with the localloc MSIL instruction, and this facility is exposed in a number of languages that target the CLR. In C#, the stack-alloc keyword can by used to allocate data types like Byte and Int32 on the call stack, and the allocated memory can be accessed and modified via pointers and unsafe code blocks. The following code snippet demonstrates the use of a stack-allocated memory block:

```
unsafe{
  const int memBlockSize = 3;
  int* pInt = stackalloc int[memBlockSize];
  for (int ix = 0; ix < memBlockSize; ++ix)
    pInt[ix] = ix;
  int sum = *pInt++;
  sum += *pInt++;
  sum += *pInt++;
}
```

NOTE VB .NET does not support unsafe code blocks, nor does it expose a keyword to explicitly allocate stack memory, and hence stack allocation techniques cannot be used with VB .NET.

The usefulness of stack-allocated memory is limited—it cannot be passed to methods that expect Array parameters, and there is very limited support for pointer types with the Framework Library. One particular area where stack-allocated memory does become useful is with unmanaged code interoperability, where a preallocated memory block needs to be passed to unmanaged code for population. A stack-allocated byte array can be used for this purpose, and various methods with the System.Runtime.InteropServices.Marshal type can be used to convert the byte array to a managed object or structure.

Like other unsafe code techniques, the use of stack-allocated memory is not verifiably type-safe, and requires a high level of trust to run. Passing stack-allocated memory to unmanaged functions also increases the possibility of the dangerous buffer overrun vulnerability, and care needs to be taken to verify data sources that are not under the immediate control of the method, and to avoid dangerous unmanaged functions that do not allow the dimensions of memory blocks to be specified.

To quantify the performance improvement of stack-allocated memory, a 50-element integer collection is defined on either the stack or the runtime heap, the collection is populated, and then each element is retrieved from the collection. The stack-allocated collection is five times faster than its heap-allocated counterpart (see Test 5.20).

Conclusion

Choosing the correct collection type to store data in is critical for achieving optimum performance. The speed that different collections can insert, append, and search data varies considerably, and a poor collection choice can result in a solution that has spectacularly poor performance. The relative performance cost of collection operations is determined by their complexity, and for frequently utilized methods, complexity is an important consideration.

Value type collections are susceptible to poor performance due to boxing. If the benefits that a specialized collection offers are only marginally better than a standard array, and performance is an important design goal, standard arrays should be employed. If the specialized collection is required, and boxing causes an unacceptable performance problem, a strongly typed collection can be used to eliminate the problem. Code generators make the implementation of strongly typed collections much easier and less error prone than cut-and-paste collection generation.

CHAPTER 6

Language Specifics

PERFORMANCE IS ONE OF THE most controversial aspects of software systems, and the performance of various languages is one of the most controversial aspects of performance. Suggestions that a particular language is slower than another often result in passionate debates that can rapidly degenerate into personal insults, with each language apostle proudly preaching the obvious superiority of his or her chosen tool. This chapter attempts to discuss the various performance aspects of the different .NET languages in a dispassionate and balanced manner, and it is worth stating at the outset that performance is a small factor when choosing a language to produce code targeted for CLR execution.

The comparative speed of various .NET languages is an issue that confuses many. The root of the confusion is that all languages that target the CLR compile down to Microsoft Intermediate Language (MSIL), which is then JIT-compiled to native code prior to execution. The common intermediate representation leads to the reasonable conclusion that all languages should have identical performance characteristics. The "common MSIL" argument is countered by the marketing spin put on languages that have a C heritage like Managed C++ and C#, which have "high-performance" features like unsafe code and unchecked arithmetic blocks. In contrast, Visual Basic .NET has legacy features like unstructured error handling and the ability to avoid strong typing that raises obvious performance questions.

The truth lies somewhere between the two positions. The "common MSIL" argument is correct as far as it goes, but the whole point of having multiple languages is that they offer different ways to accomplish the same task, and syntactic differences make up a small proportion of the features that differentiate a language. If every language was simply "C# with different syntax," the .NET platform would be in the same situation as the Java platform, in that the Java language is clearly dominant, and other languages that produce Java byte code are more an academic exercise than a legitimate commercial offering.

The "language features make me quicker" argument is also true to an extent, but the argument misses the bigger picture. To appreciate the bigger picture, it is necessary to consider what makes up a language, and how traditional compiler and language packages like Visual Basic 6 are different from .NET-targeted languages like Visual Basic .NET. A compiler package has two essential elements— a language with a set of syntax rules that define how functions, modules, and classes are built and accessed, and a set of libraries that perform certain common tasks, like displaying a message box to the user, or calculating the square root of a number. The syntax rules that define a language have no real performance consequences—a compiler can convert the high-level language statements into a fast or slow set of machine instructions, depending on the compiler's optimizing capabilities. It is the runtime libraries that are the dominant influence on the speed of an application built by a particular language.

The .NET Framework changes the situation that existed with previous Visual Studio releases by shipping a huge runtime library that is accessible from all languages. This drastically reduces the need for a compiler to ship with a large runtime library, and libraries that do ship are usually only needed to preserve backwards capabilities with previous unmanaged versions of a compiler or to offer shortcut methods relevant to a particular language. If code is a written in a language like Visual Basic without using the legacy features that exist to support Visual Basic 6 code, performance will be practically identical to a new language like C#.

Not all languages expose CLR features equally, and only one language allows absolute control over the MSIL produced, and that language is IL itself. The exposure by C# of performance features like unsafe code (discussed in Chapters 5 and 13) does allow performance wins in some specific scenarios, just as the MC++ features like manual boxing control offer some performance advantages over C#. For most applications, use of these special-purpose features will not make any noticeable difference to the performance of an application, particularly for a Web-based distributed application, where network round-trips between the application tiers are orders-of-magnitude more significant than a boxing operation.

For special-purpose applications like numerical modelling, certain language features may make a noticeable difference in the speed of an application. An extra 50 machine instructions multiplied by billions of numeric calculations does have a noticeable effect, but even for applications like this, the low cost of high-performance hardware means that the optimal solution may be to develop in the preferred language of the developer, and use the money saved on development to add extra hardware to the deployment environment.

The ability to dynamically produce and execute code that takes advantage of the most obscure or specialized CLR feature is a great equalizer amongst all languages that target .NET. This ability, which is offered through types in the `System.Reflection.Emit` namespace, allows special-purpose code to be injected where required in a running application. This functionality is not required in many situations, and some performance and working set bloat is associated with using it; but by dropping into dynamically generated MSIL, any language can claim with some truth that it can produce identical performance to that produced by any other compiler.

When analyzing language-specific performance, it is also worth considering the reduced importance of the language compiler under .NET when compared to native language compilers. The traditional role of a compiler is to convert high-level statements to machine code. Instead of performing an exact translation, an optimizing compiler performs certain modifications to the flow of one or more statements to produce machine instructions that have the same end result as the direct translation, but run faster. The unmanaged Microsoft C++ compiler is an incredibly powerful back-end compiler that sets the benchmark for producing high-performance Windows applications. In the unmanaged world, compiler optimizations still play a role in producing high-performance code, but the MSIL layer in .NET means many of the traditional compiler optimizations are no longer relevant. MSIL is a relatively high-level language, and is much higher level than assembly languages like the x86 instruction set.

The high-level nature of MSIL means that the JIT compiler now does much of the optimization work traditionally done when a high-level language is compiled. The JIT compiler is common to all languages, and this plays a great leveling role in the performance of code produced by all .NET languages.

Visual Basic .NET

After COBOL, VB is probably the world's most maligned language. A significant portion of the criticism has been unfair and irrelevant, and, at the end of the day, any language is simply a tool for producing software that meets the customer's requirements. If a developer can fulfil this requirement in VB, changing languages to a "better" alternative makes no sense. The performance criticism of previous VB versions was founded on two main areas: Language limitations prevented or hindered low-level access to the operating system, and the language runtime was slow, did not support performance-related technologies like multithreading, and was encumbered with significant amounts of legacy code.

With VB .NET, the old runtime is entirely gone, and a combination of library and language enhancements gives VB much greater flexibility and power. These enhancements mean that VB has the ability to produce code that is just as efficient and fast as any other language that targets the CLR. The difficulty in exercising this ability is the contentious point. Unlike C#, which has no backwards-compatibility requirements, VB maintains a degree of backwards compatibility with previous VB versions. This means that language features in VB have semantics that do not necessarily match those of the Framework Library and CLR, and VB code may need a conversion layer between the language and the CLR.

Backwards-compatibility support comes in two forms—directly from the compiler, and indirectly through a compatibility assembly called `Microsoft.VisualBasic.Compatibility.dll` and a language assembly called `Microsoft.VisualBasic.dll`. The `Microsoft.VisualBasic.Compatibility` assembly contains visual types like `FileListBox` that were available in Visual Basic 6, and types to support `WebClasses`, which are a Web technology superceded by ASP.NET. `Microsoft.VisualBasic.Compatibility` ensures that Visual Basic applications ported from previous unmanaged compiler versions can compile and run with minimal code modifications. In contrast, `Microsoft.VisualBasic` implements the core VB .NET language features that have no direct CLR support, such as string reversal and basic financial functionality.

There is no command-line switch that can instruct the VB compiler to turn all language-compatibility features off, and in a sense, there is little point in using Visual Basic in this mode. Compiler switches, which are discussed further in following sections, can disable some language features that negatively impact performance; but to catch all language-compatibility features, a third-party code inspection tool would be required. A number of tool vendors ship code inspection utilities that have built-in code validation rules, and most allow custom rules to be added. These products can be used to ensure that VB code is programmed explicitly against the Framework Libraries and avoid any potential performance hits, though organizations that feel it is necessary to go to such efforts should probably consider whether VB .NET is the correct language for their needs.

Strings

String equality is an example of backwards compatibility handled through the `Microsoft.VisualBasic` assembly. String equality in the VB language is defined differently from the `System.String` definition, particularly in regard to the handling of null strings. Because of this difference, VB .NET code that does not explicitly program against `System.String` results in the generation of calls to methods within `Microsoft.VisualBasic`. The performance cost of these calls is not huge, but if the calls are made repeatedly, performance can become noticeably slower, as discussed in Chapter 4.

To avoid calls to the `Microsoft.VisualBasic` assembly, ensure that Framework Library types are explicitly used in code, rather than relying on the compiler to perform the mapping for you. Fastidiously avoiding generation of calls to `Microsoft.VisualBasic` is not necessary, and in many occasions the convenience of the call will outweigh the performance impact. It is sufficient to be conscious of the fact that calls to the language assembly may have an impact, and avoid language functions in performance-critical code blocks.

The following code snippet shows the use of VB language functionality and .NET Framework functionality to achieve the same result:

```
Dim str1 As String = "abc"
Dim str2 As String = "def"

'call to Microsoft.VisualBasic.CompilerServices.StringType::StrCmp
If str1 = str2 Then
    'call to Microsoft.VisualBasic.Interaction::MsgBox
    MsgBox("Strings are equal")
End If
```

```
If String.Equals(str1, str2) Then
    MessageBox.Show("Strings are equal")
End If
```

Error Handling

Error handling is an area of Visual Basic that has changed markedly with the introduction of VB .NET. Classic VB has an unstructured error handling model that uses On Error GoTo and On Error Resume Next statements to move execution control around a method. VB .NET introduces a new structured error handling model that uses exception and try-catch blocks to handle errors detected at run-time.

On Error Resume Next and On Error GoTo support is an example of VB .NET functionality that is handled directly at the compiler. When On Error Resume Next is used, the compiler emits MSIL instructions that keep track of the logical VB statement that is executing, and, when an exception occurs, the exception is cleared, and control is transferred to the next logical statement. Chapter 8 presents a test case on the performance impact of On Error Resume Next error handling that shows a five-fold performance advantage for exception-based error handling over On Error Resume Next.

While On Error Resume Next represents a reasonably loose error handling strategy that is quite different from the exception-based model offered by the CLR, On Error GoTo is often used to implement a semistructured error handling pattern that is very similar to the exception-based model, and VB programmers who have used On Error GoTo to provide a per-method error handling code block can easily migrate to the more efficient exception-based model. Filtered exception blocks, which are exposed through the Catch When statement, allow structured exception handling to provide identical functionality to that achieved with On Error GoTo in some cases. The following code block shows two VB .NET methods, with the first using unstructured exception handling and the second using structured exception handling. The first method will cause the compiler to emit complex MSIL instructions to support the GoTo execution control, whereas the second method will use standard CLR exception-based error handling, and call methods in the Microsoft.VisualBasic assembly to convert an Exception object to the equivalent VB Err object if an exception is actually thrown.

```
    Public Sub ErrHandler()
        On Error GoTo ErrHdlr
        Dim i As Int32 = 1
        Exit Sub
ErrHdlr:
        If Err.Number = 5 Then
```

```
                'deal with type mismatch
        End If
    End Sub


    Public Sub ExceptionBased()
        Try
            Dim i As Int32 = 1
        Catch When Err.Number = 5
            'deal with type mismatch
        End Try
    End Sub
```

Boolean Logic

Previous versions of Visual Basic did not use short-circuit evaluation of Boolean statements, and all conditions in a Boolean statement were evaluated even if partial evaluation could allow the check to occur correctly in a particular case. Early beta versions of VB .NET changed the behavior of the And and Or statements so that short-circuit evaluation was used; loud protests from elements of the Visual Basic community who argued the change would cause bugs in ported code that relied on full evaluation resulted in Microsoft reversing the changes.

Short-circuit evaluation can be achieved with nested If statements, but this technique often results in excessively indented methods; in recognition of the need for a simple technique to employ short-circuit evaluation, two new keywords, AndAlso and OrElse, were introduced. All new code written in VB .NET should take advantage of these new keywords to achieve better performance, and ported code that relies on full evaluation should be rewritten. Tacking a method onto the end of a Boolean statement to perform some action based on the state of previous conditions in the statement is ugly code, and a bug waiting to happen. Calls to action-performing methods belong in the body of conditional statements, not in the Boolean statement that guards the block.

The following code sample shows an extreme example of the performance gains possible with short-circuit evaluation. While performance gains like this will not be typical in a real-world system, short-circuit evaluation takes very little extra effort to implement, and the performance benefits that it brings come essentially for free.

```
Public Sub VBLogic()
    Dim b1 As Boolean = False

    'test both conditions. ~10s to execute.
    If b1 And SlowEval() Then
```

```
            Console.WriteLine("Both true")
        Else
            Console.WriteLine("At least one condition false")
        End If


        'short circuit eval if b1 is false. very quick to execute.
        If b1 AndAlso SlowEval() Then
            Console.WriteLine("Both true")
        Else
            Console.WriteLine("At least one condition false")
        End If


        'test both condition. ~10s to execute.
        If Not b1 Or Not SlowEval() Then
            Console.WriteLine("At least one condition false")
        Else
            Console.WriteLine("Both true")
        End If


        'short circuit. very quick to execute.
        If Not b1 OrElse Not SlowEval() Then
            Console.WriteLine("At least one condition false")
        Else
            Console.WriteLine("Both true")
        End If

End Sub

Public Function SlowEval() As Boolean
    'simulate slow method
    System.Threading.Thread.CurrentThread.Sleep(10000)
    Return True
End Function
```

Arrays and Collections

VB .NET does not support the optimized array initialization of copying an array's initial state for a raw memory block stored in the binary file's metadata that is used by C#. For most applications, array initialization speed is not a significant concern, but for numerical applications that may be using large fixed arrays to represent that initial state of a complex system, the performance difference could become noticeable. Chapter 5 presents performance benchmarks that analyze the performance advantage of optimized array initialization. .NET is not a platform optimized for numerical modeling, so VB .NET's use of inline element loading is unlikely to be a large concern.

The ReDim and ReDim Preserve functionality offered by VB .NET does not have any intrinsic performance problems. ReDim simply declares a new array and discards the reference to the old array, which is a practice that would be acceptable in any language. ReDim Preserve performs a copy of the old array contents prior to releasing the reference, but this is the same technique used by ArrayList during a reallocation, and is not a performance problem if used wisely. Performance issues do arise if ReDim Preserve is used to naively increment the size of an array a few elements at a time, and this practice is used frequently. It is much more efficient to grow an array by large chunks and to keep track of the elements that are actually in use, rather than to have an array that is precisely the correct length at a given time, but which needs to be redimensioned frequently. ArrayList provides the same functionality that ReDim Preserve offers, and growth is managed automatically to achieve the best balance between reallocation cost and memory usage. VB .NET developers should use ArrayList as a preference to ReDim Preserve.

The Microsoft.VisualBasic.Collection type is a hybrid collection that offers a one-size-fits-all store of objects that can be stored and accessed by index or key. The .NET 1.x Collection type uses a Hashtable for internal storage, but also supports insertion of elements at random positions in the collection based on optional Before and After parameters. The arbitrary ordering functionality offered by Collection imparts a significant cost, even if it is not used, and for the test case of adding 100,000 integer keys mapped to their ToString equivalent, the direct use of Hashtable is seven times faster (see Test 6.01).

When Collection is used like an ArrayList, the performance is abysmal. ArrayList-like behavior is achieved by keying elements against a new instance of System.Object, which imparts a significant memory hit, and a massive performance hit. For the test case of adding 100,000 integers to a collection, then retrieving them and calculating the cumulative sum, Collection is 17,700 times slower than ArrayList (see Test 6.02). This performance difference is obviously very significant for nearly all types of applications, and Collection should generally be avoided unless the arbitrary ordering capability is absolutely required. The following snippet shows the similarity in syntax between ArrayList and Collection:

```
Dim i As Integer

Dim c As Collection = New Collection
c.Add(1)
c.Add(2)
c.Add(3)
For Each i In c
```

```
    Console.WriteLine(i)
Next

Dim al As ArrayList = New ArrayList
al.Add(1)
al.Add(2)
al.Add(3)
For Each i In al
    Console.WriteLine(i)
Next
```

Late Binding

Late bound function calls are legal in VB .NET when `Option Strict Off` is included at the beginning of a source file, or the `/optionstrict` compiler command-line option is not set. The VB .NET compiler will attempt to use early binding if sufficient type information is available, even if `Option Strict Off` is nominated, but will silently revert to late bound method invocation if call binding cannot be determined at compile time, as demonstrated in the following VB .NET sample:

```
Option Strict Off

Module LateBound
    Public Sub Late()
        Dim s As String = "123"
        Dim obj = s.Substring(2) 'early bound call
        Dim j As Int32 = obj.Length 'late bound call
    End Sub
End Module
```

Late binding is a situation where the performance cost of the VB .NET feature is not small. The performance of late bound function calls, which is handled through the `Microsoft.VisualBasic` assembly, is over three orders of magnitude slower than making the call directly for the test case of extracting the length of an `ArrayList` (see Test 6.03). While this massive performance decline is easy to avoid with compiler options, ported code can be particularly vulnerable to performance problems like this.

Optional Parameters

Optional parameters are not supported by the CLR, and are simulated using
`.param` statements that can be included with the metadata of a method. This
allows a default value to be associated with a particular parameter, but the use of
`.param` defaults is left entirely to the discretion of the compiler. Partition II of the
ECMA specification notes that "the CLI attaches no semantic whatsoever to
these values—it is entirely up to compilers to implement any semantic they wish
(e.g., so-called default argument values)."

Default parameters are resolved at compile time, so regardless of the theo-
retical arguments for and against default parameters, they impart no
performance impact.

Low-Level Execution Control

The lack of features offered by VB for low-level execution control is still a valid
concern in VB .NET, but, when compared with VB 6, the difference between its
C-family rivals has shrunk dramatically, and low-level control of execution is less
relevant with the CLR. The lack of support for unsafe code in VB is often cited as
a performance issue, but in the overall scheme of language features, unsafe code
is not an overwhelmingly important component. Types within the
`System.Runtime.InteropServices` namespace, particularly the `Marshal` class, which
offers a wide range of static methods that allow direct memory manipulation,
partially compensate for the lack of language support for unsafe constructs.

The lack of language support for switching between checked and unchecked
integer operations can be overcome by separating the code with the different
overflow checking requirements into different modules or assemblies, and compiling the code that does not require checking with the `/removeintchecks`
compiler switch turned on. In Visual Studio .NET, checking the "Remove integer
overflow checks" checkbox on the Optimizations Configuration Properties page
of the Project Properties dialog box results in `/removeintchecks` being set for
future compilations. Multiple-module assemblies are currently cumbersome to
use due to lack of Visual Studio support, but do not impose any significant performance penalties.

VB offers the ability to produce .NET code that runs just as fast as any other
language, but it tends to take more effort to produce this high-performance
code, and there are a number of potential pitfalls on the way. For devotees of the
language, these pitfalls are compensated by familiar syntax and language capabilities like easy event consumption and more flexible error handling. For
programmers with a VB background, VB .NET is usually the easiest migration
path to .NET, but for those who do not have a VB background, languages without
compatibility issues are a better option.

Managed C++

One of the great criticisms of C++ has always been that the language and its accompanying libraries offer many different ways to accomplish the same task, all of which have certain trade-offs, and none of which interoperate well with each other. From a language-centric viewpoint, the CLR and Framework Library are just another runtime that offers some benefits and has some drawbacks. The Managed Extensions to C++ and the Microsoft C++ compiler do a fantastic job of allowing CLR-targeting C++ code to interoperate with other C++ libraries in a transparent manner, but this seamless interaction does come with a performance impact.

The ability to mix managed and unmanaged code in the same source file can have a varied effect on performance, depending on how the technology is used. Dropping into unmanaged code to perform an activity that is slower in managed code is easy to achieve using MC++ and the It Just Works (IJW) managed-unmanaged code transitions. Code that makes heavy use of numerical calculations and STL collections would be a good candidate to handle in unmanaged code, where boxing performance hits, the lack of control over method inlining, and the absence of the powerful optimizing engine of the unmanaged C++ compiler can result in a significant performance hit for managed code.

The key to good performance for mixed managed and unmanaged code sections is minimizing the number of transitions that take place. The CLR has no ability to interact with unmanaged code blocks on a call stack, and must have a way of recognizing them to avoid corrupting the call stack when performing tasks like garbage collection. This means that instructions need to be emitted to mark transition boundaries, and track whether a particular operating system thread is executing managed code. These bookkeeping instructions that are emitted are fairly minimal—in the order of 50 x86 instructions—but if transitions to and from managed code are made with great frequency, the performance impact will be significant.

The degree of interoperability between managed and unmanaged code that can be achieved with MC++ is amazing, but does come at a cost. Modules compiled with the /clr switch will produce managed code if possible, but not all code that is legal within a C++ source file can be compiled into managed code, and #pragma unmanaged code blocks can instruct the compiler to generate native instructions. The full list of restrictions for managed compilation is included in the compiler documentation, with the main impediments to managed compilation being the use of C++ runtime error checks, Visual C++-style dllexport and dllimport attributes, inline machine assembly code, and function pointer comparisons.

The CLR has no knowledge of these native instructions, which becomes a problem when an unmanaged function overrides a managed virtual function. The runtime binding to the correct function cannot be handled in managed code, which means that a transition to unmanaged code to determine the correct function to call must occur, followed by a transition back to managed code to execute the function if required.

Converting classes to managed classes with the __gc keyword can reduce the transition issues with MC++. This tells the compiler that objects of this class are normal managed objects, just as those produced by the VB .NET or C# compilers are. This contrasts with simply recompiling existing C++ code with the /clr switch, which produces managed methods on unmanaged classes. This means that the C++ objects are still allocated and deleted in accordance with the rules of standard C++, but the methods of the object will be expressed in MSIL rather than native machine code if possible. The other technique to minimize excessive transitions is to simply enforce a stricter separation between managed and unmanaged code, paying close attention to where transitions occur.

Pinning of objects on the managed heap can hurt performance, as object allocation and cleanup under the CLR is optimized for a nonfragmented heap. When objects are collected, the heap is compacted and live references updated, so new objects are allocated sequentially at the beginning of the free space. C++ makes heavy use of pointers, which contain the actual address of an object, and the managed objects that these pointers reference should not be moved during the compaction phases of a garbage collection. The following code snippet shows the use of the __pin keyword to declare and allocate a String object that cannot be moved during a garbage collection:

```
#using <mscorlib.dll>
using namespace System;

int _tmain()
{
   String __pin *pString = new String("Hello from a pinned string");
   Console::WriteLine(pString);
   return 0;
}
```

This inability to compress the heap results in fragmentation, where free and allocated memory blocks are located in groupings of various sizes. This fragmentation causes a slowdown in the speed of object allocation and cleanup. Benchmarks presented in Chapter 7 show that for a heavily pinned heap, object allocation and collection takes significantly longer. Discussion of this performance outcome has resulted in some optimizations within the CLR to address the slowdown, and version 1.1 has significantly better performance compared to version 1.0.

Avoiding pinning can be achieved by the gcroot template, which adds a level of indirection via the use of the managed GCHandle type, and essentially transforms a pointer to a managed-code-style reference similar to that used in C# or

VB .NET. Using gcroot means that all object access is routed through the GCHandle.Target property, which can slow access speeds, but allows the garbage collector to work much more effectively. The following code shows the pinned String example rewritten in terms of gcroot:

```
#using <mscorlib.dll>
#include <vcclr.h>
using namespace System;

int _tmain()
{
  gcroot<String*> pString = new String("Hello from an unpinned string");
    Console::WriteLine(pString);
  return 0;
}
```

The Managed Extensions for C++ give the highest level of managed code control above MSIL. As is typical with a number of C++ features, the value of this extra control depends on the competency of the programmer. Managed C++ allows manual control of boxing operations, as shown in the following snippet:

```
void ManualBoxing(){
  Int32 i = 0; //heap allocation
  __box Int32* pI = __box(i);//moved to managed heap
  Int32 i2 = *dynamic_cast<__box Int32*>(pI);  //new copy back to heap
}
```

Manual control of runtime behavior like this can allow a few percentage points of increased performance to be achieved, but used naively, the extra control can be a source of performance loss and bugs. The extra control will have a natural feel to experienced C++ programmers, but for those new to both C++ and .NET, the extra effort required to produce even simple functionality will be frustrating and confusing.

C#

C# is often touted as the native language of the .NET platform. While it is true that C# offers the closest fit to the CLR, complete exposure of all the features offered by the CLR was not one of the design goals of C#. A number of CLR features, such as user-filtered exception handlers and indirect method calls through function pointers, have no C# support. This is neither a good nor a bad point of the language—it simply illustrates that C# is a stand-alone language that provides a very high, but not complete, level of support for the CLR.

The lack of backwards-compatibility features required for a new language like C# means that there are no dramatic performance pitfalls like those that exist in VB .NET. However, to demonstrate that not every C# keyword has been designed to correspond to a MSIL concept, consider the is keyword. The is keyword is implemented in MSIL using an isinst instruction, which determines if a reference can be legally cast to the nominated type, and places either a reference to the nominated type or a null reference on the top of the stack, depending on the legality of the cast. The instructions emitted by the C# compiler simply treat the reference as a Boolean, with zero indicating false and nonzero indicating true. The is keyword offers no way to actually retrieve the cast reference, so unless the test is simply to perform conditional logic based on the object's type, another cast will be required to actually retrieve a reference of the correct type, as shown here:

```
object obj = GetReference();
if (obj is SomeType){
  SomeType st = (SomeType)obj;
  st.SomeTypeMethod();
}
```

This code contains two casts, and is 50 percent slower than the equivalent code that uses the as keyword and contains a single cast (see Test 6.04).

```
object obj = GetReference();
SomeType st = obj as SomeType;
if (st != null){
  st.SomeTypeMethod();
}
```

The code using the is statement would generally be considered more readable, and in a lot of scenarios, readability will be more important than performance. This is especially true in situations where the cast is only performed occasionally, making the performance impact negligible. The point of the argument is not that the is keyword is bad, but rather that using C#, just like any other language, does not automatically guarantee the highest level of code efficiency possible.

J#

J# has always been a bit of an odd-man-out in the Visual Studio lineup, and J# .NET is no different. J# is a dual offering—it provides the ability to develop standard .NET applications using the Java language, as well as the ability to produce Java Development Kit (JDK) 1.1.4-targeted code that will compile and run on the .NET platform. The performance of a J# application depends on the mode it is used in.

J# code that uses the Framework Library will not be significantly slower than code written in any other language. A small slowdown is likely due to extra code that is injected into objects by the compiler to provide normal Java language behavior. For example, the default behavior of ToString for normal CLR objects is to return the name of the type that they belong to, but in Java, the default behavior of toString is to return the name of the type along with the hash code. Existing Java code may rely on this fact, and System.Object's implementation may break this code. To prevent this problem, the J# compiler emits code that overrides the System.Object implementation of ToString, and adds a toString method, both of which return a string that contains the name of the object's type and the object's hash code.

The real performance variability with J# comes when using the JDK Libraries. These libraries do not sit on top of the Framework Libraries, which is good in terms of performance; but this means a lot of the material in this book is not relevant when J# is used in this mode. Several titles on Java platform performance are available, and these would be more relevant in this scenario. *Java 2 Performance and Idiom Guide* by Craig Larman and Rhett Guthrie (Prentice Hall, 1999) and *Server-Side Programming Techniques (Java Performance and Scalability, Volume 1)* by Dov Bulka (Addison-Wesley, 2000) are both good references for getting the most out of the Java platform.

Java lacks the ability to define custom value types, and J# reflects this limitation. For heavy numerical work where user-defined value types are important, J# will not perform well. Value type allocation and cleanup is an order of magnitude quicker than the equivalent reference type allocation, which will result in very noticeable performance degradation in tight loops.

The appeal of J# is limited to those who need a quick port of Java code to the .NET platform, and those with a heavy investment in J++ 6.0 code. For developers outside these groups, J# is a fairly unattractive option. From a Java perspective, it lacks the new features introduced in JDK 1.2, and even lacks features that have been strong selling points for Java since its early days, like cross-platform capabilities and the ability to produce applets. From the .NET side, J# is similar in a language sense to C#, but has the confusing option of two competing class libraries, and lacks the features of C# in quite a few areas.

Conclusion

Using the language of greatest comfort and familiarity is more likely to result in the production of high-quality, fast code than choosing an unfamiliar language for the sake of a few performance-related features. The performance of a language will be roughly proportional to the closeness of language features to MSIL and CLR abilities, so for languages with esoteric features, performance testing early in the development cycle would be a wise risk-management strategy.

The .NET Framework makes rich interaction with assemblies written in other languages seamless, which means that switching languages for performance-sensitive code sections is possible if a particular language is found to have poor performance characteristics for a given task. The Reflection API allows assemblies in other languages to be generated at runtime, which means that even the most obscure performance requirement can be met from any language as long as it can be solved using MSIL. If this is not the case, the support for calling native code is comprehensive and robust, allowing unmanaged code libraries to be utilized with little pain (again, from any language).

CHAPTER 7

Garbage Collection and Object Lifetime Management

THE MOVE FROM MANUAL MEMORY management and deterministic destruction to a garbage-collected environment represents a huge paradigm shift for most Windows developers, especially those from a C/C++ background. It has been said that one of the greatest mistakes that can be made in transition to a new language or platform is to attempt to simulate all the techniques and patterns that are available in the previous technology. This statement is especially true when it comes to garbage collection.

The CLR Garbage Collector

A number of different algorithms for garbage collection exist, and collection algorithms represent an ongoing area of academic and commercial research. The algorithm used by the CLR garbage collector, known as the *mark-and-compact* algorithm, works by first tracing through all reachable objects within an application, starting with root references, and continuing until all reachable memory has been traced through. Memory that has not been reached during the trace phase is designated as garbage and removed. The reachable memory is then compacted, which prevents the heap from becoming fragmented as further collections and allocations occur. A nonfragmented heap makes allocation of new objects much faster, as all memory requests are satisfied from the top of the heap, and no searching for a suitably sized block is required.

   The managed heap is divided into generations, and objects that survive a collection are designated as belonging to an older generation. The use of generations allows the garbage collector to conduct partial collection of the most recently allocated objects, which have a higher probability of being garbage in typical memory allocation scenarios. The youngest generation, known as *generation 0*, is collected very frequently, with a collection likely for every 0.2 to 2MB of memory allocation. The garbage collector will dynamically schedule collections of older generations based on certain memory usage statistics, with the exhaustion of memory in the younger generation being a dominant factor. Typical ratios of collection frequencies will show an order of magnitude decrease in frequency collection for each successive generation, so a generation 2 collection should be matched by 100 collections of generation 0.

The System Monitor .NET Memory object exposes counters that allow the collection count for each generation to be monitored, and the heap size counter allows the desired size before collection of each generation to be observed.

A separate heap is maintained for objects exceeding 20KB in size. The cost of moving these large objects during a compaction phase is generally more expensive than allowing the heap to fragment, and objects on the large object heap are not moved as part of a garbage collection.

The opportunity for interaction with the garbage collector is quite limited. The CLR host can set various parameters for the managed heap using interfaces defined in gchost.idl (included with the Framework SDK), and the managed System.GC type can be used to invoke collections on one or all generations. Beyond these high-level interfaces, the garbage collector is self-configuring.

In theory, a garbage-collected system can achieve a performance level that is equal to or greater than a system in which memory allocation is manually managed. A garbage-collected object is quicker to allocate than a reference-counted object, as synchronization locks do not need to be taken to increment a per-object reference count, and heap compaction makes the search for free memory blocks to allocate quicker. Mark-and-compact garbage collection means that related objects tend to end up close to each other on the heap, which reduces the number of page faults that occur.

Common Language Runtime Flavors and Concurrent Collection

Two different "build flavors" of the CLR garbage collection exist: a workstation version that favors short pause intervals during garbage collection, and a server version that favors higher throughput at the expense of longer pauses. The choice of which garbage collector to use is made by the CLR host at startup, with the limitation that the server garbage collector will only load on multiprocessor machines. The server version contains various optimizations for multithreaded code, such as separate heap areas for each thread, which limits contention during simultaneous memory allocations and also during collection.

The workstation build flavor supports concurrent collection, where a dedicated thread is used to conduct preliminary collection work that involves identifying objects eligible for collection at the same time as the CLR continues to run. After the preliminary work is finished, CLR execution is suspended, and the collection is completed. Concurrent collection results in slower overall collection speeds, but the length of CLR suspension is minimized, which is desirable for client-side applications. The runtime's garbage collection mode can also by specified using a configuration file. The default setting for garbage collection is concurrent, and this can be overridden with the following configuration file entry. For Windows Forms, Windows Service, and console applications, the configuration file needs to be located in the same directory as the executable image and have the name of the image appended with .config. For an ASP.NET application, the file needs to be named web.config, and located in the root of the virtual directory.

```
<configuration>
  <runtime>
    <gcConcurrent enabled="false"/>
  </runtime>
</configuration>
```

ASP.NET is the only CLR host currently shipped by Microsoft that requests the server runtime flavor. Custom runtime hosts can use the CorBindToRuntimeEx function exported by mscoree.dll to specify the build flavor to use, but for fully managed applications, there is no supported technique that will allow the runtime flavor to be nominated.

The following code, which is stripped of all error handling for readability, shows the necessary steps needed to launch the assembly entitled "AssemblyToRun" using the server runtime flavor:

```
/*top of CPP file*/
#include <mscoree.h>
#import <mscorlib.tlb> rename("ReportEvent","ReportEventCOR")
using namespace mscorlib;

/*inside a function*/
CComBSTR assemblyName("AssemblyToRun");

//get runtime reference
CComPtr<ICorRuntimeHost> pHost = NULL;
CorBindToRuntimeEx(L"v1.1.4122", L"svr",
    STARTUP_LOADER_OPTIMIZATION_SINGLE_DOMAIN,
    CLSID_CorRuntimeHost, IID_ICorRuntimeHost, (void **)&pHost);

//start runtime
pHost->Start();

//get default application domain
CComPtr<IUnknown> pAppDomainPunk = NULL;
pHost->GetDefaultDomain(&pAppDomainPunk);
CComQIPtr<_AppDomain> pDefaultDomain(pAppDomainPunk);
```

```
//load assembly
CComPtr<_Assembly> pAssem = pDefaultDomain->Load_2(assemblyName);
//get the entry point
CComPtr<_MethodInfo> pEntryPoint = pAssem->EntryPoint;
//invoke the entry point method
pEntryPoint->Invoke_3(vtMissing, NULL);
```

The code first creates the COM object that represents the CLR, calls Start to begin the CLR, and then retrieves a reference to the default application domain, which is created automatically when the CLR begins. The assembly that contains the managed entry point for the application is then loaded, reflection is used to locate the entry point, and the method at this location is invoked. The _2 added to the Load method and the _3 added to the Invoke method represent a name decoration technique used by COM Interop to deal with overloaded methods, which are not supported in the COM world.

Unmanaged Resources, Disposal, and Finalization

The term *garbage collector* is misleading—it can imply a generic cleanup mechanism that takes care of all resource management. This is not the case. The garbage collector only deals with managed memory, and there are a multitude of resources in a typical program that are not composed of managed memory—Windows fonts, database connections, unmanaged heaps, and file handles, to name a few. To ensure that unmanaged resources are freed as soon as possible, a consistent and unambiguous pattern must be adopted for the types that wrap these resources so that the need for manual cleanup is obvious, and tools can be written to detect missed cleanups. The IDisposable interface provides this consistent cleanup pattern. The interface has a single method, Dispose, which is responsible for freeing any unmanaged resources that the object holds and ensuring that base and member objects implementing IDisposable are also disposed. Types that implement the IDisposable interface should also have a finalizer that can free the unmanaged resources if a Dispose call is missed.

A pattern has been established for implementing a Dispose method, and a minimal implementation of this pattern is shown in the following snippet. Noteworthy points of the implementation include the call to GC.SuppressFinalize in the public Dispose method body, which is discussed further in the following section, and tracking of whether the protected Dispose method is being called as a result of finalization or a Dispose call. Object finalization is not ordered according to any relationship between objects, which means that any referenced object may already be finalized before the finalizer on the referencing object is called, and calling methods of any other object during finalization is not supported. The protected Dispose method uses the calledFromDisposeMethod parameter to track whether calls to other objects are permitted within the method.

```
public class NonMemoryResourceHolder: IDisposable {
  private IntPtr _handle = new IntPtr();
  private bool _beenDisposed = false;

  //finalizer
  ~NonMemoryResourceHolder(){
    Dispose(false);
  }

  public void Dispose() {
    Dispose(true);
    GC.SuppressFinalize(this);
  }

  protected virtual void Dispose(bool calledFromDisposeMethod){
    if (_beenDisposed)
      return;

    _beenDisposed = true;

    if (calledFromDisposeMethod){
      //legal to Dispose references to other IDisposable objects here
    }

    //free object referenced by _handle
  }
}
```

For objects that have a single owner, the timing of Dispose calls is simple to determine, and will usually be as soon as the object is no longer needed. The C# using statement is a syntactic shortcut that will generate try-finally blocks with a Dispose call in the finally block, guaranteeing that an object will be disposed at the end of the scope; this pattern is easy to implement in other languages. The following C# code block shows the shortcut using syntax and the extended try-finally technique. Both techniques generate identical MSIL code.

```
public class DisposeUser{
  public void UsingMeth(){
    using (NonMemoryResourceHolder rh = new NonMemoryResourceHolder()){
      rh.GetHashCode();
    }//call to Dispose automatically generated here
  }

  public void ExplicitDisposeMeth(){
```

```
NonMemoryResourceHolder rh = new NonMemoryResourceHolder();
try{
  rh.GetHashCode();
}
finally{
  if (rh != null)
    ((IDisposable)rh).Dispose();
}
  }
}
```

For objects shared across multiple threads, or even for a single-threaded scenario where a number of independent references to the same IDisposable-implementing object exists, a count of active clients can be maintained and Dispose called when the active client count goes to zero. Reference counts can be error prone, and in some cases it will be preferable to simply leave cleanup to the garbage collection, particularly for resources that are not overly finite in nature.

The Cost of Finalizations

Despite their syntactic similarities in some languages, finalizers and destructors are two very different concepts. The most obvious difference between a destructor and a Finalize method is their timing—a destructor is guaranteed to be called immediately after a class goes out of scope, whereas a Finalize method will be called at some indeterminate point in the future. Performance cost is another major difference between destructors and finalizers. Although a C++ destructor has no major administrative overhead associated with it, a Finalize method makes object allocation and collection over 20 timers slower for the test case of a simple object that contains no methods or member variables except a Finalize method (see Test 7.01). This is a huge performance hit, but for real-world types that incur the expense of managing resources, the relative cost may not be as high.

The performance impact of finalizers is caused by the following factors:

- At object creation time, a reference to the object is placed on a finalizer list to ensure the finalizer is run after the object is no longer reachable.

- When the object is no longer reachable, the garbage collector must place the object in a finalizer queue, which runs on a low-priority background thread. In contrast, a nonfinalized object can simply have its memory reclaimed at this point with no further processing.

- The next run of the garage collector can then reclaim the object's memory. In effect, two garbage collection cycles are needed to fully reclaim the object. The CLR is suspended during the compact phase of a garbage collection, and if concurrent garbage collection is not enabled, the CLR will also be suspended during the mark phase. This means that it is critical for overall performance that the time spent in garbage collection is minimized, and this serves as the motivation for the separate finalization phase.

If an object is disposed, finalization will no longer be required, and GC.SuppressFinalize can be called to stop the Finalize method being called. Suppressing finalization helps reduce the performance impact of finalization, but still results in an order of magnitude decrease in allocation and collection speed (see Test 7.01). As discussed previously, when an object with a Finalize method is created, a pointer to the object is placed on the finalization queue. Calls to SuppressFinalize do not remove the pointer from the queue; they merely set the BIT_SBLK_FINALIZER_RUN bit in the object's header data, indicating that the Finalize method should not be called. If a particular type changes its implementation and no longer needs finalization, the Finalize method should be removed altogether, rather than relying on runtime suppression.

Leveraging the Garbage Collection for Resource Cleanup

There are two basic categories of unmanaged resources: generic and specific. Generic nonmanaged resources can be exhausted if too many objects are allocated and not freed but each instance of the resource is essentially interchangeable. A database connection with a given connection string is an example of a generic resource. Two calls to an allocating method will return a resource that is logically identical. Repeated allocation without corresponding calls to free the resource will eventually result in the inability of the system to supply a new connection.

Specific nonmanaged resources represent an identifiable entity that cannot be interchanged with another instance of the same type. A file and its corresponding file handle comprise an example of a specific resource, and a file handle left in an open state can block access to a particular file until the handle is closed or the process that owns the handle exits.

The garbage collector cannot provide support for the management of specific resources. Managing these types is largely the responsibility of application code. A Finalize method can perform cleanup specific to a particular object, but this Finalize method may not be called for a significant amount of time; and because objects are not finalized in any particular order, data loss may occur, as shown in the following sample. Do not be tempted to leverage the garbage collector to free nonmanaged specific resources—it will not work. Disposal is a must for these objects.

```
using System;
using System.Text;
ASCIIEncoding ae = new ASCIIEncoding();
FileStream fs = new FileStream("MyFile.txt", FileMode.Create);
BufferedStream bs = new BufferedStream(fs);
byte[] data = ae.GetBytes("I should have gone out to file");

//bytes written to BufferedStream buffer, but never flushed to disk
bs.Write(data, 0, data.Length);

//force full cleanup
GC.Collect();
GC.WaitForPendingFinalizers();
GC.Collect();
```

The garbage collector can manage generic resources, but it needs some help. The .NET runtime has no idea how many instances of a resource can be allocated before the system is exhausted, and even if it did know, it would not really care—it already has a job, and that is satisfying requests for managed memory. Leveraging the garbage collector therefore involves two problems: identifying when the resource is exhausted, and making the garbage collector care about this exhaustion.

Identifying resource exhaustion is not hard—it is sufficient to know how many instances of a particular resource can be allocated, and how many instances are currently allocated. The total number of instances that can be allocated is dependent on the resource, and various tests can be run to determine an approximate figure. To determine the current number of resources allocated, the constructor of the type that wraps the unmanaged resource can increment a static variable, and a Finalize method can decrement the count. Using a Finalize method in this case has no major performance implications, as the type will already have a Finalize method defined that cleans up the unmanaged resources.

The final step involves using the garbage collector to identify objects that are no longer referenced and ensure that the Finalize method of these objects is called, which will free the underlying unmanaged resources and document the allocation count. Calling GC.Collect will invoke a garbage collection and result in unreferenced objects ending up on the finalization queue, and GC.WaitForPendingFinalizers will block the calling thread until all Finalize methods have run.

The System.Windows.Forms assembly uses this technique to manage various Graphical Device Interface (GDI) resources. If a user allocates GDI objects without explicitly cleaning them up using the `Dispose` methods, the `System.HandleCollector` type triggers a collection in an attempt to prevent the resource from being exhausted.

`HandleCollector` adds a further enhancement to the collection scheme. A type, such as a window, is associated with an expense value as well as a threshold. The expense value is used to gradually increase the threshold at which garbage collection is invoked. For expensive items, the expense value is set so as to prevent the threshold from increasing, whereas for cheap items the expense value allows for significant threshold growth.

A simple implementation of the collector pattern is shown in the following snippet. The collector in the example is specific to a certain resource, but can be extended to keep a per-resource count in an internal collection if required.

```
using System;
using System.Threading;

public class CollectorPattern {
    private static readonly float GROWTH_RATE = .1F;
    private static int _maxCount = 1000;
    private static int _count = 0;

    public static void IncrementCount(){
        Interlocked.Increment(ref _count);
        if (_count > _maxCount){
            lock(typeof(CollectorPattern)){
                _maxCount = (int)(_maxCount + (float)_maxCount * GROWTH_RATE);
            }
            GC.Collect();
        }
    }

    public static void DecrementCount(){
        Interlocked.Decrement(ref _count);
    }
}

public class GenericResource: IDisposable{
    public GenericResource(){
        CollectorPattern.IncrementCount();
    }
    ~GenericResource(){
        Dispose();
    }
```

```
public void Dispose() {
  CollectorPattern.DecrementCount();
  GC.SuppressFinalize(this);
  //free unmanaged resource
}
}
```

This technique is clever and neat, but may result in a performance hit. All types managed by `HandleCollector` will typically implement `IDisposable`, and performance gains may be won by calling the `Dispose` method when the object is no longer needed. If the type has a low threshold, calling `Dispose` is advisable to prevent an excessive number of manually invoked garbage collections.

Optimizing Memory Usage

The garbage collector does everything it can to prevent memory leaks. With the exception of a few types within the `System.Runtime.InteropServices` namespace that allow unmanaged memory to be allocated, leaking memory is not possible directly from managed code. This does not mean that developers can take a carefree attitude to memory usage—allocating objects takes time, and holding references to objects longer than necessary may result in garbage collections occurring with increased frequency.

Managed-memory loiterers have been identified as a problem in garbage-collected environments. *Loiterers* are objects that are reachable, but have served their purpose, and are no longer required for any useful activity. The garbage collector cannot differentiate between useful and useless objects, and no reachable object will have its memory reclaimed. Loiterers have been classified into four distinct categories in Java research:[1]

- *Lapsed listener:* Objects referenced in a delegate invocation list that have no other active references.

- *Lingerer:* Temporary object associated with a long-lived object that has served its purpose, but still has an active reference. Newer temporary objects will release the current object, but until this occurs, the temporary object cannot be collected.

- *Laggard:* Occurs when expensive objects are cached as part of a type's state, but changes to other member variables make the cached object invalid. The expensive object is recalculated the next time it is required, but until this time, the old version remains in memory.

---

1. Ed Lycklama, "Does Java Technology Have Memory Leaks?," Java One Developer Conference, 1999

- *Limbo:* Object reference still on call stack, but no longer needed. A code sample demonstrating limbo is presented later in this section.

Of the four types, the lapsed listener is both the most likely to occur and the most serious. In long-running GUI programs, lapsed listeners have the ability to slowly exhaust all available memory. Short-lived objects that register themselves in a delegate chain should always remove their registration at the end of their useful lifetime. If objects fail to do this, performance is impacted in two significant ways—valuable memory is never reclaimed, and invocation of the delegate chain will becoming increasingly slower. System.Delegate exposes a Remove method, which should be called at the end of an object's life cycle. The following snippet shows the conditions necessary to create a lapsed listener, and the code necessary to fix the problem:

```
//inside a form
private void btnLapsed_Click(object sender, System.EventArgs e) {
   TempListener tl = new TempListener();
   EventHandler eh = new System.EventHandler(tl.ListenerMethod);
   this.BindingContextChanged += eh;
   //processing that may change binding context
   // ….
   // if event listener is not released here, it is lapsed
   this.BindingContextChanged -= eh;


}
//outside Form class
//this class may want to take some action if binding context changes
public class TempListener{
   public void ListenerMethod(object sender, System.EventArgs e) {
   }
}
```

The lingerer and laggard are more benign problems, and although they consume memory without serving a useful purpose, the magnitude of the problem does not increase the longer the program runs, and the offending code is usually easy to identify. Setting the offending reference to null is all that is required to fix the problem.

Limbo is not a problem with the commercial version on the CLR that runs on the 32-bit Windows operating systems. Neither the generated x86 code nor the garbage collector need to respect the scope rules of high-level languages, and an object can be collected while still logically in scope. The code that follows illustrates the typical situation where limbo could occur:

```
{
ExpensiveObject eo = new ExpensiveObject();
eo.UseOnceAndOnlyOnce();
//heaps of code not using eo
//..
// eo will be collected if a garbage collection occurs here
//..
//leave scope
}
```

The absence of limbo as a problem with the current CLR makes setting a stack-allocated object reference to null (C#) or Nothing (VB .NET) after the object is no longer required a pointless activity. The Common Language Infrastructure specification makes no guarantees that objects can be collected while still in scope, so setting a reference to null may result in better performance on some future CLI implementation; however, optimizing for some future runtime behavior that may never exist is not an overly worthwhile undertaking.

Weak References

A *weak reference* is a reference to an object that the garbage collector can collect if memory is tight, but if memory is plentiful, the reference can be recast to the underlying object and used as normal. The System.WeakReference type allows weakly referenced objects to be created and converted back to strong references, as demonstrated in the following snippet:

```
object o1 = new object(); //normal strong reference
WeakReference wr = new WeakReference(o1); //convert to weak reference
//object referenced by o1 can be collected here
object o2 = wr.Target; //get a strong reference
if (o2 != null){//check for collection
  //use o2
}
```

Weak references provide an excellent mechanism for use with caching. The use of caching can result in significant performance wins in a program, but can also result in the creation of many objects in memory that are only used occasionally. For example, caching file contents in memory can alleviate the need for an expensive hard disk read, but when memory is tight, performance can suffer by requiring more garbage collection operations and more memory pages swapped to disk.

Object Recycling and Weak References

Many objects, including some in the Framework Libraries, are expensive to create, but cheap to reset to their original state. Collection classes that contain a large number of elements are a prime example of this—the data in the collection can be cleared after it has been used, leaving the memory, which has been allocated at a significant cost, reusable. If a section of code is constantly using expensive objects that can be recycled cheaply, it would be good to have some mechanism to keep these objects around in case they are needed again, but only if memory is plentiful.

An object pool, which uses weak references to store the pooled objects, provides a solution to this problem. Client code requests an object from the pool manager, which satisfies the request by either returning an object from the pool, or creating a new object if the pool is empty. When client code is finished with the object, it returns the object to the pool, which stores a weak reference to the object.

Using weak references in the pool has the added benefit of allowing the garbage collector to deal with pool clients who neglect to return objects. If the pool uses a normal reference, an object that is not returned to the pool will always have the pool's reference, keeping the object from being collected. Using a weak reference, an object that is never returned to the pool and is out of scope can still be collected.

The following code sample shows a basic implementation of an object pool using weak references. The code is reasonably simple, with the only interesting implementation detail other than weak references being the use of reflection to create new objects if the pool is empty. Reflection is an expensive process, but objects worth pooling will be expensive to create, and the reflection hit will typically be a small component of the overall object creation cost.

```
public class ObjectPool {
  private readonly System.Type objectType;
  private int objectsInPool;
  private readonly int growthFactor;
  private WeakReference[] pool;

  public ObjectPool(System.Type objectType,
    int intialCapacity, int growthFactor) {
    this.growthFactor = growthFactor;
    this.objectType = objectType;
    pool = new WeakReference[intialCapacity];
  }

  public System.Object GetObject() {
    if (objectsInPool == 0) {
```

```
        return Activator.CreateInstance(objectType);
      }
      else {
        while (objectsInPool != 0) {
          WeakReference w = (WeakReference)pool.GetValue(--objectsInPool);
          System.Object o = w.Target;
          if (o != null)
            return o;
        }
        return System.Activator.CreateInstance(objectType);
      }
    }

    public void ReturnObject(System.Object obj) {
      if (obj.GetType() != objectType) {
        throw new ArgumentException("Wrong type returned to pool");
      }
      if (objectsInPool >= pool.Length) {
        IncreasePoolSize();
      }
      WeakReference w = new WeakReference(obj);
      pool.SetValue(w, objectsInPool);
      ++objectsInPool;
    }

    private void IncreasePoolSize() {
      WeakReference[] newPool = new WeakReference[pool.Length * growthFactor];
      Array.Copy(pool, 0, newPool, 0, pool.Length);
      pool = newPool;
    }
}
```

It is important to note that the pool management code incurs a performance overhead. If the objects are cheap to create, as most objects are, pooling will have a negative impact on performance. Similarly, if recycling is as expensive as creation, pooling serves no benefit. Be sure that any use of pooling is properly profiled to ensure that it has the desired effect.

A test case is included where a 5000-element array of 32-bit integers is used with and without pooling. For the nonpooled case, the array is simply declared, and then goes out of scope. For the pooled array, an array is retrieved from the pool, reset to its initial state by iterating through every element and resetting it to zero, and then returned to the pool. The pooled case is twice as fast as the nonpooled case (see Test 7.02).

Pinning

Interoperating with unmanaged code imposes some restrictions on the garbage collector. Managed code does not directly interact with the address of an object, rather it uses the address indirectly through references, which allows the garbage collector to move objects to free space at the start of the heap during the compaction phase of garbage collection. This heap compaction significantly boosts performance by preventing heap fragmentation. Fragmentation hurts performance in two ways: Heap allocation is more complex, and object locality is diminished, which causes more page faults as memory is accessed.

When a reference to a managed type instance is given out to unmanaged code, the address of the object needs to be pinned, as the unmanaged code deals directly with the memory address of an object, meaning that the garbage collector cannot move the object during a collection. Frequent pinning of objects can lead to heap fragmentation, and this can have dramatic performance consequences. Object allocation and collection speeds can be reduced by an order of magnitude and more by pinning a significant percentage of the objects in a program (20 percent heap pinning is used for Test 7.03). Pinning should be minimized in performance-critical programs, and the time that objects are pinned should be kept as short as possible.

The major performance hit of pinning many objects on the managed heap is not the cost of conducting the pin, but the cost of dealing with pinned objects during collection and subsequent allocations; the technique of moving objects that need to be pinned to an unmanaged heap ends up seven times quicker than the equivalent pinning strategy for the case where one in every five objects is pinned (see Test 7.03).

There are a few strategies to combat pinning-related performance problems. Aside from removing the interoperation code from an application, the simplest technique is to allocate the memory used for interoperation from outside the managed heap using Marshal.AllocHGlobal. The contents of managed objects can then be copied into this unmanaged memory using the various Marshal.Copy and Marshal.WriteXXX overloads. This technique is demonstrated in the following snippet, which also illustrates the normal pinning technique using the GCHandle type. The StructLayoutAttribute is applied to the type that will be passed out as a raw memory pointer to prevent any reordering that may occur during compilation.

```
using System;
using System.Runtime.InteropServices;

[StructLayout(LayoutKind.Sequential)]
public class DataHolder{
    public int i = 3;
    public int j = 4;
```

```
    }

    public unsafe class InteropUser {
      //unmanaged function expecting some raw memory block
      [DllImport("MyWin32DLL.dll")]
      public static extern void UnmanagedFunction(IntPtr pMem);

      public void CopyToUnmanagedHeap(){
        DataHolder dh = new DataHolder();
        IntPtr mem = Marshal.AllocHGlobal(sizeof(int)*2);
        Marshal.WriteInt32(new IntPtr(mem.ToInt32() + sizeof(int)*0), dh.i);
        Marshal.WriteInt32(new IntPtr(mem.ToInt32() + sizeof(int)*1), dh.j);
        UnmanagedFunction(mem);
        Marshal.FreeHGlobal(mem);
      }

      public void PinAndPassOut(){
        DataHolder dh = new DataHolder();
        GCHandle handle = GCHandle.Alloc(dh, GCHandleType.Pinned);
        UnmanagedFunction(handle.AddrOfPinnedObject());
        handle.Free();
      }
    }
```

Although this technique is more tedious to code than using automatic marshalling and memory pinning, the managed heap collection speed is greatly improved. The cost of allocating the memory on an unmanaged heap and copying the contents of a 20-byte object into that memory is similar to the cost of performing a pinning operation (see Test 7.03). Once the copying has occurred, the managed object can have all references to it released if the parameter is not bidirectional, allowing the garbage collector to recover the object's memory, and preventing any heap fragmentation. For bidirectional parameters, retraining a reference to the managed object and copying the data returned from the unmanaged call back to the managed object will generally be the best option.

For managed C++ code that uses the __pin keyword to pin memory so that the address of a managed type can be stored in a variable, the use of the gcroot template can eliminate the need for pinning. The gcroot template stores a private GCHandle object that is converted to the appropriate type at access time via the GCHandle.Target property. This technique is viable in C++-style programming where strongly typed pointers are used; but for more primitive C-style functions that operate on raw memory blocks, pinning or copying to an unmanaged heap will be required. Chapter 6 presents a sample on using gcroot to avoid pinning.

If the use of AllocHGlobal is too tedious to implement and gcroot is not appropriate, moving the bulk of the interoperability to unmanaged code and exposing a wrapper method that does not require heap pinning can be achieved in a number of scenarios. At a minimum, it is worth being conscious of the amount of time that objects on the managed heap are pinned and release pinned objects as soon as possible.

Controlling Process Memory Usage

The runtime host can provide a COM object that implements the IGCHostControl interface to control the amount of memory the runtime will allocate. IGCHostControl::RequestVirtualMemLimit will be called by the runtime before calls to the operating system's memory allocation functions, which allows these allocation calls to be blocked if the runtime memory consumption has exceeded some arbitrary limit. To use this technique, the runtime must be hosted using a C/C++ unmanaged application that utilizes the hosting interfaces, and a COM object implementing IGCHostControl needs to be available. The Active Template Library (ATL) can be leveraged to provide all the standard code that makes up a COM object, and the only method that needs to be implemented is RequestVirtualMemLimit. The following sample shows a simple implementation of the memory limitation technique that effectively denies memory requests above a certain limit, with the limit stored in the m_memLimit member variable and set via a COM property accessor. A small memory allocation increase is permitted to allow objects like OutOfMemoryException to be created, which gives the CLR an opportunity to gracefully handle the memory exhaustion condition.

```
virtual HRESULT STDMETHODCALLTYPE RequestVirtualMemLimit
   (SIZE_T sztMaxVirtualMemMB, SIZE_T *psztNewMaxVirtualMemMB){

  if (sztMaxVirtualMemMB < m_memLimit)
    *psztNewMaxVirtualMemMB = sztMaxVirtualMemMB;
  else{
    m_memLimit = (SIZE_T)(m_memLimit * 1.02);
    *psztNewMaxVirtualMemMB = m_memLimit;
  }
  return S_OK;
}
```

To pass this COM object to the runtime, IGCHostControl.SetGCHostControl is used, as shown in the following code block. If the CLR has not had an IGCHostControl-implementing COM object passed to it, memory will be allocated to the maximum extent permitted by the operating system.

```
//create runtime - server flavor of 1.1 runtime with single domain
//loading nominated
```

```
CComPtr<ICorRuntimeHost> pHost = NULL;
HRESULT hr = CorBindToRuntimeEx(L" v1.1.4322", L"svr",
   STARTUP_LOADER_OPTIMIZATION_SINGLE_DOMAIN, CLSID_CorRuntimeHost,
   IID_ICorRuntimeHost, (void **)&pHost);

//get runtime configuration interface
CComPtr<ICorConfiguration> pConfig;
pHost->GetConfiguration(&pConfig);

//create COM object implementing IGCHostControl and set memory limit
MemLimitLib::IMemControlPtr pMemControl;
pMemControl.CreateInstance(__uuidof(MemLimitLib::MemControl));
pMemControl->MaxMem = memLimit;
CComQIPtr<IGCHostControl> pGCHost(pMemControl);

//pass COM object to runtime
pConfig->SetGCHostControl(pGCHost);

//start runtime
pHost->Start();
```

To the runtime, `IGCHostControl::RequestVirtualMemLimit`'s refusal to allow further memory allocation will appear the same as a failed call to `VirtualAlloc`, and an `OutOfMemoryException` is likely to be raised. The code accompanying the book (available for download from `http://www.apress.com`) contains the full memory limitation sample.

Memory Monitoring Tools

System Monitor (Perfmon.exe) contains a performance object dedicated to providing data on .NET CLR memory, and the various counters of this object can be used to track a number of statistics on the performance of the managed heap. For more in-depth analysis, Allocation Profiler, which can be downloaded from the User Samples area of the GotDotNet site (`http://www.gotdotnet.com`), is an excellent tool for investigating all aspects of the managed heap. To investigate the managed and unmanaged memory usage of a process, the Virtual Address Dump (VADUMP) utility that ships with the Windows Platform SDK and SciTech Software's .NET Memory Profiler are both viable options. Chapter 15 presents a more comprehensive discussion on tracking memory problems in .NET applications.

Conclusion

Moving to a garbage-collected environment is a significant transition. While problems such as memory leaks and access violations caused by accessing invalid pointers are no longer a concern, deterministic destruction and many of the resource management patterns that it supported are also no longer feasible. It is possible to leverage the garbage collector to assist with the release of non-managed memory resources through `Finalize` methods and the Handle Collector pattern, but this leveraging can cause the performance of an application to suffer. For many applications, this performance decrease will be acceptable, but it is important to be aware of the cost, and avoid it for performance-critical code paths.

Excessive pinning of the runtime heap can cause significant performance degradation. By copying the data from the managed heap to a heap that uses manual memory management, the pinning performance hit can be avoided, but significantly more code is required, and the problems of unmanaged code like memory leaks and access violation are possible.

Developers will rarely need to interact with the garbage collector, and, ideally, they will be blissfully unaware of its activities. The main assistance that developers can lend to the garbage collector is to be conscious of holding on to object references past the object's useful lifetime. In addition to the simple act of setting member variables to null when an object is no longer needed and removing delegates from a delegate invocation list, weak references provide the ability to maintain a tenuous hold on an object, and allow for collection when memory pressure is high.

CHAPTER 8

Exceptions

THE CONSISTENT AND UNIFORM error handing model within the .NET Framework is a welcome innovation for developers on the Windows platform. Over the years, Windows has evolved various error handling models, and this has made implementing error handling within an application tedious and error prone. The use of exceptions is uniform across the CLR and Framework Libraries, and unmanaged function failures are translated to CLR exceptions. This allows a clean and consistent approach to error handling for all .NET code in all languages.

The performance consequence of an exception-based error handling model is a contentious topic. The overuse of exceptions can cause significant performance problems, and the cost of setting up exception handling blocks can have a noticeable performance impact in some technologies like unmanaged C++. To counter these negative impacts, exceptions can bring performance benefits by forcing errors to be handled, which eliminates the problem of silent method failures that can cause an application to fail unexpectedly, or continue to operate but at a reduced rate. Exceptions also result in cleaner code, with error handling logic separate from the main logic of a method, and this makes optimization easier.

Without exceptions, error conditions must be checked every time a function is executed, but with exceptions, the amount of post-call error checking is reduced or eliminated. Less post-call error checking reduces the working set size of an application and can result in faster execution speed.

CLR exceptions are lighter weight than unmanaged C++ exceptions due to the different life cycle management strategies that exist in the two technologies. When an exception is thrown in C++, the destructor of local variables must be called as the stack unwinds, and this overhead makes C++ programs compiled with exception handling enabled slower than an equivalent C++ program that does not use exceptions. The CLR does not offer the same deterministic destruction guarantees available in C++, which makes setting up exception handling blocks much cheaper.

At the end of the day, there is little point in worrying about whether exceptions or return codes offer the fastest error handling model, as no option exists for removing exceptions from the CLR and Framework Library. The support and use of exceptions is deeply rooted within the CLR, and the European Computer Manufacturer's Association (ECMA) specification, which serves as the formal definition of the features that are required within a Framework implementation, mandates that exceptions be supported.

Exceptions and Exception Handling

Blocks of code within an exception handler are known as *protected blocks*, although they are colloquially referred to as *try blocks* in various sources. A protected block of code is associated with one of the following four types of handlers:

- *Type-filter exception handlers*, which will handle exceptions if they are of a particular type. A type-filtered exception handler is implemented at MSIL level with try-catch statements, and high-level languages generally use a similar pattern.

- *User-filtered exception handlers*, which will handle exceptions if the execution of certain user-defined methods returns true.

- *Fault handlers*, which will execute if exceptions are thrown, but will not clear the exceptions.

- *Finally handlers*, which always execute, regardless of whether an exception occurs.

Different languages offer varying degrees of support for the four exception handlers. C# and Managed C++ provides support for type-filtered exception handlers (in the form of catch blocks) and Finally handlers (in the form of the finally and __finally keywords respectively), and VB .NET adds support for user-filtered exceptions with the Catch When statement. Fault handlers are not supported by VB, C#, or Managed C++, but can be simulated with a catch block that rethrows the exception that was originally caught.

Every method with a protected code block contains an Exception Handler Table that describes the protected regions and handlers within the method. Nested protected blocks are supported, and the runtime will transverse the Exception Handler Table of a method in an attempt to find a handler for a particular exception. If a particular method does not handle an exception, that execution stack is unwound a level, and, if present, the Exception Handler Table of the calling method is examined to determine if the current exception can be handled. This exercise is repeated until a handler is found, or the stack is fully unwound.

Protected Code Block Handler Efficiency

Of the four different categories of exception handlers, user-filtered and type-filtered exception handlers are the only two that have functionality that is logically similar. The performance of the filtered exception handlers is very similar, with any extra cost of user-filtered handlers being proportional to the cost of executing the filter block. For the test case of catching an exception using a type-filtered and a user-filtered exception block, with the user-filtered block using a simple integer comparison as the handler entry criteria, performance is very similar between the two techniques (see Test 8.01).

For code written in higher-level languages, the translation that the language compiler performs to support a particular error handling technique is more important than the type of exception filter used. Structured exception handling techniques within a high-level language can be translated to efficient MSIL with minimal effort, and it is advisable to stick to these techniques if a language offers them.

The performance cost of language-specific error handling techniques is proportional to the complexity of translating the techniques to MSIL. VB .NET supports On Error Resume Next error handling, in which any exception raised is silently handled, and execution continues at the next line of code. There is no support for this error handling technique within the CLR, and the VB .NET compiler must emit reasonably complex instructions to allow the code to execute in the expected manner.

The current implementation of the On Error Resume Next functionality is to use a local variable to keep track of the VB .NET statement that is about to be executed, and to implement a user-filtered exception handler to catch any exception that occurs. The handler clears any exception raised, and execution resumes at the MSIL instruction that represents the next line of Visual Basic code. The bookkeeping instructions needed to achieve this functionality have an obvious performance overhead, and in a test case of two logically identical methods, one of which uses try-catch blocks and the other of which uses On Error Resume Next functionality, the try-catch method is five times faster (see Test 8.02).

Execution Interruption

Exceptions are used to communicate much more than errors that are detected in managed code. The CLR uses exceptions as the preferred means of notification for any unexpected event or any requests for interruption. This ubiquitous use of exceptions is beneficial from a performance perspective, as it allows code to be written that is entirely focused on completing a particular task efficiently, and alleviates the need to constantly make peripheral checks for memory exhaustion, unmanaged code problems, and thread termination requests. The paths that can lead to an exception are quite varied, as detailed in the following list:

- Managed code can raise an exception with the MSIL throw or rethrown instructions, or higher-level language equivalents.

- The runtime Interop services can translate an unmanaged return code, such as E_FAIL, into a managed exception. This is really a special case of the first case.

- The runtime can throw an exception, such as OutOfMemoryException or ExecutionEngineException.

- An unmanaged call can raise a Windows structured exception, which the runtime will translate to the appropriate managed exception.

- Thread.Abort can be called, which will result in the runtime raising a ThreadAbortException within the referenced thread. A ThreadAbortException can be caught, but it will automatically be thrown again at the completion of a catch block.

- A thread in a WaitSleepJoin state may be awoken by an Interrupt call, which will result in ThreadInterruptedException being thrown.

Protected Code Blocks

The lack of deterministic destruction within the CLR makes the implementation of protected code blocks a lot simpler than the unmanaged C++ equivalent. Once an exception has been raised, the runtime simply needs to locate the appropriate handler for the protected block, and there is no requirement to call the destructor of any objects that were created from within the block.

This simplified model means that making a block of code protected is not overly expensive. For a test method that assigns new values to elements in a character array, which is a very cheap operation, adding a try-catch block in C# increases execution time by 30 percent. For a try-finally block, execution time is increased by 39 percent (see Test 8.03). As the complexity of a method increases, the addition of protected code blocks becomes less and less significant, but setting up protected code blocks inside loops should be avoided if an alternate implementation is possible. The following class contains two methods that set up try-catch blocks, with the TooGranular method setting up the block inside the loop (which has the potential to cause performance problems):

```
public class TryGranularity {
  public TryGranularity() {
    SomeArrayPopulationMethod();
  }

  private int[] _arr = new int[100];
```

```
private void SomeArrayPopulationMethod(){
  //fill arr
}

public void TooGranular(){
  foreach(int i in _arr){
    try{
      //some processing
    }
    catch(Exception){
      //handle exception
    }
  }
}

public void RightGranularity(){
  try{
    foreach(int i in _arr){
      //some processing
    }
  }
  catch(Exception){
    //handle exception
  }
}
}
```

Rethrowing Exceptions

It is not uncommon for a method to rethrow an exception that has been caught. It is important to appreciate that throwing the exception that was caught and rethrowing the original exception are two distinct activities. The runtime will reset the StackTrace property of an Exception object each time an exception is thrown, but will not perform a reset if the original exception is simply rethrown. The MSIL syntax for the two different actions is clearly distinct—an exception is thrown with the throw instruction, and an exception that has been caught is rethrown using the rethrow instruction. Higher-level languages provide syntax that is slightly more confusing: In C# and VB .NET, rethrowing the original exception is accomplished by executing the throw statement in an exception handler without specifying any expression, as shown in the following VB snippet:

```
Catch ex As Exception
  'deal with exception
  Throw 'Throw ex would have reset the stack trace
End Try
```

Resetting the StackTrace property is rarely an intentional consequence of catching and rethrowing an exception, and is also pure overhead that can easily be avoided.

At times, a method will want to catch an exception of a particular type, and throw a different exception. The motivation to do this comes from various sources, but it is most often done to maintain the encapsulation. A reference to the original exception can be placed inside the new exception to allow the actual cause of the problem to be investigated and solved, and the stack trace for the new exception will begin at the point the original exception is caught. The following sample shows a simple example of this technique:

```
using System;
using System.IO;

[Serializable]
public class LoggerException: ApplicationException{
  public LoggerException(){}
  public LoggerException(string msg): base(msg){}
  public LoggerException(string msg, Exception innerEx): base(msg, innerEx){}
}

public class Logger {
  public Logger(){
    try{
      FileStream fs = new FileStream("myLog.txt",
        FileMode.Create, FileAccess.Write);
    }
    catch (IOException ex){
      throw new LoggerException("Logger could not open the log file", ex);
    }
  }
}
```

The performance cost of this technique is not great, with a 56 percent increase in execution time compared to the case of not catching and repackaging the exception (see Test 8.04). Given the infrequency at which exceptions should be thrown, this is not a significant performance impact.

Coding to Avoid Exceptions

Raising and catching exceptions should not routinely occur as part of the successful execution of a method. When developing class libraries, client code must be given the opportunity to test for an error condition before undertaking an operation that can result in an exception being raised. For example, `System.IO.FileStream` provides a `CanRead` property that can be checked prior to calling the `Read` method, preventing a potential exception being raised, as illustrated in the following code snippet:

```
Dim str As Stream = GetStream()
If (str.CanRead) Then
  'code to read stream
End If
```

The decision of whether to check the state of an object prior to invoking a particular method that may raise an exception depends on the expected state of the object. If a `FileStream` object is created using a file path that should exist and a constructor that should return a file in read mode, checking the `CanRead` property is not necessary; the inability to read the `FileStream` would be a violation of the expected behavior of the method calls made, and an exception should be raised. In contrast, if a method is documented as returning a `FileStream` reference that may or may not be readable, checking the `CanRead` property before attempting to read data is advisable.

To illustrate the performance impact that using a "run until exception" coding technique can cause, the performance of a cast, which throws an `InvalidCastException` if the cast fails, is compared to the C# as operator, which returns nulls if a cast fails. The performance of the two techniques is identical for the case where the cast is valid (see Test 8.05), but for the case where the cast is invalid, and using a cast causes an exception, using a cast is *600* times slower than using the as operator (see Test 8.06). The high-performance impact of the exception-throwing technique includes the cost of allocating, throwing, and catching the exception and the cost of subsequent garbage collection of the exception object, which means the instantaneous impact of throwing an exception is not this high. As more exceptions are thrown, frequent garbage collection becomes an issue, so the overall impact of the frequent use of an exception-throwing coding technique will be similar to Test 8.05.

Throwing Exceptions

Determining when it is appropriate to throw an exception can often be a difficult decision. The well-worn cliché that an exception should be thrown when an exceptional circumstance occurs does not provide any real guidance about whether a particular section of code should throw an exception in a particular circumstance, primarily because it is hard to determine if a circumstance is exceptional, especially from the viewpoint of type designers.

Approaching a method as a consumer rather than a producer generally gives a better perspective about which actions are appropriate to deal with using exceptions. Adding header documentation to a method, which is particularly easy in C# with XML documentation, will make the exceptions that a method should throw self-evident. The documentation should include the assumptions and responsibilities of the client code when calling the method, and violation of these conditions will be grounds for an exception. The following C# sample demonstrates this technique in practice—notice that a property is made available so that a client that is handed an object for external code can check if the state is valid for the particular call, which means that an exception never needs to be raised for the client to determine information that could be made available through other means.

```csharp
/// <summary>
/// This method completes task X.
/// The object that this method is called upon should be in states A or C.
///<param name="portNumber">Nominates the port that the method is
/// completed on. The minimum legal value is 1000, and the maximum
/// legal value is 5000</param>
///<param name="auditMessage">Text to record in audit log for task X.
///Cannot be null or empty</param>
///<exception cref="System.ArgumentException">Thrown if rules
/// for parameters are not met</exception>
///<exception cref="System.InvalidOperationException">Thrown if
/// object is not in state A or C</exception>
/// </summary>
public void DocumentedMethod(int portNumber, string auditMessage){
  const int MIN_PORT_NUMBER = 1000;
  const int MAX_PORT_NUMBER = 5000;
  if (portNumber < MIN_PORT_NUMBER || portNumber > MAX_PORT_NUMBER)
    throw new ArgumentException("The port number must be between " +
    MIN_PORT_NUMBER.ToString() + " and " + MAX_PORT_NUMBER.ToString(),
    "portNumber");
  if (auditMessage == null || auditMessage.Length == 0)
    throw new ArgumentException("The audit message cannot be null or empty",
      "auditMessage");
```

```
  if (_objectState != "A" || _objectState != "C")
    throw new InvalidOperationException("The caller must be in states A" +
      " or C");

  //processing logic - not common to explicitly throw in here
}

//let client check object state to see if call to DocumentedMethod is legal
public string ObjectState{get {return _objectState;}}
```

The use of the `param` and `exception` XML documentation elements forces the developer to explicitly think through the legal states for parameters, and to explicitly nominate why an exception would be thrown. While not as formal as the Java language `throws` clause, full nomination of exceptions before writing a method reduces the uncertainty that can confront the developer deep within a method.

Monitoring Exceptions

Windows System Monitor (formally known as Performance Monitor [Perfmon.exe]) contains a .NET CLR `Exceptions` performance object that can be used to view exceptions thrown, exception filters executed, `finally` blocks entered, and the stack depth that needs to be covered to find an exception handler. The rate at which exceptions are thrown (`# of Exceps Thrown / sec`) is the most important counter, and using this counter makes tracking down exception-related performance problems straightforward. When monitoring managed code in an attempt to track down performance problems, it is worthwhile adding this counter, and watching for correlations between system slowness and excessive exception throw rates. The explanation text that accompanies the counter comments that "exceptions should only occur in rare situations and not in the normal control flow of the program; this counter was designed as an indicator of potential performance problems due to large (>100s) rate of exceptions thrown."

 NOTE   Chapter 15 presents a full discussion on the use of System Monitor to diagnose performance problems. For introductory material, the help documentation that ships with System Monitor should be consulted.

Conclusion

The error handling model in .NET is extremely simple. The CLR goes to great lengths to ensure that all error conditions and interrupt requests are communicated to code though exceptions, which makes dealing with the exceptions in a consistent and performant manner reasonably simple. The techniques required to extract the best performance in relation to exceptions are straightforward: Avoid code that throws an excessive number of exceptions, and understand the mapping that a high-level language performs to match its natural error handling syntax to the CLR's exception-based model.

CHAPTER 9
Security

SECURITY AND PERFORMANCE are often conflicting priorities in program design and implementation. Each new security feature typically decreases performance, and the balancing act between the two conflicting priorities is often complex. The problem is frequently exacerbated by a haphazard software development process, where security and performance considerations are both left until the end of a project and have to be tacked on to an existing code base.

When making design decisions that impact both security and performance, it is usually best to err on the side of slower, more secure operation. The embarrassment and potential economic losses of slow software are nearly always less severe than the consequences of security breaches.

While secure operations are critically important for many applications, blindly throwing security features at a system hurts performance, usability, and security. Secure features must be designed to combat identified threats, and the security layers that protect an application should be uniformly applied across risk categories. Correct and thorough design is much more important than implementation techniques in achieving secure software. With this design information available, making designs about performance optimizations is possible, as it is clear what threat a security feature addresses, and whether this threat is also dealt with by other security measures.

Security, Application Design, and Performance

Security features should not cause a major performance impact in a well-designed application. The security systems available in .NET, the Windows platform, and the .NET Servers have been designed and implemented to impart a minimal performance impact, and by themselves will not pose significant problems if employed correctly. One of the main difficulties with designing a security infrastructure for a particular application is determining which security features to use from the overlapping functionality offered by the various systems components, such as the .NET Framework, the operating system, and enterprise servers. For an ASP.NET application, the security infrastructure in IIS, Windows, SQL Server, and the CLR can all be used to secure the application, and choosing the appropriate tool to implement security policy aspects can be difficult.

The most efficient system element to use for security enforcement is the one that allows the security check to be completed with the lowest cost at the earliest point in time. If security checks can be performed at two or more different levels, the most efficient check can be determined by considering the cost of the actual check, and the processor time taken to get to the check multiplied by the probability that check will fail. Formulaically, this approximate efficiency rating can be expressed as:

> Performance of check = 1 / (Cost of check + (Cost of processing required to get to check * Probability that check will succeed))

If there is a reasonable probability that the check will fail, it will be worthwhile terminating the action as close as possible to the system's entry point, rather than wasting system resources getting to a check point deeper inside the system. To continue the ASP.NET example, using IIS IP address restrictions to limit access to the site would be much more efficient than undertaking full processing on a request through to the database layer, only to fail based on SQL Server security settings.

Deciding on the security safeguards that are appropriate within a system is a matter of risk management. By applying a methodical analysis to the security of a system, areas where the level of security is inappropriately high and low can be identified, and, if possible, redundant security layers can be removed, improving performance.

The performance cost of security is usually the most severe in the routing of calls through application layers to the code that actually implements the business functions of the system, rather than within the business layer itself. Chunky APIs that complete a lot of work per call within a trusted or semitrusted environment will deliver the best mix between security and performance, but care needs to be taken that data entering the secure part of the application is fully validated.

Security analysis, design, and implementation cannot be covered adequately in a single book, let alone a single chapter. For an overview of security design and implementation on the Windows platform and .NET Framework, *Writing Secure Code, Second Edition* by Michael Howard and David C. LeBlanc (Microsoft Press, 2002) is an excellent text. *.NET Framework Security* by Brian A. LaMacchia et al. (Addison Wesley Professional, 2002) provides a comprehensive description of security features of the .NET Framework.

CLR Security Model

The CLR introduces a new security model in which the unit of application deployment (the assembly) becomes an important member of the security-granting process. This is in contrast to the Win32 security model, where the Windows user was the dominant player in the permission-granting process. The new model is based on the premise that executable code comes from a number of different sources having varying degrees of trust associated with them, and that security permissions should reflect this.

The permissions that will be available to an assembly are calculated in the following manner:

1. An assembly belongs in one or more code groups, as determined by the evidence known about the assembly. The default code groups are similar to the security zones used by Internet Explorer, and include My_Computer_Zone and Internet_Zone. Example of evidence includes the strong name of an assembly and the application directory.

2. Code groups have associated permissions, and the permission of every code group that an assembly belongs to is combined to form the permission set of the assembly.

3. An assembly can refuse certain permissions, which are subtracted from the permission set in step 2.

4. The result is the final set of permissions that is granted to an assembly.

The CLR also contains numerous checks that prevent an assembly circumventing the permission-granting process. When an assembly is loaded, the strong name of the assembly is verified to prevent an assembly impersonating a more trusted assembly, and slipping into a code group that will be granted more permissions. A series of load-time checks, which are discussed further in the following section, guard against deliberate flaws being used to circumvent security policies. At runtime, stack walks prevent an assembly with limited permissions using a more trusted assembly to access system resources that it would not have direct access to (the so-called luring attack).

Validation and Verification During the Loading Process

When a module containing managed code is loaded, the Portable Executable (PE) file and managed metadata are validated to ensure the various sections within the file format do not contain inaccuracies that could be used to trick the runtime into allowing the loaded assembly access to data or functionality it would otherwise not have access to. The checks ensure that information in header sections is consistent with the data contained in the main sections of the file.

Once the native and managed metadata of the module that houses the managed code has been validated, the MSIL is validated to ensure it has no physical flaws, such as invalid byte sequences. On successful completion of this check, verification of the MSIL is carried during the JIT compilation process if an assembly does not have the SkipVerification permission, which is discussed shortly. The MSIL verification checks focus on type safety, which is critical in ensuring that code does not read or modify memory locations it does not have the permission to access directly. Every IL instruction has a particular set of conditions that allow the instruction to be deemed verifiable, and these are listed in Partition III of the ECMA standard. Verification includes checks such as ensuring that the argument passed to a call instruction is a method reference and checking that the correct number of arguments have been placed on the stack.

Certain languages that target the runtime can produce code that is not verifiably type-safe. For assemblies produced in this manner to be successfully loaded, the permission to skip verification must be granted. The default security policy will give this permission to code that belongs to the My_Computer_Zone code group, but not to any other zone code group. This means that code loaded across an intranet or over the Internet will take a MSIL verification performance hit, which will be in addition to the performance hit of copying the Win32 module that houses the MSIL across the network. Assemblies loaded from remote locations are cached between uses, but even though they can be physically loaded from disk, they will logically remain part of a remote code group, and will experience MSIL verification each time they are loaded and JIT compiled.

NOTE   The term *module* has been overloaded to mean a number of different things. In Win32, an executable image loaded into memory is known as a module, and this term applies to both DLLs and EXEs. In .NET, an assembly is made of one or more .NET modules, all of which are Win32 modules; an assembly can also contain files such as JPEG images, which are not Win32 modules, even when they are loaded into memory.

Assemblies

Assemblies are the basic unit to which permissions are granted within the CLR. The permissions that are granted to an assembly are resolved at load time by examining the code groups that an assembly belongs to, and by summing the permissions that have been granted to each of these code groups. Executing code has a limited opportunity to modify these permission grant sets, by either refusing to use a certain permission (through the CodeAccessPermission.Deny method), or by accepting responsibility for using a permission even if the other assemblies present in the call stack do not have this permission (through the CodeAccessPermission.Assert method). The following snippet shows both techniques in use:

```
FileIOPermission fileIOPerm =
  new FileIOPermission(FileIOPermissionAccess.AllAccess, "c:\\");
fileIOPerm.Assert();
//code here that needs assert
CodeAccessPermission.RevertAssert(); //deactivate assert

RegistryPermission regPerm =
  new RegistryPermission(RegistryPermissionAccess.Read,"HKEY_LOCAL_MACHINE");
regPerm.Deny();
//code here protected by deny operation
CodeAccessPermission.RevertDeny();
```

The evidence-gathering process is not influenced by an assembly's contents in most cases. The cost of computing the assembly's hash, which can be used as evidence to determine if an assembly belongs to a code group, is dependent on an assembly's size, but most evidence, such as application directory, publisher, site, URL, and zone, is implementation independent. The hash code of an assembly is not used as evidence for any of the default code groups, meaning that hash code calculation cost will not be overly important for most scenarios. The cost of accessing evidence is largely dependent on the number of assemblies that are loaded, and larger assemblies will have a smaller per-type performance hit when determining assembly evidence. Large assemblies will cause some working set increase, but Windows NT-based operating systems will share the memory associated with the assembly image across all processes that load the assembly, and the CLR only JIT compiles methods on demand, which minimizes the working set hit.

The manifest of an assembly may contain a permission set request, which can *declaratively* detail the permissions an assembly would like to reject, permissions that are required for an assembly to function correctly, and optional permissions that an assembly would like to have in order to offer maximum functionality. Permission set requests are not mandatory, but make it easier for system administrators to determine the consequences of refusing certain permissions. Refusing a required permission will result in the assembly failing to load, while refusing an optional permission will result in slower or more limited functionality from an assembly.

As discussed previously, the location from which an assembly is loaded has an impact on the security overhead that is experienced at load time. Loading of remote assemblies can have certain deployment advantages, but it is important to realize that the security policy overhead is higher for these loads. In many situations, the performance overhead will be less of a concern than the deployment benefit, but security overhead is worth investigating if load times become excessive.

Stack Walks and Permission Demands

Stack walks are the runtime security feature that attracts a lot of attention in relation to their performance impact. Consider a benchmark of an unmanaged code transition that compares performance with and without a stack walk in place. With the stack walk in place, an eightfold decease in performance occurs for the test case of calling a C-style DLL function that returns a constant 32-bit integer (see Test 13.05). Despite this cost, stack walks are a critical element of Code Access Security (CAS), and without them, the CAS model is weakened to the point of uselessness, as methods in assemblies that lack permissions can simply call into code in more trusted assemblies to perform unauthorized activities. Certain techniques can be used to minimize the impact of stack walks, which are discussed next.

One of the easiest and most efficient techniques to reduce the performance impact of stack walks is to make chunky calls that perform a high volume of work per invocation in situations where stack walks are triggered. In the unmanaged code transition scenario, this means that instead of calling an unmanaged method for every element in a collection, better performance is possible by calling out to a single unmanaged function to do the call for every element, package the results, and send them all back together.

In some situations, combing the calls that result in a permission demand, which in turn triggers a stack walk, is not possible. In this scenario, the best performance scenario is to move the stack walk outside the loop, and to suppress that stack walk being made inside the loop. Suppressing the stack walk can only be done in special cases, such as with the SuppressUnmanagedCodeSecurityAttribute type, so this technique will not always be viable. The SuppressUnmanagedCodeSecurityAttribute type is discussed in Chapter 13.

It is possible to combine a demand and an assert on a method to "cache" the permissions at a position in the stack close to the demand, and this results in a modest performance boost of 8 percent for the test case of reducing stack walk depth from two assemblies to one (see Test 9.01). Code to cache the permission for unlimited reflection is shown in the following snippet. The Demand attribute ensures that all assemblies in the call stack have the permission, and the Assert attribute terminates the stack walk at this location. For a call stack that is walked frequently, and contains many assemblies, caching may be a feasible optimization technique.

```
[ReflectionPermissionAttribute(SecurityAction.Demand, Unrestricted=true)]
[ReflectionPermissionAttribute(SecurityAction.Assert, Unrestricted=true)]
public void PermissionCacheExample{}
```

The permission caching improvement represents only a small percentage of savings in the overall cost of the CAS stack walks. For the permission caching test case from the benchmark described previously, the execution time of this test case was 170 times slower than the test case that did not include a stack walk at all. This dramatic slowdown is heavily influenced by the simplicity of the test method (an integer addition), but highlights that the cost of CAS is not trivial, and the haphazard or overly eager application of permission demands can severely impact performance. In most cases, proper security design within an application can allow these performance problems to be avoided, but in some situations, the cost of the stack walk will be too high.

In these scenarios, an alternative to removing the check completely is to move the check from runtime to JIT time. These JIT-time checks occur when the methods are linked together, and are implemented by placing a declarative link-time check on the method. This LinkDemand *only* checks that the immediate caller of a method has the appropriate checks to call a method, so the possibility of a luring attack is still possible, but the attacker must find an intermediate method that satisfies the link demand to conduct the attack through. LinkDemands are very cheap, impacting less than a 1 percent performance hit compared to the no-demand case in the benchmark discussed earlier. The following code illustrates a LinkDemand for the permission to use unrestricted reflection for a method:

```
[ReflectionPermissionAttribute(SecurityAction.LinkDemand, Unrestricted=true)]
private void LinkDemandMethod(){
 //implementation of method
}
```

As the code sample illustrates, the demander of the permission makes the decision on the use of a link versus runtime demand. This means that the choice is left to the permission consumer, who may not be in the best position to make the decision. To overcome this problem, a declarative link demand can be placed on a method, and based on a parameter or custom attribute, an optional imperative check can be conducted. This technique offers a degree of security—the immediate caller, who is responsible for determining whether the runtime stack walk is conducted, must have been granted the permission to pass the link check; but callers lower in the call stack, which may not have the permission, can explore various code paths in an attempt to convince the caller not to conduct the runtime demand.

In the test case, a single permission is used in the demands and asserts. If multiple permissions are required within a certain method, the permissions can be grouped together in a PermissionSet object, and the demand for all permissions can occur together. This single demand should, in theory, improve performance by reducing the number of stack walks needed. Benchmarking of the current CLR and Framework Library implementation indicates that combining two permissions and conducting a demand operation is about three times slower than performing the two demands individually (see Test 9.02). Future releases may reverse this performance disparity, but if stack walk speed is critical, be sure to investigate whether this anomaly still exists.

The MSDN Library recommends that permission asserts are made declaratively, and demands are made imperatively. Benchmarking indicates that imperative demands are 2.3 times quicker than declarative demands (see Test 9.03), and declarative asserts are 8.7 times quicker than imperative asserts (see Test 9.04). Unless performance is critical, choose the most natural demand or assert technique, which is usually declarative checks when the security action is always performed and imperative checks when performing the action is conditional.

The figures presented in this section show the worst possible case for code access checks, and highlight the importance of not being dismissive of the potential performance impact of access checks. If security checks are properly designed and implemented, they will not typically be a major source of performance problems, and it is worth emphasizing the critical roles correct analysis and design play for security and performance issues.

Cryptography and Encryption

Secure data transfer and identity validation are the challenges that cryptography addresses. Cryptography is a large and complex topic, and the subject of many great books. The MSDN Library provides a good high-level overview of the topic (`http://msdn.microsoft.com/library/default.asp?url=/library/en-us/cpguide/html/cpconcryptographyoverview.asp`), as well as covering the cryptography support offered by the .NET Framework. This section is intended only to complement these resources, and address some of the performance issues relevant to the subject.

As with Code Access Security, optimum performance is strongly dependent on good design. Security features that are thrown into a system late in the implementation phases are often haphazard, with overlapping functionality to cover risks in one area, and no protection in others. Before performance optimizations are even considered, the ability of the security system to address identified threats needs to be ensured. Without this, the whole security system is simply overhead, as it decreases performance without fulfilling its intended purpose.

The level of operating system and Framework Library support for encryption is so powerful and easy to use that it is possible to hurt performance by being overeager in the application of encryption. To take an example, the remoting infrastructure of .NET allows encryption channel sinks to be applied using the configuration file; so for situations where remote communications have variable encryption needs, performance gains can be achieved by removing encryption applications from code elements and allowing configuration settings to control the scope and strength of encryption techniques. For sensitive data written to disk, some users and administrators will prefer to leverage operating system encryption features, while other users on stand-alone machines may prefer no encryption at all. By allowing the level of encryption to be adjusted using settings in a configuration file, the performance characteristics of a system can be tuned without code modification.

When offering adjustable encryption levels, the "out-of-the-box" configuration should support a high level of secure operation, which can then be adjusted down if a user wishes. Default installation configurations with low security thresholds have been the source of many security breaches, and are an area where security is usually a much higher priority than performance.

The technique through which users are offered the option to relax the security settings is dependent on the application, but for consumer applications, offering a more user-friendly experience than manual configuration file editing is preferable. A possible technique is to allow the user to pick between various typical usage patterns, such as home user and corporate environment, and use this information to install an appropriate security policy configuration.

Most recent discussions on encryption focus heavily on public key encryption, which uses asymmetric algorithms to encrypt data. The asymmetric nature of these algorithms is the reason for their popularity—an organization can freely publish its public key, which anyone can use to encrypt data with, and only the holder of the private key can decrypt the data. This encryption differs from private key encryption, which allows encryption and decryption with the same key. This requires an out-of-band exchange of the private key, and obliges both parties to keep the key secret. Both these requirements mean private key encryption has logistical scalability problems when a large number of parties are involved, but for local or two-way encryption, private key encryption is feasible, and has a definite speed advantage.

To put some sort of quantitative measure on the speed difference between the two different encryption methods, a benchmark using the `RijndaelManaged` symmetric encryption class and the `RSACryptoServiceProvider` asymmetric encryption class is defined, and a 10-element byte array is encrypted and decrypted a number of times with both classes. The maximum key length of 256 bits is used with the `RijndaelManaged` type, and the minimum key length of 384 bits is used with the `RSACryptoServiceProvider` class. The asymmetric algorithm is 65 times slower in encrypting and decrypting the byte array, which gives some indication of the significant performance differences that can be expected (see Test 9.05)

To combat the high performance cost of public key encryption, a symmetrical session key can be exchanged using asymmetric encryption, and this new key can be used to provide fast encryption for the rest of the session. This technique is usually implemented by the security infrastructure of a server product or operating system, and application code rarely needs to go to the trouble of implementing this method. Secure Sockets Layer (SSL) uses this symmetric session key-exchange technique, and leveraging the effort that has gone into optimizing technologies like SSL is preferable to attempting to code a manual key-exchange security infrastructure.

The key length used in encryption determines how safe the encrypted data is from brute-force attack. The vulnerability to brute-force attack is proportional to the result of two raised to the power of the key length, so an increase in key length by 1 bit doubles the number of key combinations that have to be attempted to guarantee the success of a brute force attack. Key lengths in the 40 to 56 bit range have been shown to be vulnerable to brute-force attack, but most legal key lengths offered in the `SymmetricAlgorithm`-derived classes are above this. Benchmarking of the 10-element byte array encryption-decryption test with symmetric algorithms shows only a 22 percent increase in execution time when using the maximum key length of 256 bits offered by the `RijndaelManaged` type, compared to the minimum of 128 bits (see Test 9.06). The choice of a key length somewhere between 128 and 256 bits is the best compromise between performance and guaranteed data security.

Encryption has become a vital element in computer and communication systems, and many companies now offer specialized hardware for the task. These hardware devices have processors specially designed for their particular encryption task, and typically outperform software-based encryption techniques. For very high encryption loads, specialized hardware devices can offer a better cost-performance ratio than a combination of general-purpose software and hardware. Most large hardware vendors have material available on their Web sites describing hardware-based encryption solutions. The article at `http://www.dell.com/us/en/biz/topics/power_ps1q02-ssl.htm` provides a good overview of the interaction between software- and hardware-based solutions.

Monitoring Security

A dedicated System Monitor performance object exists to allow the performance impact of CLR security checks on a process to be monitored. The % Time in RT Checks performance counter allows the overall impact of .NET security checks to be monitored, and the Total Runtime Checks and Stack Walk Depth counters can be used to diagnose the cause of a problem if the percentage time counter is excessively high. The Total Runtime Checks counter is a cumulative total of all the Code Access Security checks that have been conducted since the application started, and Stack Walk Depth is the depth from the last observed stack walk. A very deep stack walk will obviously be a performance problem if it occurs too frequently, and techniques such as combining assemblies to reduce the number of permission groups that need to be accessed during a stack walk can be used.

Spikes in the percentage time above 20 percent indicate that a significant amount of time is being spent in runtime checks, and it is worth investigating the code that causes the spikes if overall application performance is unacceptable in these areas.

Conclusion

At the risk of overemphasis, the most critical aspect in achieving optimum performance and security is through thorough risk analysis and design. These activities allow an appropriate level of defensive depth to be put in place to protect an application, and the rationale for various security decisions will be available when optimization work needs to occur. By knowing the risk that a security feature is countering, any decision on how to optimize, replace, or move the vulnerability protection can be made with confidence.

The Code Access Security model gives designers and implementers a new tool to combat security problems. CAS targets a specific aspect of the security issue—the permission that an assembly will be given based on various characteristics of that assembly, such as its origin, strong name, and hash value. CAS is not designed to work in isolation, and the security services offered by the operating system and server software need to be used in addition to CAS to fully secure an application.

Security checks are best applied as close to the boundary of a system as possible. This benefits both system security, as invalid requests are prevented from entering a system, and performance, as no time is wasted processing a request that will eventually be denied. It is only when boundary checks are infeasible or prohibitively expensive that a potentially invalid request should enter the system.

Encryption is a powerful technique for securing data, but encrypting data, particularly using public key encryption, comes at a performance cost. Data encryption should be applied with a specific purpose in mind, with the appropriate algorithm, and with the appropriate key length.

CHAPTER 10

Threading

THREADING AND PERFORMANCE ARE two topics that are often closely related. The motivation for employing multiple threads in a program typically originates from two distinct origins: the need to keep the user interface of an application responsive while a lengthy task is being performed in the background, which is a problem usually experienced in client-side applications, and the need to service multiple requests at the same time, which is a requirement commonly experienced in server-side applications.

Achieving correct thread synchronization and preventing data corruption is a concern for both client-side and server-side applications, but high-performance multithreading is more critical at the server side. Most client-side applications operate at the speed of the user's thought process, which is many orders of magnitude slower than software; and on most occasions when the user is waiting for the software, such as when a large file is being compressed, employing additional threads is only useful to keep the user interface responsive. In contrast, a server-side application will be servicing many requests simultaneously, and threads can provide an ideal tool for ensuring that requests are serviced in the fastest time possible.

Thread Synchronization

The CLR does not alleviate the need to synchronize access to shared resources in a multithreaded application. In fact, the conceptual application of thread synchronization is largely unchanged from Win32, with the requirement to safely guard resources against simultaneous access still very much in existence. At the implementation level, threading in .NET adds a number of new synchronization primitives that makes the application of multithreading simpler, and reduces the need for a considerable amount of the boilerplate code required for safe multi-threading in previous technologies.

The thread safety of all types within the Framework Library is documented in the MSDN Library, with built-in thread safety for static functions and no thread safety for instance functions being the dominant pattern. The lack of built-in thread safety for instance functions is motivated by performance, and the likelihood of deadlock that would occur from locking every object for all operations. To support safe multithreaded operations, the Framework Library supports three common patterns:

- The most prevalent pattern is to simply allow the client code to deal with thread safety, either by not sharing the object across multiple threads, or by using synchronization primitives to lock the object before concurrent access can occur. For objects shared across threads, the use of the Monitor type (which is discussed later in this section) to prevent simultaneous access is the most common option.

- System.String adopts a different technique for thread safety, and is intrinsically thread-safe due to its immutable state. Immutability prevents concurrent modification by definition, and means that no synchronization locks need to be taken out to complete any operation on a string. Any modifying method on a string returns a new instance, leaving the original string, which may be concurrently accessed by another thread, unmodified. Locking of string references to prevent logic bugs due to race conditions may be required in some situations, but this is the case with all thread-safe objects.

- A third technique that can be used to provide thread safety is the Just-In-Time synchronization wrapper, which is used by the Framework Library's collection types. These types are not thread-safe by default, but a call to their Synchronized method returns an object reference that is logically identical to the reference passed in, and will provide the necessary locking before allowing any function calls to be invoked. A nested type derived from the thread-unsafe base type implements the Just-In-Time wrapper, with the derived type maintaining a reference to the original parent object, which it locks before passing function calls through. By deriving the Just-In-Time wrapper from the type that it wraps, the wrapper can be used in all situations where the wrapped type is expected. The following snippet demonstrates the use of ArrayList, which implements this technique:

```
public void UseArrayList(ArrayList al){
}

public void SyncWrapper(){
   ArrayList al = new ArrayList();

   UseArrayList(al); //single-threadeded use

   //pass array list to another thread

   //get a sync wrapper
   al = ArrayList.Synchronized(al);
```

```
    UseArrayList(al); //safe use across mutiple threads
}
```

Implementing Thread-Safe Code

Thread safety can be implemented manually with synchronization primitives and declaratively using attributes. Manual synchronization involves writing code that acquires a lock on a resource, performs the required operations on the resources, and then releases the lock, while declarative synchronization simply involves placing an attribute on a method to indicate that concurrent execution by multiple threads is not permitted.

Declarative Synchronization

The Framework Libraries and CLR offer two declarative synchronization options: the System.Runtime.CompilerServices.MethodImplAttribute with the MethodImplOptions.Synchronized enumeration specified and the System.Runtime.Remoting.Contexts.SynchronizationAttribute. Using the MethodImplAttribute results in the generated MSIL method having the synchronized method modifier applied, which instructs the CLR to take out a lock on the object reference prior to invoking an instance method, and to lock the type reference for static methods. The CLR will release the lock at the completion of the method call. The following snippet shows the application of this technique:

```
// using System.Runtime.CompilerServices;
[MethodImpl(MethodImplOptions.Synchronized)]
public void SyncMethod(){}
```

The SynchronizationAttribute is implemented via a context sink, which intercepts calls made on an object, applies a lock, and then passes control to the next sink in the context sink chain. The SynchronizationAttribute can also intercept outgoing calls if the IsReEntrant property is set to true, which allows other threads access to the method, increasing throughput. To use SynchronizationAttribute, a type must be derived from MarshalByRefObject, which adds the necessary interception layer to allow the context sink to be successfully applied. The MarshalByRefObject-derivation requirement can be a significant obstacle if a complex type hierarchy based on logical relationships has been developed.

Manual Synchronization

The simplest synchronization primitive for manual synchronization is the `Monitor` type. `Monitor` has static `Exit` and `Enter` methods that take an object parameter and can be used to ensure that a single thread is within a code block at a particular time. When implementing thread-safe methods, it is common to call `Monitor.Enter` with the `this` reference (`Me` reference in VB .NET), perform the required access of the type's member variables, and then call `Monitor.Exit`. Wrapping the call to `Monitor.Exit` in a `finally` block guarantees that the lock will be released even if an exception is thrown.

Both VB .NET and C# offer syntactic shortcuts for dealing with the `Monitor` type. The C# `lock` and VB .NET `SyncLock` statements both allow a `Monitor` lock to be acquired in the context of a try-finally block, making exception-safe lock use extremely easy. The `lock` and `SyncLock` statements are fully resolved at compile time, and there is no performance motivation for shying away from their use. The following snippet shows the use of the `SyncLock` statement:

```
Dim o As Object = New Object
'pass o to another thread
SyncLock (o)
    'safe multithreaded use of o here
End SyncLock
```

In terms of raw performance, managing synchronization manually will always allow for the best performance to be achieved. Lock granularity can be manually adjusted to achieve the optimum balance between lock acquisition and contention, and multiple resources can be grouped into types to allow a single lock to be taken out over a group of objects that will be used together. Manual lock management also allows for use of a `ReaderWriterLock`, which is discussed in the "ReaderWriterLock" section.

Synchronization Performance

To illustrate performance differences, a test case involving an `ArrayList` where the value of an integer element needs to be retrieved, incremented, and then stored back in the collection is conducted. Table 10-1 shows the results of normalizing all test results to a value of 1 for the case with no synchronization (see Test 10.01).

Table 10-1. Synchronization Performance

Test Case Description	Result
No synchronization	1.00
System.Monitor lock for entire operation	1.00
System.Monitor lock once per element	1.19
Synchronized wrapper	1.49
Context bound wrapper with no synchronization	1.35
Context bound wrapper with synchronization	185.9

The results show that using context attributes for synchronization is extremely slow compared to the other methods, and the fastest synchronized case is to acquire a lock for the entire test. Holding a lock for long periods blocks other threads that need to access the resource, and can cause significant bottlenecks within a system. The test case of taking a lock out once per element and holding it for a read-write cycle is only slightly slower than the case where the lock is held for the entire test, and gives the best compromise between performance and scalability in this scenario. The synchronized wrapper test case is slower than the lock-per-element test case, as the synchronized wrapper will actually take out a lock twice per element—once for the read operation and once for the write operation.

For general-purpose thread safety in situations where performance is not a critical priority, the use of synchronized wrappers represents a good compromise between performance and a simplified programming model. Synchronization can be tedious to code and a common source of bugs. The C# lock statement and VB .NET SyncLock statement reduce the possibility of a lock failing to be released by placing Monitor.Exit calls in a finally block, but these statements still require client code to have an awareness of the thread safety of a particular type. The Synchronized wrapper pattern allows Just-In-Time thread safety to be achieved, and it is also possible to provide an overloaded constructor that can return a fully thread-safe object reference without the need to later call the Synchronized method. The use of the synchronized wrapper is only marginally slower than the equivalent synchronization locks added directly to an object. For the test case of incrementing a virtual public property, employing the synchronized wrapper is 12 percent slower than direct synchronization (see Test 10.02).

A Visual Studio .NET add-in that can add a Synchronized wrapper to any reference type is included with the code samples for the book (available for download at http://www.apress.com).

Synchronization Primitives

The System.Threading namespace includes equivalents for most Win32 synchronization primitives. A Monitor is the .NET equivalent of a Win32 critical section, the Mutex type is a wrapper around a Win32 mutex object, and the Win32 event object is represented by AutoResetEvent and ManualResetEvent. The Win32 semaphore is missing, but its functionality can be simulated using Mutex objects and a count variable.

The Mutex type and Monitor type have characteristics that are superficially similar, but the most fundamental difference is the scope of the lock. A mutex lock is globally visible to all processes running on a machine or Windows session, depending on whether the name of the mutex is prefixed with Global\ or Local\. A Mutex is required to synchronize access to resources shared across multiple processes, such as memory-mapped files, whereas a Monitor is application domain-specific. The extra overhead of the system-wide locking is very high—acquiring and releasing a Mutex is around 50 times slower than a Monitor (see Test 10.03). If a machine- or session-wide lock is required, the only option available is to use kernel objects like Mutex, but be aware of the cost of acquiring these locks in tight loops. If profiling indicates that acquiring kernel-level locks is a significant performance strain on an application, architectural changes to alleviate the need to lock so frequently or widely are required, and code-level technique is unlikely to fix the problem.

The System.Threading namespace also exposes an Interlocked type that supports optimized increment, decrement, and exchange methods, as shown in the following code. The methods exposed by the Interlocked type offer faster execution than applying a Monitor lock and performing the equivalent function. In a test case, incrementing an integer member variable of an object is five times quicker using Interlocked.Increment compared to using a Monitor lock (see Test 10.04).

```
Dim i As Integer = 0, j As Integer = 0
'pass i and j to another thread
System.Threading.Interlocked.Increment(i) 'i = 1
System.Threading.Interlocked.Decrement(j) ' j =-1
System.Threading.Interlocked.Exchange(i, -2) 'i = -2
```

Thread Coordination

In a multithreaded application, having all worker threads completing the same activity is the simplest scenario to cater for. Worker threads are those threads that are completing processing activities not related to keeping the application in a state of responsiveness, and will either be manually created threads or thread pool threads (the thread pool is discussed later in this chapter). Worker threads are not synonymous with background threads, which are defined as threads that will not prevent a process from terminating. The following snippet demonstrates the various relationships between background and worker threads:

```
using System;
using System.Threading;

public class ThreadTypes {

  static public void ThreadTypesDemo(){
    Console.WriteLine("main thread is background: {0}",
      Thread.CurrentThread.IsBackground);
    //main thread is background: False

    //create foreground worker
    Thread workerThread = new Thread(new
      ThreadStart(ThreadTypes.WorkerThreadMethod));
    workerThread.Start();
    //worker thread is background: False

    //create background worker
    Thread workerThread2 = new Thread(new
      ThreadStart(ThreadTypes.WorkerThreadMethod));
    workerThread2.IsBackground = true;
    workerThread2.Start();
    //worker thread is background: True

    //schedule for thread pool
    ThreadPool.QueueUserWorkItem(new WaitCallback(ThreadPoolMethod));
    //worker thread is background: True

  }

  public static void WorkerThreadMethod(){
    Console.WriteLine("worker thread is background: {0}",
      Thread.CurrentThread.IsBackground);
  }

  public static void ThreadPoolMethod(object state){
    Console.WriteLine("thread pool thread is background: {0}",
      Thread.CurrentThread.IsBackground);
  }
}
```

When all worker threads are completing the same task, the amount of coordination that needs to occur between the threads is minimal. Each thread completes its task blissfully unaware of other threads, and the only concern is preventing simultaneous access of shared resources. The main performance issue that can arise in this situation is excessive locking caused by shared resources that are accessed frequently across multiple threads. Excessive locking can prove to be a performance problem, and the inability to share a resource effectively can be a scalability problem.

To solve this issue, some type of replication or courser-grain resource allocation can be used. Replication is the simplest solution, and involves adding further resources to the system to avoid the lock contention problem. If this solution is not feasible, using a better resource sharing strategy is required. Thread locks are often taken out to acquire a single unit of a shared resource, but lock contention can be reduced by taking multiple units of the resource at a single time and storing these on the call stack or thread-local storage for future use.

NOTE *Thread-local storage* is "globally" accessible memory like static variables that can have unique values for each thread. The AllocateNamedDataSlot, GetNamedDataSlot, SetData, and FreeNamedDataSlot method of Thread and the ThreadStaticAttribute type support thread-local storage.

When multiple worker threads are completing different tasks, the coordination implementation becomes more complex. The scenario where a method acquires a lock, checks on some condition, and if this condition is met, schedules a task that is completed by another thread is a common occurrence in many types of applications. A real-world example is an application that has a thread that is monitoring a port for requests from a hardware device, and placing the requests on a queue for other threads to service. Both the listener thread, which needs to add items, and the worker threads, which need to remove items, modify the queue, and this means a thread-safe implementation is required.

Minimizing the amount of time that each thread locks the queue is critical in achieving maximum system throughput. This means that a thread should surrender a lock as soon as it determines that there is no work to complete, and for threads that are required to complete work, the length for which the lock is held should be kept to a minimum. For smaller data items, copying the data and releasing the lock should be used to minimize lock duration if application logic allows this to occur. In some cases, simply copying the entire data structure will not be possible due to size or logic constraints, but it is worth attempting a redesign of the overall logic in this case to see if the partial copying or temporary locking can be used without compromising thread safety or application logic. Long-term thread locking kills scalability, and the concern is particularly relevant for server applications, which are more likely to be running on hyper-threaded or multiprocessor machines.

NOTE *Hyper-threading* is an Intel processor technology that allows a single processor to act like a multiple processor. A hyper-threaded processor can achieve some parallelization of thread execution, and will deliver an approximate speed boost of 10 percent over a non-hyper-threaded processor running at the same clock speed.

A thread is regularly allocated a block of processor time, called a *time slice*, and the number of times that this time slice is allocated is dependent on the thread's priority. In a multithreaded application, it is possible that a thread will run out of work to do before its time slice expires. In the example described earlier, a processing thread can discover that there are no items in the queue, and hence no useful work needs to be done. This thread has two options—it can continue to poll the queue for items until its time slice expires, or it can surrender its time slice. Polling always hurts performance, and it is wise to surrender the remaining time slice. The simple way to do this is to call Thread.Sleep, and pass in a parameter of zero.

The problem with the Sleep technique just described is that worker threads will be constantly loaded, and they will check the queue and then sleep if there are no items, which takes time away from the listener thread. Loading and unloading threads requires a switch from application mode to kernel mode under the current CLR implementation, which is a moderate performance hit, and best avoided if possible. A better solution would be to suspend the processing threads until the listener adds an item to the queue. The Monitor.Wait and Monitor.Pulse methods are purpose-built to support this technique. When a thread calls Monitor.Wait on an object, it is telling the thread scheduler that it can't do anything useful until the object it is waiting upon changes. Threads that have an interest in an object are normally in one of two states—they either hold the lock on the object, or they are ready to acquire it. Threads that have called Monitor.Wait are in a third category. They neither hold the lock, nor are they ready to do anything if they get the lock—they are inactive until something else happens.

When the listener thread adds an item to the queue, it must call Monitor.Pulse to allow a thread to be moved from the waiting queue to the ready queue. This reactivates one of the processing threads, which can then process the new request once it acquires the lock. The following snippet shows the two techniques:

```
//wait and pulse
public void EnqueueWorkWithPulse(){
  //add work item
  Monitor.Pulse(this);
}

public void UseWaitAndPulse(){
  lock(this){
    if (/*cannot do anything*/){
      Monitor.Wait(this);
    }
    else{
      //do work
    }
  }
}

//sleep
public void EnqueueWork(){
  //add work item
}

public void UseSleep(){
  lock(this){
    if (/*cannot do anything*/){
      Monitor.Exit(this);
      Thread.Sleep(0);
    }
    else{
      //do work
    }
  }
}
```

The choice between using the Sleep technique, which simply forfeits the current time slice, and the Wait/Pulse technique, which allows a processing thread to forfeit all time slices until a pulse is received, depends on the probability that there will be an item in the queue when a thread acquires a lock. Moving threads to the waiting queue and signaling these threads with a Pulse method call incurs a certain overhead, so for the case where it is likely a processing thread will have work to do once a lock is acquired, the use of the Sleep technique is optimum. Conversely, if the queue is mostly empty, the Wait/Pulse technique is best. A test case where a listener thread adds an integer to the queue and a single processing thread removes the item is used to test the optimum ratio. The Sleep technique gives the system greater throughput until the probability that the queue contains an item falls below 10 percent (see Test 10.05).

NOTE The CRL thread pool, which is discussed later in this chapter, presents an alternative to this technique.

Thread.Sleep vs. Thread.SpinWait

The Sleep and SpinWait methods of the Thread type appear to offer the same functionality. Both suspend the calling thread's execution for a certain time period, as specified by the method's parameters. The critical difference between the two methods is that while the Sleep method causes the thread to surrender the remainder of its processor time slice, the SpinWait method will cause the thread to remain active on the processor until preemptively removed.

This means that if a resource is expected to become available very soon, SpinWait has the potential to increase performance by reducing context switches. The method is only useful on systems where other hardware devices are capable of making the resource available, and where excessive context switches cause performance issues. Under most circumstances, the employment of SpinWait should be left to the optimization phases of development. Premature employment is likely to hurt performance by wasting processor cycles waiting for locks or resources that will not become available in the thread's time slice.

Resource Contention and Thread Locking

Lock granularity refers to the length of time and number of resources that a particular lock holds. A lock on a single object that spans a few lines of code is highly granular, while locking an entire method or a large block of code is a low-granularity locking strategy. Code that has a high-lock granularity sacrifices absolute speed for scalability, and on multiprocessor machines, system through-put is maximized. On single-processor machines, the effect of low-lock granularity is not as pronounced, as threads that are blocked while waiting on a resource will not consume processor time waiting for the lock to become available. On a multiprocessor machine, holding a lock for a long time can prevent work from being completed on all other processors that do not hold the lock, and this can significantly impact both performance and scalability. As a general rule, it is advisable to hold a lock for the minimum amount of time possible to perform the required work.

The performance figures related to synchronization in Test 10.01 show that decreasing lock granularity from a per-method lock to a lock held for the entire test case results in only a minor improvement in raw performance, indicating that the raw speed benefit of low-lock granularity is not pronounced.

ReaderWriterLock

Threads that modify an object must apply locks to prevent concurrent data modification. Threads that simply retrieve data from an object, and do not modify it, must still apply locks to prevent writers modifying the data that they are reading. However, in most circumstances, there is no need for a lock held by a reader to prevent other readers from accessing the data, but this is the consequence of using simple locks like Monitor and Mutex. In situations where a significant reader population exists, adopting a Reader-Writer lock pattern can improve system throughput by reducing resource contention. A Reader-Writer lock allows multiple concurrent readers, but acquiring the Writer lock prevents all other threads from acquiring a Reader or Writer lock.

 NOTE At times, the reader should exclusively lock data. If the reader is going to read the data, perform a calculation based on the data, and then store the calculation results back in the original source, the lock may need to be held for the entire operation, depending on the isolation levels required. Isolation-level concerns are typically more prevalent with data access code, but it is beneficial to be aware of the issues when dealing with thread locks.

Prior to .NET, developers had to resort to homegrown or third-party solutions to implement a Reader-Writer lock pattern. In recognition of the general usefulness of the pattern, the ReaderWriterLock has been incorporated into the System.Threading namespace, and can be easily accessed from any .NET language. The ReaderWriterLock type is easy to use—an instance of the type is created, and the AcquireReaderLock and AcquireWriterLock methods can be used to acquire a lock of the appropriate type.

The current implementation of ReaderWriterLock is much slower than using a Monitor lock, and it is worth measuring system performance using both lock techniques to ensure that the use of ReaderWriterLock results in an overall increase in system throughput. A Writer lock on a ReaderWriterLock instance is five times slower than acquiring a Monitor lock (see Test 10.06), and a Reader lock is six times slower to acquire. To allow easy switching between ReaderWriterLock and Monitor locks, the acquisition of a lock can be contained in conditional compilation blocks, and a #define can be used to switch between two techniques, as shown in the following sample:

```
#define RWLOCK
using System;
using System.Threading;

public class ConditionalLocking {

#if RWLOCK
   private ReaderWriterLock _rw = new ReaderWriterLock();
#endif

   public void ReadMethod(){
#if MONITOR
      Monitor.Enter(this);
#endif
#if RWLOCK
      _rw.AcquireReaderLock(-1);
#endif
      try{
         //actual logic
      }
      finally{
#if MONITOR
         Monitor.Exit(this);
#endif
#if RWLOCK
         _rw.ReleaseReaderLock();
#endif
      }
   }

   public void WriteMethod(){
#if MONITOR
      Monitor.Enter(this);
#endif
#if RWLOCK
      _rw.AcquireWriterLock(-1);
#endif
      try{
         //actual logic
      }
      finally{
```

```
#if MONITOR
        Monitor.Exit(this);
#endif
#if RWLOCK
        _rw.ReleaseWriterLock();
#endif
    }
  }
}
```

Thread Suspension

A thread executing managed code may be blocked to allow the runtime to perform some function, such as garbage collection. It is possible to use the unmanaged interface IGCThreadControl to receive notification that these events are about to happen, and it is conceivable that an application may want to make some call out to unmanaged code when execution of managed code is blocked. Using the IGCThreadControl notification to implement a compensating action in unmanaged code when a very performance-sensitive operation is being conducted is a possible scenario.

Specifying an IGCThreadControl-implementing object can only be done from an unmanaged CLR host, as the SetGCHostControl method is part of the ICorConfiguration interface, which can be retrieved only *before* the CLR starts, making it inaccessible from managed code. Chapter 7 presents a code sample that uses an unmanaged host to interact with the ICorConfiguration interface. For a managed-code-only solution, calling GC.Collect prior to a time-critical method may prove to be a possible alternative to using IGCThreadControl, but this technique is imprecise, and may hurt performance by triggering an excessive number of garbage collections.

Thread Pool

The ability to receive and queue work requests for subsequent execution is a common requirement. Creating and then discarding a thread for each request incurs an unnecessary overhead, and it is desirable to recycle existing threads to service new requests. Implementing a solution where a pool of threads is available to service incoming requests can be tedious and error prone, and in recognition of the general usefulness of thread pools, the Framework Library provides the ThreadPool type in the System.Threading namespace. The thread pool is implemented independently of operating system thread pools, and is available for use on any platform that the CLR supports.

Using the thread pool to queue work items is quite simple. The System.Threading.ThreadPool static method QueueUserWorkItem takes a WaitCallback delegate object, which represents the entry point into the work item. An overloaded version of QueueUserWorkItem allows an object containing state data to be passed to the callback method. If the process thread pool has an inactive thread that can execute the work item, the new task is assigned to this thread and executed. If an inactive thread does not exist, but the thread pool has not reached its maximum limit, a new thread is created, and the work item is assigned to this thread. If there are no inactive threads, and the thread pool maximum limit has been reached, the new work items are queued until a thread becomes available. The following sample shows the use of the thread pool for queued work items:

```
Public Sub UseThreadPool()
   ThreadPool.QueueUserWorkItem(New WaitCallback(AddressOf SubWorkerMethod))
   ThreadPool.QueueUserWorkItem(New WaitCallback(AddressOf _
     SubWorkerMethod), "state")
End Sub

Private Sub SubWorkerMethod(ByVal state As Object)
   If state Is Nothing Then
     'Do work without state
   Else
     'optionally use state for work
   End If
End Sub
```

In addition to their work-queuing functionality, thread pools also allow the number of threads in a process that are created to monitor a single event to be minimized. For example, an application may want to modify its behavior based on the setting in a registry key. The Win32 API function RegNotifyChangeKeyValue allows a handle to be supplied to the registry API that will be signaled when the requested change occurs. Although delegates and events replace asynchronous notification in .NET, at times interoperating with Win32 functions like RegNotifyChangeKeyValue will be required. Prior to thread pooling, a typical implementation would be to create a dedication thread that is blocked waiting for a change to the handle to be signaled, but with the thread pool, a single thread is dedicated to waiting for all blocked operations, and items can be added to this waiting thread with the RegisterWaitForSingleObject method. When the object is signaled, the WaitOrTimerCallback delegate that was passed to the RegisterWaitForSingleObject method is called. The code to accomplish this monitoring is shown here:

```
//see full sample in code downloads for DllImport arguments
int keyHandle;
string registryKeyName = ""; //set as appropriate
System.Threading.WaitHandle regWaitHandle =
  new System.Threading.AutoResetEvent(false);
RegOpenKeyEx((int)Microsoft.Win32.RegistryHive.CurrentUser, registryKeyName,
  0, KEY_READ, out keyHandle);
RegNotifyChangeKeyValue(keyHandle, 1, REG_NOTIFY_CHANGE_LAST_SET,
  regWaitHandle.Handle.ToInt32(), 1);
System.Threading.ThreadPool.RegisterWaitForSingleObject(regWaitHandle,
    new System.Threading.WaitOrTimerCallback(RegistrKeyChanged),
    registryKeyName, -1, false);
```

The thread pool is also used for other activities like asynchronous delegates and the System.Threading.Timer type. The proper operation of the thread pool is important for the successful operation of a process, and it is essential that work items added to the thread pool are good citizens. The work items should complete their tasks as quickly as possible, and not block for excessively long periods. If long blocking is required, the work item should call the pool's RegisterWaitForSingleObject method, and surrender the current thread, or the method should be moved onto a manually created thread.

When diagnosing application performance issues with asynchronous calls and timers, it is worth checking the thread pool's utilization. If the number of available threads, which can be determined by calling the ThreadPool.GetAvailableThreads method, is constantly low, the overall performance of the application is likely to suffer.

Modifying the Process-Wide Thread Pool

Each process has a set maximum thread pool size that is determined according to the number of processors on the system. The default setting is to use a maximum of 25 threads per CPU, but at times this default setting may not deliver the best performance. If profiling indicates that context switching is a significant performance issue, or profiling with a higher pool size is required, the unmanaged runtime API can be invoked to modify the maximum pool size.

NOTE The motivation for this section came from work and code developed by Mike Woodring of DevelopMentor. Mike has an excellent selection of .NET tools and samples located at http://www.bearcanyon.com.

The unmanaged interface that controls the thread pool is ICorThreadPool; because this interface is not included in the mscoree type library that defines many of the CLR interfaces, it must be manually added to a project. The definition for the interface is included with the code sample that accompanies this book. Once this interface has been defined using the appropriate Interop method attributes, a .NET wrapper for the mscoree.tlb COM type library can be used to create the main COM class that represents the runtime, this class can be cast to the ICorThreadPool interface, and the new thread pool limit can be set:

```
ICorThreadPool threadControl = (ICorThreadPool)new mscoree.CorRuntimeHostClass();
threadControl.CorSetMaxThreads(50,50);
```

Care should be taken when modifying the maximum thread pool settings, as it is easy to create a situation where performance suffers due to the modifications. This process should be mostly reserved for custom projects where atypical hardware configurations are likely to make the modifications successful.

Monitoring Threading

Many tools are available for monitoring thread performance within a process. The System Monitor .NET CLR LocksAndThreads performance object can be used to view information specific to managed threading, but as .NET threads are implemented using Win32 threads, any traditional thread monitoring tool can provide valuable performance data. System Monitor also contains a Thread performance object that exposes counters containing detailed statistics not available in the CLR LocksAndThreads performance object.

Identifying the underlying thread ID of a managed thread can be a tedious task. If a specific thread is being monitored, the AppDomain.GetCurrentThreadId method can be used to output the thread ID of interest so that it can be selected in System Monitor. An instance of the Thread performance object is available for each thread in a process, and the ID Thread counter can be used to match up a thread instance with a thread ID.

The Visual Studio .NET debugger can also be used to retrieve the thread ID for a particular thread. Switch between the call stacks of threads in a process when execution is paused using the Debug Location toolbar, shown in Figure 10-1. The ID of each thread appears in square brackets in the thread drop-down menu.

When unmanaged debugging is enabled for a project, the Program drop-down menu will contain one entry for the managed portion of the application, and another entry for the entire application including unmanaged threads, which will be in the form of [ProcessID] ProcessName:Native. The program entry suffixed with Native needs to be selected in the drop-down menu to observe CLR threads like the finalizer thread and the concurrent garbage collector thread.

Debug Location			▼ ✕
Program [268] PerfTest.exe ▼	Thread [3296] <No Name> ▼	Stack Frame 0000000000	▼

Figure 10-1. Visual Studio's Debug Location toolbar

NOTE Unmanaged debugging allows all threads in an application to be analyzed and stepped through. When debugging thread-related performance problems, enabling both CLR and unmanaged debugging gives the fullest range of information. For C# and VB .NET, unmanaged debugging can be enabled on the Debugging page of the Project Properties dialog box.

When attempting to identify the cause of performance problems in a background thread that is not explicitly created by managed code, it is crucial that the operating system and CLR debug symbols are installed. Microsoft Knowledge Base article 319037 describes how to configure Visual Studio .NET to download debug symbols from the Microsoft Symbol Server, which allows debug symbols to be automatically downloaded during a debugging session.

Once the symbols are installed, use System Monitor to determine the thread ID of the thread that is suffering poor performance, attach to the process using Visual Studio .NET, and pause the process when the thread is performing poorly. Switch to the poorly performing thread using the Debug Location toolbar, and determine what the thread is doing by inspecting the call stack. If the cause of the performance problem is in a thread not explicitly created by application code, and it is not evident from the name of the functions in the call stack what activities are being conducted by the thread, a newsgroup archive search using the function names is a worthwhile exercise. It is important to document the circumstances of performance problems as thoroughly as possible even if the information does not appear readily usable. At worst, the exact function name causing performance problems will assist in reducing the turnaround time when submitting a support request to Microsoft Product Support or the developer of a third-party component.

Conclusion

Threads can significantly increase the performance of an application if implemented properly, and can allow many tasks to be conducted in parallel. Poor implementation can cause deadlocks and sluggish performance, and add greatly to application complexity. The .NET Framework offers some new patterns for implementing thread safety, but conceptually, the topic has not changed greatly with the introduction of .NET. Solid design is a critical element in successful development of a multithreaded application—shared resources need to be identified early, and common locking strategies need to be applied across an application to prevent deadlock and excessive waits for locked objects.

Identifying the correct synchronization primitive to use when implementing thread safety is important from a performance perspective. The different synchronization primitives are optimized for different usage patterns, and using the wrong primitive will result in code that is slow and awkward. The `Monitor` lock will be sufficient for most requirements, whereas the other locking structures are suited to special-purpose scenarios.

CHAPTER 11

IO and Serialization

As with other areas of functionality within the Framework Libraries, the System.IO namespace replaces a multitude of APIs that exist in the unmanaged world for file and directory management. The types in the IO namespace offer most of the functionality available through Win32, with some notable exceptions such as multistream and memory-mapped files. Streams play an important role in the IO namespace, and they allow services to be transparently applied to data flow, which can be used to boost performance in a number of scenarios.

Serialization is the process of transforming the data of an object from its in-memory form into a representation that can be stored or transported. The support for and awareness of serialization in the Framework Libraries is quite pervasive, which means that effort spent in optimizing serialization is likely to result in performance wins across many areas of an application.

IO Performance Background

Reading and writing from hard disk is much slower than the equivalent access of volatile memory, and when the disk is located on a remote machine, the performance hit becomes even more pronounced. Hard disk access speed has gradually improved, but the relative performance difference between volatile and disk storage has been maintained. Improving the performance of disk IO involves decoupling the speed of the disk access from the speed of the application. A number of techniques can be employed to achieve this:

- Buffered disk writes add a memory cache between the code persisting data to disk and the actual writing of the bytes onto a disk sector. In buffered writes, data can be flushed to disk asynchronously, allowing application code to perform other tasks.

- Hard disk drivers can prefetch disk data into a memory buffer based on the patterns of previous data requests from a file. Synchronous reads are generally required for successful prefetching of data, so splitting data reads between random and synchronous reads can result in increased performance.

- Asynchronous IO can be used to place a request to retrieve data from disk, and allow the application to execute other code while waiting for the data to become available.

- The speculative reading of data from disk on worker threads can be performed so that frequently required data is available before it is requested. When using this technique, the potential for excessive memory usage exists, and the use of a caching framework to allow the data to be discarded if memory pressure is high is advisable. ASP.NET has a built-in caching engine, and the Caching Application Block (`http://msdn.microsoft.com/library/default.asp?url=/library/ en-us/dnpag/html/Cachingblock.asp`) can be used in any .NET application.

- A tightly packed binary file format can be used instead of a more verbose format like XML, particularly if the amount of data in the file is large. The use of a binary file format can dramatically reduce the amount of data that needs to be read from disk, but can limit the ability to interoperate with other systems, and the provision of XML export functionality may be needed to overcome this limitation.

A number of the factors affecting IO performance are outside the control of .NET applications. Hardware, drivers, and file systems all have a significant impact on IO speed, and disk fragmentation can slow down disk access considerably. Investigating these factors should be the first step in investigating IO-related performance problems, as any code modifications are unlikely to solve the problem. The `PhysicalDisk` and `Network Interface` objects in System Monitor allow for many low-level aspects of IO to be monitored, and the Disk Defragmenter tool can analyze a disk and identify whether defragmentation is required. DiskMon and FileMon from Sysinternals (`http://www.sysinternals.com`) can also serve as useful tools when investigating IO-related performance issues. FileMon is a file system monitoring tool that displays information on all read, write, delete, open, and create operations that occur on a file system, and can also monitor named pipe and mail slot activity. DiskMon offers similar functionality to FileMon, but where FileMon is focused on providing information on a per-file basis, DiskMon collects and displays the information on a per-disk basis.

The System.IO Namespace

In addition to various helper and exception types, the `IO` namespace contains two basic groups of types: those that deal directly with files and folders, and the stream types, all of which derive from the abstract `System.IO.Stream` type. The stream types provide an abstraction from the physical medium that stores the data, and also allow services to be layered on top of standard streams. The

`BufferedStream` type is an example of a service-only stream, and it allows data to be written or read from another stream in a buffered manner. `BufferedStream` requires another stream, such as `FileStream`, to sit between it and the object representing the storage medium. This layered approach to streams makes it extremely easy to write code that takes advantage of various stream services. The client code simply writes data to the stream at the top of the layer; this stream provides the required processing and passes the modified data to the next stream in the layer. Figure 11-1 shows an example of stream layering.

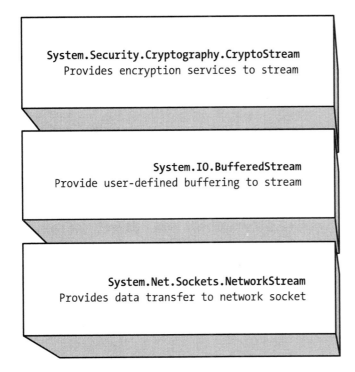

Figure 11-1. Layered streams allow pluggable services to be applied to a stream of data.

Different types of streams have different abilities, such as the ability to move to an arbitrary position in a stream and to move backward through a stream. The abstract `System.IO.Stream` class provides various properties that can be queried to determine the supported operation on a particular stream.

Layered streams can be used to optimize an application's performance. If the speed of a distributed application is bound by network latency, compressing data before transport makes sense. Streams make implementing this encryption trivial—a stream that offers compression simply needs to be inserted above the network stream on both the client and server side. The code samples that accompany this book (downloadable from `http://www.apress.com`) provide a compressed stream type based on the LZW compression algorithm, and the following code block demonstrates the simplicity of using the layered stream approach:

```
public void WriteCompressedData(System.Net.Sockets.Socket Soc, byte[]
DataToWrite){
  using(System.IO.Stream netStream = new System.Net.Sockets.NetworkStream(Soc)){
    using (System.IO.Stream compStream = new
      DotNetPerformance.IO.CompressedStream(netStream)){
    compStream.Write(DataToWrite, 0, DataToWrite.Length);
   }
  }
}
```

NOTE The LZW algorithm is covered by various patents, and is the algorithm at the heart of the GIF file format controversy. Check with your favorite legal department before using this technology in your code.

Reading and Writing to Disk

The IO namespace contains various types for achieving stream and disk access, and each of these types has different capabilities and performance characteristics. Table 11-1 summarizes the basic types and their uses.

Table 11-1. System.IO Core Types

TYPE	CHARACTERISTICS
Stream	Abstract type that defines the interface for all inherited streams and provides a number of common methods that derived streams can access.
FileStream	Sits at the bottom of the IO stack and is the lowest-level managed type for disk access.
MemoryStream	Similar to FileStream, with the exception that the stream stores its data in volatile memory.

Table 11-1 System.IO Core Types (Continued)

TYPE	CHARACTERISTICS
BinaryReader and BinaryWriter	Optimized for persisting data of primitive types, such as Byte and Int32, to a stream. The data is converted to the equivalent byte array, and passed on to a stream for persistence or transport. Neither type can read or write directly to disk, and both require an intermediate stream object.
TextReader and TextWriter	Abstract types that define semantics of types that read and write character-based data.
StringReader and StringWriter	Types that implement TextReader and TextWriter abstract types respectively, and support reading from and writing to a string. The StringWriter type uses a System.Text.StringBuilder object for internal storage.
StreamReader and StreamWriter	Types that implement TextReader and TextWriter abstract types, respectively. Neither type can read from or write directly to disk, and both require an intermediate stream object. A number of the overloaded constructors will create a Stream object internally.
File	Provides static methods for manipulating a file. All reading and writing to the file is supported through returning objects of other types, such as FileStream and StreamReader. Typically used to perform a single operation on a file.
FileInfo	Provides instance methods for manipulating a file. All reading and writing to the file is supported through returning objects of other types, such as FileStream and StreamReader. Typically used to perform multiple operations on a file.
Directory	Provides static methods for manipulating a directory. Typically used to perform a single operation on a directory.
DirectoryInfo	Provides instance methods for manipulating a directory. Typically used to perform multiple operations on a directory.

System.IO.FileStream

As the FileStream type is so pervasive in disk access, it is worth drilling down into its specific performance characteristics. In the current version of the Framework Libraries, all constructors of FileStream eventually resolve to a call to the Win32 CreateFile function, and the read and write functionality methods are implemented using ReadFile and WriteFile functions, respectively. FileStream does not expose the full functionality of the Win32 CreateFile function, and when porting existing applications that have been pretuned with some of the hint flags that can be passed to CreateFile, it may be necessary to use P/Invoke to call CreateFile to open the file and then use the FileStream constructors that accept a file handle. The hint flags can inform the operating system and hardware drivers about the typical access pattern of a file, and this can allow optimized preloading of data to occur. The following sample shows the creation of a FileStream object with the FILE_FLAG_SEQUENTIAL_SCAN hint:

```
using System;
using System.IO;
using System.Runtime.InteropServices;

public class FileIOHints {
  [DllImport("kernel32.dll")]
  static extern IntPtr CreateFile(string lpFileName, uint dwDesiredAccess,
    uint dwShareMode, IntPtr lpSecurityAttributes,
    uint dwCreationDisposition,
    uint dwFlagsAndAttributes, IntPtr hTemplateFile);

  const uint GENERIC_READ             = 0x80000000;
  const uint FILE_SHARE_READ          = 0x00000001;
  const uint FILE_ATTRIBUTE_NORMAL    = 0x00000080;
  const uint FILE_FLAG_SEQUENTIAL_SCAN = 0x08000000;
  const uint OPEN_EXISTING            = 3;

  public void CreateFileObjectWithHints(){
    //open file handle with FILE_FLAG_SEQUENTIAL_SCAN hint
    IntPtr fileHandle = CreateFile(@"c:\myFile.txt", GENERIC_READ,
      FILE_SHARE_READ, IntPtr.Zero,
      OPEN_EXISTING, FILE_ATTRIBUTE_NORMAL | FILE_FLAG_SEQUENTIAL_SCAN,
      IntPtr.Zero);
    //create file stream based on this handle
    using (FileStream fs = new FileStream(fileHandle,
      FileAccess.Read, true)){
      //use fs;
    }
  }
}
```

The optimization settings that are accessible through the FileStream type are the buffer size, and whether the file is opened for synchronous access. For FileStream objects that are created with support for asynchronous IO, CreateFile is passed a FILE_FLAG_OVERLAPPED flag to indicate that IO should be conducted asynchronously, but this is only done if the underlying operating system supports overlapped IO. On Windows 98 and Windows ME systems, the request to open the file with asynchronous IO is ignored, and the file is opened with the FILE_ATTRIBUTE_NORMAL flag.

The flag passed to CreateFile has a significant effect on the performance of asynchronous calls to FileStream. For asynchronous calls on a FileStream object that was opened for synchronous IO, the call is actually completed synchronously. When a synchronous Read or Write method is called on a file that has been opened in asynchronous mode, the call must be completed asynchronously due to the underlying operating system requirements. Translating between synchronous and asynchronous calls adds overhead to IO operations, and should be avoided where possible.

FileStream maintains an internal buffer with a default size of 4096 bytes, but this buffer size can be set using a number of constructors. The buffer size is used to construct an internal byte array that is employed when making requests through to the Win32 functions. When a read or write request is made to a FileStream, an attempt is made to satisfy the request from the internal buffer before actually issuing a read or write operation to the underlying file.

Modifying the file buffer size can have a moderate impact on performance—in tests conducted that involve reading a large file from disk, increasing the buffer size from the default 4KB value to 64KB gives a speed increase of 16 percent (see Test 11.01). This increase in speed comes at the expense of greater memory usage, and is not appropriate when processing many files or files that are small. The test result is also heavily dependent on the hardware in use, so unless an application is being tuned to a particular hardware environment, leaving the buffer size at the default will be sufficient for most applications.

System.IO.BufferedStream Type

The BufferedStream type supports the buffering of data in an internal memory store prior to passing the data through to the underlying stream, which allows requests to the underlying stream to be merged before transmission. As described previously, FileStream provides its own internal memory buffer, but other streaming types, such as System.Net.Sockets.NetworkStream, do not provide built-in buffering capabilities. As with the internal buffer of FileStream, the BufferedStream buffer size can be specified via the use of an overloaded constructor, and defaults to 4096 bytes.

Large, infrequent read and write operations have better performance than small, frequent operations for most stream types, and this is particularly true for network connections. Employing a BufferedStream is a simple way to improve performance in applications when the frequency of read and write operations on a stream is too high, and as with all stream-layering techniques, the changes to the code are minimal.

Migrating code to use a BufferedStream, or any other service-only stream, is made much simpler if code accessing the stream uses references to the System.IO.Stream abstract type rather than the concrete type that performs the IO. Using streams in this manner means that employing a new stream-derived type for data services is simply a matter of adding a single line of code to layer the stream, and all other code will be unaffected. The following code sample shows the use of BufferedStream:

```
using System;
using System.IO;
using System.Net;
using System.Net.Sockets;

public class BufferedStreamUser {
  public static void UseBufferedStream(){
    using (Socket s = new Socket(AddressFamily.InterNetwork,
      SocketType.Stream, ProtocolType.Tcp)){
      IPEndPoint endpoint = new IPEndPoint(IPAddress.Any, 80);
      s.Connect(endpoint);
      using (Stream str = new NetworkStream(s)){
        using (Stream buffStr = new BufferedStream(str)){
          buffStr.WriteByte(0x00);
        }
      }
    }
  }
}
```

Sparse, Compressed, and Memory-Mapped Files

Sparse files represent a feature of the NT File System (NTFS) that allows files containing a large percentage of unoccupied space to minimize disk space wastage by only storing nonzero data in the physical disk file. Read operations on sections of the file that consist entirely of null data do not need to access the hard disk, and depending on the percentage of the file that is empty, a significant performance improvement is possible.

The .NET Framework Libraries provide no support for writing or creating sparse files. The SetAttributes method of the System.IO.File type advertises the possibility of designating a file as sparse, but this method simply forwards the call to the Win32 SetFileAttributes function, which is insufficient to create a sparse file. The functionality to write sparse sections to a file is also missing in the .NET Framework Libraries.

Sparse files that have been created using Win32 functionality can be accessed using the FileStream type. The fact that a file is sparse has no impact on the Win32 ReadFile function used by FileStream to read files. For write operations using FileStream, all data, including zeros, will be written to disk. Setting a section of the file to contain zeros that will not be stored on disk requires a P/Invoke call to DeviceIoControl with a FSCTL_SET_ZERO_DATA control code.

Compressed files on a NTFS file partition have the same level of support in .NET as sparse files—they can be read using the FileStream type, but the compressed attribute cannot be set without using P/Invoke function calls. The following code shows the necessary calls needed to create a compressed file:

```
using System;
using System.IO;
using System.Runtime.InteropServices;

public class CompressedFile {
  [DllImport("kernel32.dll")]
  static extern IntPtr CreateFile(string lpFileName, uint dwDesiredAccess,
    uint dwShareMode, IntPtr lpSecurityAttributes,
    uint dwCreationDisposition,
    uint dwFlagsAndAttributes, IntPtr hTemplateFile);

  [DllImport("kernel32.dll")]
  static extern bool DeviceIoControl(IntPtr hDevice, uint dwIoControlCode,
    ref ushort lpInBuffer, uint nInBufferSize, [Out] byte [] lpOutBuffer,
    uint nOutBufferSize, out uint lpBytesReturned, IntPtr lpOverlapped);

  static uint CTL_CODE(uint DeviceType, uint Function, uint Method,
    uint Access) {
    return ((DeviceType) << 16) | ((Access) << 14) | ((Function) << 2) |
      (Method);
  }

  static readonly uint FSCTL_SET_COMPRESSION =
    CTL_CODE(FILE_DEVICE_FILE_SYSTEM,
    16, METHOD_BUFFERED, FILE_READ_DATA | FILE_WRITE_DATA);
  const uint METHOD_BUFFERED           = 0;
  const uint FILE_DEVICE_FILE_SYSTEM   = 0x00000009;
  const uint FILE_READ_DATA            = 0x0001;
  const uint FILE_WRITE_DATA           = 0x0002;
  const uint GENERIC_ALL               = 0x10000000;
```

```
const uint FILE_SHARE_WRITE              = 0x00000002;
const uint FILE_ATTRIBUTE_COMPRESSED = 0x00000080;
const uint CREATE_ALWAYS                 = 2;

public unsafe static void CreateCompressedFile(){
  //open file handle
  IntPtr fileHandle = CreateFile(@"c:\myFile.txt", GENERIC_ALL,
    FILE_SHARE_WRITE, IntPtr.Zero,
    CREATE_ALWAYS, FILE_ATTRIBUTE_COMPRESSED, IntPtr.Zero);
  //compress file
  uint retBytes;
  ushort COMPRESSION_FORMAT_DEFAULT = 0x0001;
  bool res = DeviceIoControl(fileHandle, FSCTL_SET_COMPRESSION,
    ref COMPRESSION_FORMAT_DEFAULT, sizeof(ushort), null, 0,
    out retBytes, IntPtr.Zero);
  //create file stream based on this handle
  using (FileStream fs = new FileStream(fileHandle,
         FileAccess.Write, true)){
    fs.WriteByte(0x45);  //write uppercase E to file
  }
}
}
}
```

Memory-mapped files (MMFs) allow disk-based files to be mapped into memory and accessed using the same functions and techniques that are normally used to access memory locations with an application's address space. Mapping a file's data into an address range alleviates the need to read the data into a volatile memory buffer. MMFs can also be used to create a file that is backed by the operating system's paging file, meaning that two separate processes can map the same file into memory and exchange data between themselves, which is an extremely efficient, but limited, form of interprocess communication.

The .NET Framework provides no built-in support for memory-mapped files, though third-party managed wrappers from the MMF API do exist. Tomas Restrepo's FileMap assembly, available at http://www.winterdom.com/dev/dotnet/index.html, is a free wrapper available in C# source-code form.

Target Platforms

The IO performance of .NET is heavily dependent on the operating system that the CLR is operating on top of. A paper produced by Microsoft Research[1] shows

---

1. "Study of Random and Sequential IO on Windows 2000," Chung et al.,
   http://research.microsoft.com/BARC/Sequential_IO/

significant performance improvements between different service packs of NT 4. The performance improvements came from various bug fixes and optimizations, and highlight the importance of applying service packs and being conscious of the underlying operating system that .NET applications are deployed on.

The file system of logical disks will also impact performance. Although the FAT16 and FAT32 file systems are becoming less common as the Windows 9x product line dies out, consumer applications still need to be conscious of the existence of FAT file systems and ensure that the IO sections of an application perform adequately when utilizing a FAT disk partition. Various methods within the System.IO namespace will behave differently on lower-end operating systems, and some types, such as System.IO.FileSystemWatcher, will not work at all on Windows 9x/Windows ME systems. If an application makes use of any advanced IO functionality, functional and performance testing on all target operating systems is crucial.

Serialization

Serialization is the process of converting the state of an object from a "living" representation to a "dehydrated" form, which can be used to reconstitute the object in an identical state at some later stage through *deserialization*. A type that wishes to support serialization must be marked with the SerializableAttribute and may optionally implement the ISerializable interface. Frequently used custom attributes within the Framework Libraries have been grouped together into a single TypeAttributes bit flag, which reduces the storage space associated with applying the attribute. The SerializableAttribute is one of the type attributes that form part of TypeAttributes, which means that no storage cost is associated with annotating a type as supporting serialization. As with all other custom attributes, no runtime cost is associated with applying a custom attribute until the attribute is actually used.

The SerializableAttribute gives a type automatic serialization support, whereas implementing the ISerializable interface in addition to using the SerializableAttribute requires a type to provide methods that handle the movement of data to and from a serialized state. Automatic serialization through the SerializableAttribute will generally be sufficient for most types, and it is only for unusual type implementations, such as a type for which the order of member variable population is significant, that it is necessary to implement ISerializable.

Formatters are responsible for converting the raw bytes of a serialized type into a form that can be transported or stored and later converted back to the raw byte format. Two formatters ship with the .NET Framework Libraries: System.Runtime.Serialization.Formatters.Binary.BinaryFormatter and System.Runtime.Serialization.Formatters.Soap.SoapFormatter. Both formatters handle issues such as circular and recursive relationships that can make serializing objects a difficult task, and this means that any object can safely use automatic serialization regardless of the relationships that it may have with other objects.

Member variables that simply cache values and can be recalculated from other member variables within an object, as well as member variables that do not make sense in a different application domain (such as Windows handles), can be marked with the NotSerialized attribute; this tells formatters to ignore this member variable when serializing the object.

Automatic serialization through SerializableAttribute uses reflection to retrieve the state information of an object. Reflection is a complex activity, and raises the question whether implementing ISerializable and handling the transfer of state information manually can improve performance. A test case of two types containing a 32-bit integer and a string is defined, and the performance of one implementation that handles serialization manually is compared with another implementation that simply applies the SerializableAttribute. When using the BinaryFormatter, the ISerializable type shows a slight performance boost, and is about 5 percent faster than the attributed type (see Test 11.02). Deserialization performance shows no significant variation between the two test cases (see Test 11.03). Similar results are obtained for the SoapFormatter (see Tests 11.04 and 11.05). The following snippet shows the ISerializable-implementing type:

```
[Serializable]
public class ISerializableImpl: ISerializable{
  public ISerializableImpl(int x, string y){this.x = x; this.y = y;}
  public ISerializableImpl(SerializationInfo info, StreamingContext context){
    x = info.GetInt32("x");
    y = info.GetString("y");
  }
  public void GetObjectData(SerializationInfo info,
    StreamingContext context){
    info.AddValue("x", x);
    info.AddValue("y", y);
  }
  public int x;
  public string y;
}
```

The small performance hit that automatic serialization imparts is testament to the optimizations that exist in the formatters. Significant caching of type data occurs, which means that the bulk of the reflection's performance hit occurs once per type, not once per object.

Custom Serialization Optimization Techniques

Custom serialization can deliver significant performance gains when the member variables of a type are expensive to initialize, and may not be used in all scenarios. Just as it is possible to lazily initialize member variables, it is also possible to lazily deserialize an object. To implement lazy deserialization, it is necessary to store the SerializationInfo object that contains the serialized data and also keep track of which member variables have been deserialized. When a member variable is needed, it can be retrieved from the cached SerializationInfo object, and when all the member variables have been retrieved, the reference to the SerializationInfo object can be released to allow its memory to be collected.

Custom serialization gives a type the opportunity to decide at runtime whether a member variable is worth serializing, or whether the destination object should regenerate it. Automatic serialization with the SerializableAttribute means that the choice of whether to serialize a member variable must be made at compile time, but for types implementing ISerializable, the determination can be made at runtime based on any relevant parameter. The StreamingContext object passed in to the GetObjectData method allows an object to determine the logical distance that the serialized bytes will travel, and it is possible to serialize different data for cross-application, cross-process, and cross-machine calls.

Different data packaging can also be implemented depending on information available at runtime. For example, a type that keeps a large data structure may decide to compress the structure for cross-machine calls, but transport the data uncompressed when the object is being transported to an application domain on the same machine. The following code shows a simple implementation of this technique. Note the use of the SerializationInfo object that is passed into the overloaded constructor and the GetObjectData method. SerializationInfo acts as an opaque state bag that allows data to be stored and retrieved in a formatter-independent manner.

```
[Serializable]
public class LargeDataStructureHolder: ISerializable{
  object _lotsOfData;
  public LargeDataStructureHolder(){}
  public LargeDataStructureHolder(SerializationInfo info,
    StreamingContext context){
    if (info.GetBoolean("compressed")){
      object compressedData = info.GetValue("data", typeof(object));
      //expand compressedData - see the CompressStream demo code for a possible
      //compression library, or visit
      //http://www.icsharpcode.net/OpenSource/SharpZipLib/Default.aspx
      //for a free .NET zip library
```

```
      _lotsOfData = compressedData;
    }
    else
      _lotsOfData = info.GetValue("data", typeof(object));
  }
  public void GetObjectData(SerializationInfo info, StreamingContext context){
    if (context.State  == StreamingContextStates.CrossMachine){
      info.AddValue("compressed", true);
      //compress data here - see earlier comment
      object compressedData = _lotsOfData;
      info.AddValue("data", compressedData);
    }
    else{
      info.AddValue("compressed", false);
      //compress _lotsOfData
      info.AddValue("data", _lotsOfData);
    }
  }
}
```

Formatter Options

The two formatters that ship with the .NET Framework Libraries have very different design goals and roles within the serialization framework. The System.Runtime.Serialization.Formatters.Binary.BinaryFormatter type has its conceptual origins in COM marshal-by-value objects, where an opaque byte array representing an entity could be passed across execution boundaries and a cloned object could be created. In contrast, the System.Runtime.Serialization.Formatters.Soap.SoapFormatter is designed to format CLR objects into a SOAP-compliant representation that can be parsed by different types of client applications running on different platforms.

Producing SOAP-compliant, XML-encoded data is more expensive than producing an optimized byte stream containing the same data. The extra processing and memory needed by the SoapFormatter will clearly cause a performance hit, and for the test case of serializing an Int32 object, using the SoapFormatter is five times slower than using the BinaryFormatter (see Test 11.06).

Conclusion

Good architecture is critical in achieving high-performance IO, and retrofitted optimizations at a code-level are unlikely to solve performance problems caused by excessive IO usage. IO is an inherently slow process, and if an application is consistently waiting for IO activities to complete before it can conduct other activities, an architectural redesign is appropriate. Asynchronous IO can alleviate some of the problems caused by application performance suffering due to IO speed, but operating system limitations restrict this option to NT-based operating systems.

The IO namespace does not offer the full range of disk access optimizations that are available under Win32, and if these optimizations are required, an unmanaged wrapper that exposes this functionality to .NET is the best option. For applications that are extremely sensitive to IO performance, such as multimedia applications that are reading and writing large amounts of data for the entire process lifespan, using an optimized IO library like the Windows Multimedia File I/O Library may be required (see `http://msdn.microsoft.com/library/default.asp?url=/library/en-us/multimed/mmio_4jvz.asp` for further details).

The choice of using `SerializableAttribute` or `ISerializable` when adding serialization support to a type has no major performance impact for most types. `ISerializable` allows types with unusual characteristics to apply some special-purpose optimization techniques, but for most types, the benefits of automatic serialization through `SerializableAttribute` will outweigh the small performance boost that manual serialization through `ISerializable` will deliver.

CHAPTER 12

Remoting

UNLIKE OTHER AREAS OF .NET, which have strong similarities with their Win32 and COM ancestors, remoting is an entirely new section of the Framework, and shares few similarities with DCOM, its logical predecessor. The newness of remoting means that it is critical for developers and architects to gain an understanding of the qualities and features that remoting offers to allow for efficient system design. No amount of tuning on a poorly designed distributed system can bring the performance level up to that of a well-designed system, meaning that up-front architectural design is critical in achieving good performance.

Remoting revolves around the flow of data, and the first step in achieving a high-performance distributed system is determining where the data is to reside, and identifying which pieces of data need to be transported across application domain, process, and network boundaries. By identifying the data flow characteristics of a distributed system, opportunities for reducing the volume of data flow and for caching data usually present themselves. In addition to performance considerations, identifying data security requirements and risks is a critical element of this step, as security is likely to be a higher priority than performance for distributed systems.

Cross-Application Domain Data Movement

Employing the correct form of cross-application domain data access is crucial for both the performance and functional quality of a system. In terms of cross-application domain accessibility, objects fall into three distinct categories: those that cannot be accessed from outside an application domain, those that may be passed by value to other application domains, and those that can be passed by reference to other application domains. The nonapplication domain agile objects are the simplest to deal with—any data that such an object owns can only be accessed from other application domains by passing it to an object in the other two categories.

Objects that can be copied to other application domains are known as *marshal-by-value* (MBV) objects. These objects must have the Serializable attribute applied to them, and may optionally implement the ISerializable interface. The performance considerations for serialization of objects are discussed in Chapter 11. Marshal-by-value objects will typically form the parameters in a remoting call, and should be designed to ensure the minimum amount of data required is transmitted.

Passing a reference to an object to remote application domains resembles the typical COM method of remote access. Objects that wish to use this form of remoting must inherit from System.MarshalByRefObject, which provides the services necessary for proxy and object lifetime management. The inheritance requirement has significant implications for type design, as the CLR does not support multiple inheritance. Marshal-by-reference (MBR) behavior must be identified and designed early in the type design phase, as retrofitting a MarshalByRefObject inheritance to a type deep in the class hierarchy can be a difficult exercise.

The characteristics of remotable types dictate that MBR objects will fall into the role of data managers, whereas MBV objects will be data transmitters. The different responsibilities of the objects indicate their characteristics for optimum performance will be quite different. MBV objects, which will form the parameters in a remoting call, should be designed to ensure the minimum amount of data required is transmitted. MBR objects need to support an interface that allows for a logical unit of work to be completed in the minimum number of calls necessary. In a sense, the design goals of MBR and MBV are in conflict. An MBV object aims to be as compact as possible and avoid carrying any data that is not absolutely necessary, whereas an MBR object aims to provide an interface that includes the maximum amount of data in a single call.

The balance between the two competing goals is system specific, but it is generally worth leaning towards the "more data" approach rather than the "more calls" approach. In a test case of moving string data across a LAN using the HTTP channel and a singleton remoting object, moving strings in 5000-character clumps is three times faster than moving the same amount of data across the network 1000 characters at a time. When the number of cross-network calls is the same, the increase in time for the 5000-character calls is only 84 percent compared to the 1000-character calls, despite the fivefold increase in data transmitted (see Test 12.01).

Remoting Channel Selection

Channels are the lowest level in the .NET Remoting stack. They handle the transport of data between application domains once formatters have transformed the data into a format suitable for transmission. The .NET Framework Library ships with two channels, HttpChannel and TcpChannel, and the Framework provides support for the development and use of any arbitrary channel that may be required. The TcpChannel is generally recommended as the high-performance alternative, but it is worth exploring the issue further to understand the reasoning behind the recommendation, and the performance differences that can be expected.

Systems that support data transport over a network have a modular, layered design. Each layer communicates with the layer below using a defined interface, and provides a higher level of abstraction to the layer above it. The Open System Interconnection (OSI) protocol stack is an ISO standard that defines seven protocol layers for data transport on a network. The layers are shown in Figure 12-1.

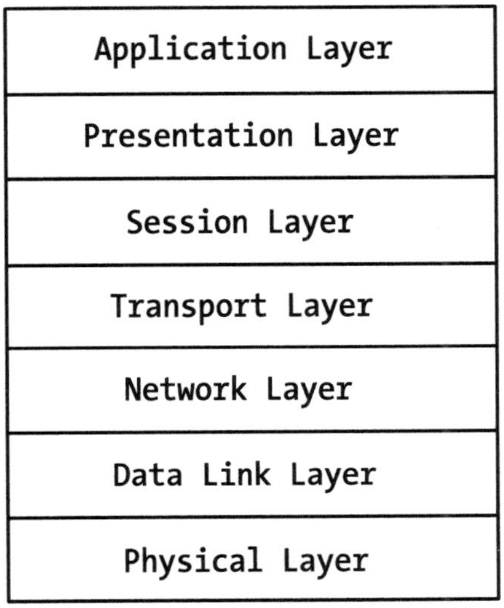

| Application Layer |
| Presentation Layer |
| Session Layer |
| Transport Layer |
| Network Layer |
| Data Link Layer |
| Physical Layer |

Figure 12-1. OSI protocol stack

When a call is made over a network, the data starts at the protocol layer that is being employed by an application, transverses down the layers to the physical layer, and then undergoes the reverse process on the receiving end. For code that is making direct use of a transport-layer protocol, the amount of processing that is required before data reaches application code is minimized, but the amount of processing required within application code may negate any performance benefit unless domain- or problem-specific optimizations can be applied.

TCP and HTTP sit at different levels of the protocol stack. TCP is a transport-layer protocol, which means that it concerns itself with features like data flow control and data delivery reliability. In contrast, HTTP sits at the top of the protocol stack, at the application layers, and provides a high-level model for accessing remote resources. The level that a protocol occupies on the protocol stack results in certain characteristics—the lower-level layer protocols perform better, but provide fewer services. Both these characteristics come from the same source—the number of levels that a particular protocol has beneath it. Each protocol level provides certain services, which is what they are there for, but these services naturally come at a performance cost.

Looking at the individual protocols, TCP is clearly more performance oriented in its design compared to HTTP. TCP headers are a fixed size, which allows for fast processing, and the data in the header is tightly packed into binary structures. In contrast, the header size for HTTP is not fixed, which slows parsing speed, and data is encoded as plain text for transport, which imparts a significant hit. HTTP's performance weaknesses are also its interoperability strengths, allowing protocols like SOAP to be easily transportable over HTTP.

In general, HTTP will be the best choice for remoting interoperability, and TCP will give the best performance. To qualify the performance benefits to some degree, a test case is defined where a server-activated singleton exposes methods that return small (10 bytes), medium (100 bytes), and large (1000 bytes) result sets. The results for cross-network calls over a 100 megabits per second (Mbps) LAN using the default formatters for each channel are shown in Figure 12-2. The results demonstrate that the size of the data transported across the network has a very small impact on performance, and that the TCP channel outperforms the HTTP channel by a factor exceeding five (see Test 12.02).

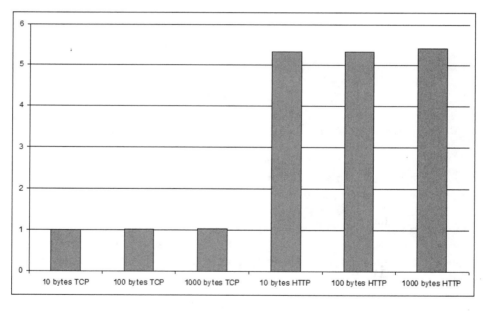

Figure 12-2. TCP vs. HTTP remoting channels (results normalized to the fastest test)

As well as slowing execution speed, the use of the HTTP channel imparts a heavy burden on memory usage. Executing Test 12.02 using the TCP channel alone results in the memory usage for the remoting server increasing from 8940 kilobytes before the test is conducted to 13,908 kilobytes at the end of the test. The same test conducted using the HTTP channel alone results in a memory usage increase from 8940 kilobytes to 45,416 kilobytes. The test case involves the transmission of a 1000-byte message over a 100 Mbps LAN 6000 times.

Allocation profiling on the server application shows that the majority of the allocated memory for the HTTP channel test is composed of character arrays (23 percent), byte arrays (19 percent), and `String` objects (18 percent), and the `SoapServerFormatterSink.ProcessMessage` method is responsible for 97 percent of the memory allocated.

The preceding comparison is biased by the use of the default formatters for the channels. The TCP channel will use the binary formatter by default, whereas the HTTP channel will use the SOAP formatter. The binary formatter has superior performance compared to the SOAP formatter, which is reflected in the overall results presented earlier. The channels can be configured to use either the binary or SOAP formatter, and the tests rerun using the same formatter for both channels. Although the SOAP formatter's speed is significantly less than that of the binary formatter, the SOAP formatter offers greater interoperability with other systems, and it is important to consider all factors when designing and implementing a distributed system.

With the binary formatter, the performance difference between the two channels is much closer, with the TCP channel being faster by a factor of two. Using the SOAP formatter on both channels, the result is even closer, with TCP speed being greater by a factor of only 1.5 (see Tests 12.03 and 12.04). The similarity in speed between the TCP and HTTP results with the use of the SOAP formatter highlights the performance impact of producing the XML-encoded SOAP packets for this test.

For .NET-to-.NET Remoting applications, the TCP channel will deliver the best performance. When an application is interoperating with non-.NET clients, exposing objects on the HTTP channel will often be required. It is possible to expose the same remoting object on multiple different channels simultaneously—the only requirement is that the channels must be listening on a different port. This technique allows high interoperability and high performance to be achieved simultaneously.

Object Activation

Remoting supports three basic kinds of object activation: singleton, singlecall, and client-activated objects. Singleton and singlecall objects are both server activated. The lifetime of server-activated objects (SAO) is managed by the server in most cases,[1] whereas the server or the client can manage the lifetime of client-activated objects (CAO). Each different category of remotable object has different life cycle patterns. The life cycle of a singlecall object is the simplest—it is created to serve a call from a client, after which it is unreachable, and available for collection by the server's garbage collector. A singleton object is created to service the first client request for an object of that particular type, and will stay

---

1. Registering a client-side sponsor for a singleton object is possible, but it is hard to think of a situation where this makes sense.

alive for a certain period of time based on the settings in the ILease-implementing object returned from the singleton's GetLifetimeService method.

The life cycle of a CAO is similar to the life of a traditional DCOM object, in that the object is created based on a client request, the object has a stateful existence only accessible to the client, and the object is released when the client is finished using it.

The various activation schemes have different performance characteristics. Client-activated objects require an extra network round-trip to create an object before any meaningful work can be accomplished. This means that, other things being equal, the performance of CAOs will be worse than that of SAOs. Client activation has a cleaner, more object-oriented feel to it, but the extra round-trip can easily be avoided by passing the state-initialization parameters with the other parameters in a method call to a SAO.

The long living object-per-client characteristic of CAO is not present with either SAO activation model. There are three options for dealing with the stateless nature of SAOs:

- The type's interface can be designed to accomplish a full unit of work in a single call.

- Objects that define a SAO's state can be serialized and transported backward and forward to the client for each call.

- State data can be stored in a database, and the client can pass an identifier to allow that state to be retrieved for each call.

The third technique will typically require another network round-trip per call, and should generally be avoided unless data persistence is crucial. The first option is preferable, but the second option offers a good compromise, and is not hard to implement with the serialization support available in the Framework Library.

For some situations, the extra initialization cost of a CAO may be negated by reducing the quantity of data that needs to be transferred between the client and server, and the overall performance of a CAO may be higher than that of a SAO. When considering CAOs, the potential scalability impacts should also be analyzed. In a load-balanced environment, subsequent method calls on a CAO need to be routed to the original server, and this can add an administrative and performance overhead to the use of CAOs.

The two SAO activation models appear similar, and for small deployments, the performance will be comparable. As load on the server increases, the performance of singleton objects is likely to degrade, as any shared state must be locked before each thread-servicing client request can access the data. A more scalable solution is to use singlecall objects and attempt to limit or eliminate the need for shared state between clients. Data that would normally be maintained by a singleton can be serialized to a byte stream or XML document and maintained by the client between requests.

The choice between stateless singleton and singlecall objects is not overly significant in terms of performance (see Test 12.05). Profiling of a remoting server shows that processing a single remote call on the HTTP channel with the SOAP formatter results in the allocation of 3 kilobytes of managed memory, making the allocation cost of the singlecall remote object insignificant.

In high-load scenarios, standard scale-out techniques like software and hardware load balancers can be used to share the load across a farm of servers hosting the singlecall and stateless singleton objects. For stateful singleton objects, the load balancer may need to be configured to redirect the client back to the original server for subsequent requests, which can reduce overall system throughput.

Calling Methods

Calling a remote method will block the calling thread until a message is received back indicating the success of the method call, or until the method call experiences a timeout error. The current default timeout value is –1, which means that the client will wait until the server responds or is disconnected. The timeout period for a remote call can be configured by setting the timeout property of the ChannelSink type, as demonstrated here:

```
RemoteObject remoteObject = new RemoteObject();
System.Runtime.Remoting.Channels.ChannelServices.GetChannelSinkProperties(
  remoteObject)["timeout"] = 10000;  //10000ms timeout
```

In some situations, the client does not care about the result of the remote call. The call may be a simple notification or logging call, and the client has no interest or capability to deal with any return values or exceptions thrown by the server. If this is the case, a method may be decorated with OneWayAttribute, which informs the remoting runtime not to wait for the call processing to finish before returning. Using OneWayAttribute increases the speed of remote calls considerably—in a test case of a cross-network call, applying the OneWayAttribute to the method increases the call speed by a factor of over 30 (see Test 12.06).

If the results of a remote call are required, or if the client wants to confirm that the server does not throw any exceptions when executing the method call, OneWay methods are not appropriate. For situations where blocking the calling thread is not desirable, but retrieving the results of the remoting call is required, making an asynchronous call is a good solution. Asynchronous calls are particularly useful in GUI-based applications, where blocking the main thread gives the appearance of a slow and buggy application. However, *always* remember that callbacks will not be made on the UI thread, and the use of Control.Invoke or

`Control.BeginInvoke` is usually required to safely update the UI. See "Safe, Simple Multithreading in Windows Forms" by Chris Sells in the MSDN Library (http://msdn.microsoft.com/library/default.asp?url=/library/en-us/dnforms/html/winforms01232003.asp) for further details.

Making asynchronous method calls is easy, and it is possible to call any method on a reference type asynchronously. The first step is to define a delegate with the same signature as the method that needs to be called asynchronously, create an instance of this delegate, and then call the `BeginInvoke` method of the delegate. The following code demonstrates calling the `System.String IndexOf` method asynchronously:

```
private delegate int FindIndexDelegate(char c);

private void MakeAsyncCallWithEndInvoke() {
  string s = "abc";
  FindIndexDelegate stringIndexMethod = new FindIndexDelegate(s.IndexOf);
  IAsyncResult ar = stringIndexMethod.BeginInvoke('b', null, null);
  //do other stuff here
  int res = stringIndexMethod.EndInvoke(ar);
}
```

The `BeginInvoke` method for the delegate will be created by the compiler based on the delegate's signature. IntelliSense for the generated method was not available in Visual Studio 2002, but Visual Studio 2003 fixes this problem. To retrieve the results of an asynchronous call, the `EndInvoke` method of the delegate can be called. `EndInvoke` is a blocking call, so when this call is made, the asynchronous nature of the call comes to an end. The timing of the call to `EndInvoke` is up to the client code—the code sample simply calls `EndInvoke` when other processing has been completed. If this technique is not desired, casting the `IAsyncResult` reference returned by `BeginInvoke` to an `AsyncResult` reference and inspecting the `IsCompleted` property can determine the status of the call.

The `BeginInvoke` method also allows for an `AsyncCallback` delegate instance to be specified. When the asynchronous call has completed, the delegate method will be called, and the `ref` parameters, `out` parameters, and return value of the method call can be accessed, as well as any exceptions that have been thrown.

```
// using System.Runtime.Remoting.Messaging;

private delegate int FindIndexDelegate(char c);

private void MakeAsyncCallWithCallback() {
  string s = "abc";
  FindIndexDelegate stringIndexMethod = new FindIndexDelegate(s.IndexOf);
  IAsyncResult ar = stringIndexMethod.BeginInvoke('b', new
```

```
      AsyncCallback(FindIndexResults), null);
}

private void FindIndexResults(IAsyncResult ar){
  FindIndexDelegate fid = (FindIndexDelegate)((AsyncResult)ar).AsyncDelegate;
  int res = fid.EndInvoke(ar);
}
```

It is important to note that making a call asynchronously does not make the actual method call any faster; it simply allows the calling thread to perform other work while the call completes. For local asynchronous calls where the overall performance of the application is constrained by the CPU, making the call asynchronously will have no performance benefit.

IIS Hosting

Remote objects can be hosted in IIS via the use of a web.config file. Using IIS simply piggybacks the remoting infrastructure on top of ASP.NET, and the `RemotingConfiguration.Configure` call that launches server-side remoting is made when the ASP.NET application is launched. Using IIS to host remote objects has some advantages, especially in relation to security, where encrypted channels (HTTPS) and client authentication is supported. IIS-based remoting does have some limitations, especially in relation to channel selection. IIS only supports the use of the HTTP channel, but will support either the SOAP or binary formatter, depending on the formatter used on the client side. The following sample shows the web.config contents required to expose the `RemotingPerfLibrary.DataManager` type from the `RemotingPerfLibrary` assembly as a singlecall SAO at a Uniform Resource Identifier (URI) of `DataManager.rem`:

```
<?xml version="1.0" encoding="utf-8" ?>
<configuration>
  <system.runtime.remoting>
    <application>
      <service>
        <wellknown mode="SingleCall" objectUri="DataManager.rem"
        type="RemotingPerfLibrary.DataManager,RemotingPerfLibrary" />
      </service>
      <channels>
        <channel ref="http" />
      </channels>
    </application>
  </system.runtime.remoting>
</configuration>
```

Using IIS hosting can provide a number of scalability benefits that a custom host is unlikely to deliver. The ASP.NET worker process (aspnet_wp.exe) will launch a separate application domain for each virtual directory, whereas a custom host will handle all remoting processing within the default application domain by default. The IIS model makes it easy to place high-traffic remote types in their own application domain—all that is required is the creation of a new virtual directory and web.config file.

ASP.NET has been built with scalability and performance as one of its main goals, and IIS hosting allows non-ASP.NET applications to take advantage of these features. Memory usage on the server is one of the main areas where IIS can outperform a custom host. The CLR does not allow types to be unloaded from an application domain, but shutting down an application domain will release the memory associated with any types that have been loaded in it. IIS can choose to shut down an application domain that contains types that have not been used recently to free memory. Excessive memory usage within an application domain can also trigger IIS to recycle the ASP.NET worker processes, so memory leaks within unmanaged components and Framework code can be worked around.

The actual call timing of IIS-hosted remote objects compared to the same object hosted in a custom host is fairly similar. In tests to transfer a 100-character string, the call to the IIS-hosted object is 39 percent slower (see Test 12.07). The size of the HTTP response received from IIS is 50 percent larger than the equivalent custom host response due to extra call context metadata contained in the SOAP header, which will account for a portion of the call timing increase. The number of application layers through which data must travel on the server side is greater for IIS-hosted objects—the call is received by IIS, mapped to ASP.NET, and then travels through the remoting framework before reaching the remote object, which also has an impact on call timing.

Sink Chains

The focus up until this point has been primarily on channels and hosts, but sinks also play an important role in the remoting performance picture. Sinks sit between the transport layer and the proxy, and provide various services, such as formatting method calls. The remoting framework allows custom sinks to be specified, and these sinks can actually modify the contents of the data that is sent over the wire. In terms of performance, compression is an obvious service that can be provided through sinks, and this technique is illustrated in *Advanced .NET Remoting* by Ingo Rammer (Apress, 2002).

Sinks also allow additional metadata to be associated with a method, and this metadata can be used to add performance hints and optimizations to a remote call. Remoting has no native support for caching the result of method calls, but this functionality can be easily added with sinks. A sink can be added to the client side to keep track of remote calls that the server side indicates are cacheable, and if a call with the same parameters is sent to the server, the cached result can be returned to the client, avoiding the cost of a cross-network trip. The use of the caching sink is completely transparent to both the client and server, and can be retrofitted to any remoting application. A caching sink sample is included with the book's sample code (downloadable from the Apress site at `http://www.apress.com`), and its implementation and use is described in the following section.

Implementing a Channel Sink

Two separate interfaces, `IServerChannelSink` and `IClientChannelSink`, define a sink. These interfaces have minor differences, but both provide the same message processing methods necessary to prepare messages for the data transport layer. For synchronous method calls, the `ProcessMessage` method on both interfaces performs the bulk of the functionality for the channel sink. `ProcessMessage` takes in a sink property bag (`IMessage`), the request headers, and the request stream, and, after processing the call, returns the response headers and response stream. Processing the message simply involves performing the sink-specific processing and passing the message onto the next sink.

Implementing a caching channel sink is achieved by determining if the same message has already been processed, and if it has, determining if the message is still valid. Implementing the check for previous method invocations is discussed in the following section; the focus of this section is on the implementation of message validity checks. Checking with the server to determine if a response is still valid is technically feasible, but defeats the whole purpose of the sink. Having the client control response validity is equally problematic, as encapsulation and distribution of business rule principles are violated. For the client to make the decision, it has to make some assumptions about whether the response will still be valid at some future point, and in most distributed application architectures, the client does not have the background information to make this call.

The solution to the problem is using a combination of server- and client-side processing logic. The remoting server returns a response header when it processes a call, and various call metadata can be easily inserted into this header, which allows a timespan representing the maximum cache duration of a message to be transmitted back to the client. This header metadata can be retrieved within the client sink and stored in the message cache along with the response streams. When a remote call is made, and the client channel sink is searching for a valid response, the maximum cache duration is a factor in determining whether a cached message can be used or a new response should be fetched for the client.

The caching logic is shown in Figure 12-3. Code that implements this logic is contained in the code samples for the book.

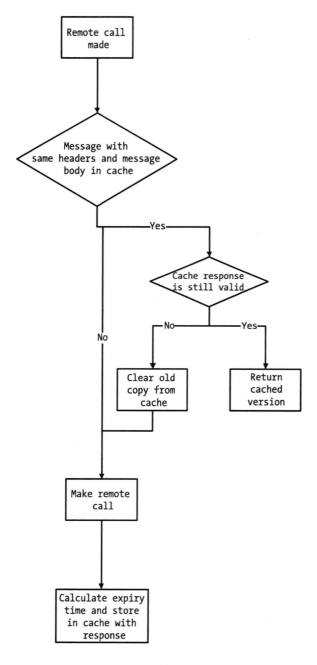

Figure 12-3. Processing a remote call with the caching channel sink

Collections, Equality, and Serialization

Implementing the actual cache is made relatively simple thanks to the Hashtable class in the System.Collections namespace of the Framework Library. A hash table is a dictionary-like collection that maps a key to an element in the collection, which in this case is a map of a remoting request to a response. The use of the Hashtable class makes it simple to check if a particular request has been seen before, and retrieve the response if it has been seen. To locate a response in the collection, the Hashtable uses two pieces of information—a hash code to locate a region in the collection to look in, and once this region is found, the Hashtable then uses equality checks to identify the exact object. Every object exposes a GetHashCode and Equals method through inheritance from System.Object, but some objects may override the default implementations to provide different equality and hash definitions.

The equality checks inherited from System.Object implement a form of equality known as *reference-based equality,* which means that two objects are only considered equal if they are the same physical object on the heap; two objects that have identical member variables, but are two distinct objects, are not considered equal. In a similar way, the GetHashCode implementation in System.Object returns a value that is loosely based on an object's physical address, and is unrelated to the values held in member variables.

Reference-based equality is clearly not the correct form of equality for the caching sink. The check on the request objects must consider the values in the objects, not whether they are the same physical object, as it is almost guaranteed that they will not be. The other form of equality is value-based equality, where equality is determined by checking whether all the member variables of an object are equal.

Hash codes and equality share a special relationship due to the way the Hashtable algorithm locates objects within its internal data structures. The hash code indicates the general area within the Hashtable to begin a detailed search, so to locate objects for which Equals returns true, they must both be located within the same hash code locality. This requirement leads to the rule that if two objects are Equal, they must have the same hash code.

To successfully use the Hashtable to store the request-response collection, the remoting requests must be modified to implement value-based equality, and the hash code calculation must reflect the change in equality definition. Deriving from the classes that make up a request to achieve value-based equality is an option, but as discussed previously, remoting is a highly configurable framework, and it is possible that the caching sink will be dealing with custom classes that are outside the .NET Framework. The method used to implement value-based equality must be successful even if the classes that make up the requests are unknown when the caching sink is developed and compiled.

When the data that makes up a remoting request is considered, it is apparent that the information contained in the remoting packet is irrelevant for caching purposes—all that is required is a binary comparison of the two objects, and a hashing algorithm that operates on the same binary data. This simplifies the requirements down to two challenges: the ability to accomplish a binary dump of an arbitrary object, which can be used for comparison purposes, and the ability to hook the results of this binary comparison into the Hashtable lookup logic.

The .NET Framework has excellent support for converting an object into a binary blob in the form of serialization. Binary serialization is perfect for the value-based checks that the caching sink requires. Once the remoting request is in the form of a byte array, an element-by-element comparison can be used to compare two remoting requests, and a hashing algorithm can compress the byte array into a single 32-bit hash code.

Hooking this data into the Hashtable is extremely easy—an overloaded version of the Hashtable constructor has IHashCodeProvider and IComparer parameters, which are two interfaces that define a hash code and equality algorithm provider respectively. To allow the alternative value-equality-based lookups to be used by the Hashtable, the code that works with the serialized byte-array representation of the remoting response simply needs to be located in classes that implement these interfaces, and passed into the Hashtable constructor.

Using the Channel Sink

None of the cache complexity needs to be visible to the end user. The only requirement for using the caching sink is to add an entry in the client's and server's configuration files to tell the remoting plumbing to add the sink to the channel sink chain, and to add an entry to the server file's appSettings section to set the cache duration for messages. The full configuration file for a server using the caching sink is shown in the following snippet, with a cache duration of five seconds nominated for remote calls made on the HTTP channel serving requests on port 1235:

```
<configuration>
 <appSettings>
  <add key="CacheLimit" value="5" />
 </appSettings>
```

```
<system.runtime.remoting>
  <application>
   <channels>
    <channel ref="http" port="1235">
     <serverProviders>
      <provider type=
         "DotNetPerformance.Remoting.CachingSink.CachingServerSinkProvider,
            CachingSink" />
      <formatter ref="soap" />
     </serverProviders>
    </channel>
   </channels>
   <service>
    <wellknown mode="Singleton" type="Service.RemoteObject, Service"
      objectUri="RemoteObject.soap" />
   </service>
  </application>
 </system.runtime.remoting>
</configuration>
```

The configuration file for the remoting client is similar, with the only differences being the lack of a cache duration limit setting, and a remoting client declaration in contrast to the preceding server declaration.

Monitoring Remoting

As remoting generally uses standard transport channels, a wide range of tools can be used to inspect and monitor the movement of data across these channels. tcpTrace (available from http://www.pocketsoap.com/tcpTrace/) can be used to view remoting messages when the HTTP channel and SOAP formatter is in use. Figure 12-4 shows a remote message call and response for one of the test case methods discussed in this chapter.

Channel sinks can also be used to monitor remoting. Settings in configuration files can be used to add channel sinks to a remoting system without the need for source code modification, which makes them an excellent tool for monitoring deployed applications. Writing the code to intercept and display remoting messages with channel sinks can be tedious, and for those who prefer to leverage the hard work of others, a fully featured tool called Remoting Probe can be downloaded from http://www.codeproject.com/useritems/remotingprobe.asp.

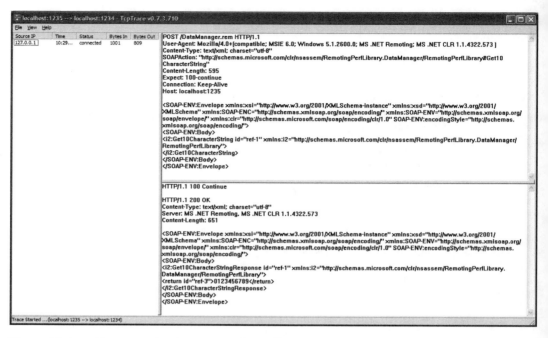

Figure 12-4. tcpTrace monitoring a remoting call

Conclusion

Efficient data movement patterns are a critical element in achieving a well-performing distributed application. Types used for remoting should be designed to minimize both the amount of data that travels between client and server and the number of calls that need to occur to accomplish a given unit of work. If an efficient cross-application domain data transfer architecture is achieved, performance problems become more of a deployment and configuration issue, and often can be addressed without code changes.

The remoting infrastructure in the .NET Framework is highly configurable, and this allows for the development and use of software components that have characteristics appropriate to a given scenario. This means that channels, formatters, and channel sinks can all be used as tuning parameters to boost the performance of a remoting solution. A server is also free to use multiple ports to expose the same services through different remoting configurations, which allows clients to determine which set of services they would like to consume.

CHAPTER 13

Unmanaged Code
Interoperability

THE .NET FRAMEWORK'S ability to interoperate with unmanaged code is not only an important and useful feature, but also the key technology that allows legacy systems built using Win32 and COM to continue to be accessible in the .NET world. The performance impact of making calls to unmanaged code varies widely, and there is significant scope for tuning interoperability calls. As with performance tuning in other areas of functionality, performance improvement comes at the expense of other features, such as ease of use and security, and overeager performance optimization should be avoided.

Two distinct technologies support unmanaged code interoperability—P/Invoke and COM Interop. P/Invoke allows Win32-style (also known as C-style) DLLs to be accessed, whereas COM Interop enables the use of Component Object Model (COM) DLLs from within .NET code. COM supports a much richer definition of interfaces and types compared to the simple function-based approach of Win32 DLLs, and this wide divergence in ability is the key reason for the separate access technologies available in .NET.

P/Invoke Calls

The `System.Runtime.InteropServices.DllImportAttribute` type supports the definition of method signatures whose eventual implementation will be provided by Win32 DLLs. `DllImportAttribute` methods compile to methods decorated with the `pinvokeimpl` method attribute, and the CLR will use the information contained in the `pinvokeimpl` attribute to load and call the underlying Win32 DLL function. Parameters passed to a Win32 function may require a conversion to a different physical form, and this conversion, which is termed *interoperability marshalling,* is provided by the CLR. The following code shows a C# method that calls the kernel32.dll `Beep` function and the generated MSIL that is used by the CLR to allow the call to complete successfully:

```
//using System.Runtime.InteropServices;
[DllImport("kernel32.dll")]
static extern bool Beep(uint dwFreq, uint dwDuration);
```

```
public static void MakeABeep(){
  uint freq = 3700;
  uint duration = 1000;
  Beep(freq, duration);
}
//generated MSIL for Beep
/*
.method private hidebysig static pinvokeimpl("kernel32.dll" winapi)
  bool  Beep(unsigned int32 dwFreq,
    unsigned int32 dwDuration) cil managed preservesig
{
}
*/
```

The conversion requirements of a type when undergoing interoperability marshalling fall into two distinct categories. *Blittable data types* have an in-memory representation that is the same for managed and unmanaged code, and hence no interoperability marshalling is required. Primitive types like integers and doubles fit into this category. If a type is not blittable, the runtime must perform a conversion of the managed type to its unmanaged equivalent, and the cost of this transformation is proportional to the differences between the unmanaged and managed memory representations. For P/Invoke calls, strings and arrays are among the most common *nonblittable data types*.

Figure 13-1 shows the results of calls to an unmanaged DLL that exposes functions with varying parameter types (see Test 13.01). The call processing inside the unmanaged DLL is identical in all cases, and simply involves returning a constant 32-bit integer. Each function has a single parameter, which is indicated by the column title in the figure. The two tests that use nonblittable parameters are the Constant String Param Ansi test, which requires the runtime to convert a Unicode System.String to an ANSI string, and the Changeable String Param test, which uses a System.Text.StringBuilder parameter to support modification of the string in unmanaged code.

The call that takes no parameters is obviously the quickest, but it is interesting to note that the timing for other calls that do take parameters is quite similar. Adding a 32-bit integer to the parameter list adds less than 1 percent to the call timing, and adding a string parameter to a function that takes a Unicode C-style string as a parameter also imparts a negligible cost. When a function with the same internal processing is exposed with an ANSI string parameter, the call cost increase jumps to 256 percent. The result emphasizes the importance of keeping the managed and unmanaged parameters as close as possible to each other in terms of physical binary representation to avoid this marshalling hit.

The most severe performance penalty comes from using a nonblittable bidirectional parameter. In this case, the call is almost six times more expensive than the zero parameter call, indicating the amount of work that the runtime must perform to correctly marshal data. For a `StringBuilder` object passed to unmanaged memory, the runtime must allocate a temporary buffer, copy the contents of the `StringBuilder` to this buffer, and pass the buffer to the unmanaged function. On return, the CLR needs to check the validity of data in the buffer, and copy the new value back into the `StringBuilder` object.

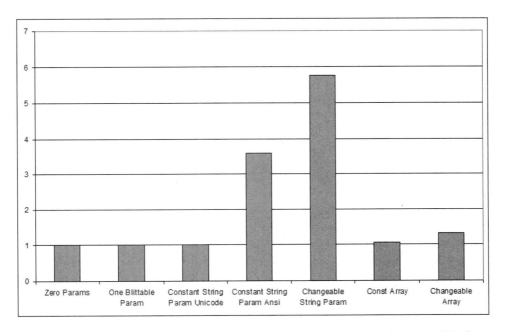

Figure 13-1. P/Invoke call speed for different parameter types (results normalized to the fastest test)

Inclusion of stack-allocated memory in unsafe code blocks and manual marshalling of the data returned from the unmanaged function can be used to avoid the performance impact of complex interoperability marshalling. Stack allocation is an order of magnitude quicker than heap allocation for the test case of allocating 100 bytes of memory (see Test 13.02), and the `System.Runtime.InteropServices.Marshal` type provides a number of static methods that can convert the raw bytes returned from unmanaged functions into types usable from managed code. The two function prototypes shown in the following snippet describe the same unmanaged function, with the `ChangeableStringParamUnsafe` prototype exposing suitable parameter declarations for a method call that uses stack-allocated memory. Code to call both functions is also shown.

```
//using System;
//using System.Text;
//using System.Runtime.InteropServices;
```

```
[DllImport("SomeDll.dll", CharSet=CharSet.Unicode)]
public static extern int ChangeableStringParam(StringBuilder s, int length);

public void ChangeableStringParamCaller(){
   const int length = 10;
   StringBuilder sb = new StringBuilder(length);
   //populate sb if required
   int i = ChangeableStringParam(sb, length);
   string s = sb.ToString();
}

[DllImport("SomeDll.dll", CharSet=CharSet.Unicode,
   EntryPoint="ChangeableStringParam")]
public static extern unsafe int ChangeableStringParamUnsafe(byte* b,
   int length);

public unsafe void ChangeableStringParamUnsafeCaller(){
   const int length = 20; //2 bytes per Unicode char
   byte* b = stackalloc byte[length];
   //populate byte array if required - see code in next line
   //Marshal.Copy(myString.ToCharArray(), 0, new IntPtr(b), length/2);
   int i = ChangeableStringParamUnsafe(b, length/2);
   string s = Marshal.PtrToStringUni(new IntPtr(b), length/2);
}
```

The ChangeableStringParam declaration relies on the runtime performing the marshalling from a StringBuilder object to the LPWSTR (long pointer to a wide string) parameter expected as the first parameter of the unmanaged function. This is done by copying the contents of the StringBuilder to a separate block of allocated memory, passing this memory to the unmanaged function, and copying the post-call contents of the separate memory block back into the StringBuilder object before returning to managed code. The caller of ChangeableStringParamUnsafe must provide manual data marshalling in both directions if required—and, as shown in the code snippet, the Marshall type provides static methods for achieving this marshalling.

The performance advantage of manual marshalling can come from two areas—the amount of marshalling performed can be customized to the documented behavior of the function, and stack-allocated memory can be used as parameters, which is quicker to allocate than the heap-allocated memory used by runtime-provided marshalling. The data marshalling provided by the runtime has no way of using hints in return parameters to marshal the minimum amount of unmanaged data to its managed equivalent, which is particularly relevant in cases where all the returned data may not need to be converted to a managed equivalent. In addition to the faster allocation of stack-allocated memory compared to heap-allocated memory, stack-allocated memory requires no pinning because it is not affected by garbage collection, unlike heap-allocated memory, which can require an explicit pin to prevent any reallocation.

The cumulative effect of manual marshalling optimizations is that calling an unmanaged function that requires a mutable string parameter is about 2.7 times quicker using a stack-allocated byte array for a buffer size of four characters (see Test 13.03). If a Marshal.Copy call is required to copy the contents of a managed String to the stack-allocated byte array before the unmanaged call, the performance improvement drops, and the stack-allocated technique is only twice as fast (see Test 13.04).

Marshalling Data to Managed Types

Efficient marshalling of data back to managed types is a critical step when stack-allocated memory is used as a parameter in an unmanaged call. Byte pointers are essentially useless in managed code—they cannot be passed to library functions that expect byte arrays, and they cannot be cast to managed types even if their in-memory representation is identical to that of the managed type. The Marshal type provides functionality to convert pointers to any value type and to strings. To convert a pointer to a reference type, a new object needs to be allocated, and data must be read from the memory block that the pointer references and copied to the reference type a member variable at a time, as shown in the following snippet:

```
using System;
using System.Runtime.InteropServices;

public class MarshalFromByteArray{
  public string s;
  public int i;

  public unsafe static MarshalFromByteArray ConvertFromRawMemory
    (IntPtr pMem){
    MarshalFromByteArray mfba = new MarshalFromByteArray();
    mfba.i = Marshal.ReadInt32(pMem);
    IntPtr pStringLoc = new IntPtr(pMem.ToInt32() + sizeof(int));
    mfba.s = Marshal.PtrToStringAnsi(pStringLoc);
    return mfba;
  }
}
```

Strings represent a particular problem for conversion due to the numerous possible representations of string data in unmanaged code. The Marshal type provides a number of methods to convert an IntPtr to a System.String object, and these methods all have an overloaded version that takes the string length as an additional parameter, with the exception of the BSTR conversion function, which gets the length as an embedded element in the string. It is critical for performance that the version of the function with the length parameter is used, as the overloaded method versions without length parameters require a further transition to unmanaged code inside Marshal to calculate the string's length. For the MarshalFromByteArray sample, if the integer member variable represents the length of the string member variable, the call to PtrToStringAnsi can be changed to include this information as shown in the following snippet, allowing better performance to be achieved:

```
mfba.s = Marshal.PtrToStringAnsi(pStringLoc, mfba.i);
```

A test case of passing a mutable Unicode string to an unmanaged function, replacing the string's contents in unmanaged code, and then converting the returned data to a System.String object in managed code is defined to test the performance of various string conversion techniques. Using a stack-allocated byte array and Marshal.PtrToStringUni call is 2.7 times faster than using StringBuilder (see Test 13.03). Converting the byte array to a string using UnicodeEncoding in the System.Text namespace is quicker than using StringBuilder, but still nearly two times slower than using Marshal (see Test 13.03). Neglecting to pass the string length to Marshal.PtrToStringUni actually makes the function slower than using StringBuilder, emphasizing the importance of employing any performance hints available. The three different techniques for converting the byte array to a managed String are shown in the following snippet:

```
const int length = 20; //2 bytes per Unicode char
byte* b = stackalloc byte[length];

int i1 = ChangeableStringParamUnsafe(b, length/2);
string s1 = Marshal.PtrToStringUni(new IntPtr(b), length/2);

int i2 = ChangeableStringParamUnsafe(b, length/2);
//still faster than StringBuilder if the UnicodeEncoding object is reused
// but slower than PtrToStringUni with length hint
System.Text.UnicodeEncoding ue = new System.Text.UnicodeEncoding();
byte[] outBytes = new byte[length];
Marshal.Copy(new IntPtr(b), outBytes, 0, length);
string s2 = ue.GetString(outBytes);
```

```
int i3 = ChangeableStringParamUnsafe(b, length/2);
//big performance hit because of no string length - AVOID IF POSSIBLE
string s3 = Marshal.PtrToStringUni(new IntPtr(b));
```

Character Sets

Most Win32 functions are present in both a Unicode and ANSI form on NT-based operating systems. Operating systems based on the Windows 9x kernel only have ANSI versions of most functions available by default, but support for Unicode functions can be added with the Microsoft Unicode Layer for Windows 9x. The version of the Win32 function that the runtime will call depends on the CharSet parameter used in the DllImport, and if this parameter is not specified, the ANSI version will be used. This behavior is tragic for performance on NT-based operating systems, as the Unicode System.String has to be converted to an ANSI string prior to the call to the unmanaged function. On the unmanaged side, ANSI calls on Windows NT–based operating systems simply forward the call to the Unicode equivalent after converting the string parameters to Unicode. This means that in the course of a call, the string data goes from Unicode to ANSI and back to Unicode before any call logic is executed.

To give some indication of the cost of these transformations, a call to the kernel32.dll function lstrlen with a 10-character string is 2.6 times slower using the default ANSI version compared to the Unicode version (see Test 13.05).

The best performance strategy in relation to the CharSet property is to use the Auto enumeration value. This instructs the CLR to choose the character set that is the default for the system that the code is executing on—Unicode for NT and ANSI for 9x. The following snippet demonstrates this technique for the kernel32.dll CopyFile function.

```
[DllImport("kernel32.dll", CharSet = CharSet.Auto)]
static extern bool CopyFile(string lpExistingFileName, string lpNewFileName,
  bool bFailIfExists);
```

Unmanaged DLL Loading and Unloading

Unmanaged DLLs that contain functions called through the DllImportAttribute are loaded when the first call is made to a function contained within the DLL. This default behavior benefits performance by minimizing application startup times, but can cause pauses in an application when the unmanaged DLL is first loaded. If these pauses are undesirable, it is possible to load the DLL before the first call by using the Marshal.PrelinkAll method. This method takes a System.Type parameter, which means that the DllImport functions that need to be loaded before they are actually required should be placed in a particular type, and PrelinkAll should be called to load the functions, as shown in the following snippet:

```
public class PrelinkExample {
   [DllImport("kernel32.dll", CharSet=CharSet.Auto)]
   static extern int lstrlenAuto(string s);
   //other methods
}


//in app startup code
System.Runtime.InteropServices.Marshal.PrelinkAll(typeof(PrelinkExample));
```

If finer control over the early loading mechanism is required, the Marshal.Prelink method should be called with a MethodInfo parameter that refers to a function exported from the DLL.

The InteropServices namespace provides no functionality to unload unmanaged DLLs that have been loaded through the DllImportAttribute. While it is possible to use the Win32 functions LoadLibrary, GetProcAddress, and FreeLibrary to dynamically load a DLL and extract an unmanaged function pointer, dealing with the unmanaged function pointer in managed code is extremely tedious. Unless the high language in use supports the generation of the MSIL calli instruction, which is not the case with C# or VB .NET, a dynamic assembly must be generated, and intermediate language code to set up the call stack and execute the IL calli instruction must be generated and then dynamically compiled and executed. *.NET and COM: The Complete Interoperability Guide* by Adam Nathan (SAMS, 2002) demonstrates this technique.

Security Attributes

Calling unmanaged code requires all assemblies in the call stack to have been granted the UnmanagedCode permission. The check that all callers have this permission is performed at runtime using a stack walk, which is an expensive operation. To move this check from runtime to link time, an unmanaged function can be annotated with SuppressUnmanagedCodeSecurityAttribute, which significantly speeds up the transition to unmanaged code. The following snippet shows a declaration with the SuppressUnmanagedCodeSecurityAttribute applied:

```
[System.Security.SuppressUnmanagedCodeSecurity()]
[DllImport("MyDll.dll")] public static extern int FunctionName();
```

For a test case of a minimal unmanaged function that takes no parameters and does no processing in unmanaged code, applying SuppressUnmanagedCodeSecurityAttribute results in an order-of-magnitude speed improvement for P/Invoke calls (see Test 13.06) and a threefold speed improvement for COM calls (see Test 13.07). The /unsafe command line switch of the Type Library Importer (Tlbimp.exe) can be used to produce a type library with the SuppressUnmanagedCodeSecurityAttribute applied within the generated Interop assembly.

Applying the SuppressUnmanagedCodeSecurityAttribute should only be done in extreme cases where the number of calls made to unmanaged code is very high. Reducing the security restrictions on unmanaged code access undermines the entire security infrastructure of the CLR, and in most cases, security will be a higher priority than performance.

COM

The level of support for COM within .NET is quite comprehensive, and is much more complex than the P/Invoke technology used to load and execute C-style DLLs. The added complexity is a reflection of the complexity of COM, which has much broader functionality than the GetProcAddress technology that it superseded. In many ways, COM's added features make it a simpler technology to deal with in .NET, especially COM's addition of the type library, which is a language-independent definition of the library's functionality; it allows Tlbimp, which is a command-line tool that ships with the .NET Framework SDK, to generate a .NET assembly that provides a complete wrapper of the COM library.

Loading COM objects can be accomplished in a number of ways. The easiest method is to use an Interop assembly that defines the metadata required for .NET to use the COM object, and this allows the runtime to forward creation calls to CoCreateInstance. If the original COM component vendor has shipped a Primary Interop Assembly (PIA), it is preferable to use this instead of a Tlbimp-generated Interop assembly. A PIA is an Interop assembly produced by the original vendor of the COM component, and has the main purpose of providing a consistent .NET identity for COM objects.

In terms of performance, a PIA can have two benefits: All code within a process will use a single Interop assembly, which reduces working set size, and any optimizations that the original component vendor has made to the Interop assembly are employed. A PIA can be identified by the PrimaryInteropAssemblyAttribute, which will be stored in the assembly's manifest if it is applied.

The current version of the CLR loader is implemented as a COM object, so any process that has the CLR loaded will have the COM runtime loaded as well. This means that CoInitializeEx has already been called by the time the first line of managed code is executed, and by default, the threading model will be set to `COINIT_MULTITHREADED`. To override this setting or set it explicitly, `STAThreadAttribute` and `MTAThreadAttribute` can be applied to the entry point of the managed application. For Visual Basic .NET programs, failing to set the threading model explicitly will result in the compiler adding `STAThreadAttribute`. The following snippet shows the use of the `MTAThreadAttribute` on a VB .NET application entry point:

```
<MTAThread()> Shared Sub Main()
    'app entry point
End Sub
```

COM marshalling, which is unrelated to interoperability marshalling, is handled entirely in unmanaged code, and the CLR simply acts as a normal unmanaged client when calling COM objects. Marshalling objects between COM apartments is an expensive task, and should be avoided if possible. COM marshalling can be avoided by matching the threading model of the unmanaged and managed code, or by using a COM component that has a threading model of `Both`, which means that it can be loaded into any apartment. At times, it will not be feasible to change the default apartment model of the application, or a number of COM components with incompatible threading models will need to be used. In this case, it is possible to move the COM calls to secondary threads, and set the `Thread.ApartmentState` property to the appropriate value prior to the first call to unmanaged code, as shown in the following snippet:

```
<STAThread()> Shared Sub Main()
    'COM calls that need STA here
    Dim mtaThread As New Thread(AddressOf MTAThreadProc)
    mtaThread.ApartmentState = ApartmentState.MTA
    mtaThread.Start()
    'other processing
    mtaThread.Join()
End Sub
```

```
Public Shared Sub MTAThreadProc()
    'COM calls that benefit from MTA here
End Sub
```

COM and .NET have different lifetime management techniques, and this can be a source of performance problems with Interop. COM objects can legally assume that they will be freed as soon as client code is finished using them, which is not the case with .NET objects, which will not be freed until a garbage collection has occurred. The lack of deterministic destruction within the CLR means that COM components won't be released until a garbage collection occurs, which can cause serious problems if the COM component has ownership of scarce resources.

The only solution to the problem is to manually call the Release method of the COM object when the managed code has finished with the object. This can be achieved with the Marshal.ReleaseComObject method, but be aware that this method decrements the reference count of the COM Runtime Callable Wrapper (RCW), *not* the underlying COM object. The RCW reference count is only incremented when a COM interface is passed from unmanaged code, and most RCWs will have a reference count of one. This means a call to Marshal.ReleaseComObject will typically result in the underlying COM object being freed, and an exception will be raised if the RCW is used again, as shown in the following snippet:

```
using System;
using System.Runtime.InteropServices;
using ADODB;

public class COMInterop {
  public static void CreateRecordset(){
    Recordset rs = new RecordsetClass();
    UseRecordset(rs);
    object o = rs.ActiveConnection;   //null reference exception here
  }

  public static void UseRecordset(Recordset rs){
    //use rs
    Marshal.ReleaseComObject(rs);
  }
}
```

The traditional method of COM programming that uses AddRef on creation and copy, and Release when the pointer to the COM object is no longer needed, is not available using Interop. ReleaseComObject acts in a similar way to the IDisposable interface discussed in Chapter 7, and this makes the release of a COM object that is shared by many clients a difficult task. The garbage collector will collect RCW objects that no longer have any active references, which will in turn allow the release of the COM object, but this can mean that COM objects are maintained in memory a lot longer than required. Keeping the scope of a COM object as small as possible, and not passing COM object references to other methods, is the best strategy for allowing a safe call to ReleaseComObject to be made as early as possible.

Making unmanaged calls to COM components is more expensive than calls to DLLs loaded through P/Invoke. A call to a COM method, which simply returns S_OK, is about 50 percent slower than an equivalent call to a C-style DLL function that returns a 4-byte integer to simulate the COM HRESULT (see Test 13.08).

(HRESULTs are discussed further in the next section.) The extra call cost relates to increased indirection in locating that actual address of the function to call, and increased processing requires providing extra services like automatic error checking that are offered by COM Interop.

COM Error Translation

The physical success of a call to a COM object is communicated through a 32-bit return value known as *result handle* (HRESULT). HRESULTs may also communicate the logical success of the call, but due to the varying level of support for accessing result handles in unmanaged technologies, separating the logical and physical success of a COM call gained popularity. The logical success of the method is determined by the "business rules" of the object, whereas the physical success is determined by the ability to execute the call without assembly, server, and application domain failures.

Expressed in IDL, the two techniques look like this:

```
//traditional technique - HRESULT returns all error conditions
HRESULT BillClient([in] ClientID, [in] ITransactionDetails* pDetails);

/*modern technique - HRESULT indicates physical success of the call,
   retval indicates if the "business rules" allowed the call to proceed */
HRESULT BillClient([in] ClientID, [in] ITransactionDetails* pDetails,
   [out, retval] VARIANT_BOOL* pSuccess)
```

The default behavior of Tlbimp and the CLR Interop layer is to remove the HRESULT for the method signature exposed to .NET, and to translate any HRESULTs that indicate failure into an equivalent exception.

The separation of the physical and logical call success in COM results in a better mapping of the COM component into .NET, where failure of the physical method call due to system problems like memory exhaustion, or unexpected conditions like null parameters, result in exceptions, and the more common logical failures are translated using the method's return value. This technique ensures that exceptions are only thrown occasionally, and are not thrown during the normal execution of a method, which is beneficial for performance.

Avoiding COM-Generated Exceptions

Not all COM components follow the convention of separating logical and physical call success, and the use of components that frequently return non-S_OK HRESULTs will result in an excessive number of exceptions being thrown, which can hurt performance. Unfortunately, Tlbimp does not expose the option of maintaining the IDL signature of the COM interface, which means that the interface has to be manually transformed.

Transforming the COM Interop Assembly can be accomplished by round-tripping the Tlbimp-generated assembly through the MSIL Disassembler (Ildasm) and the MSIL Assembler (Ilasm) to modify the interface. Tlbimp will remove the HRESULT and replace it with the method's retval if present, and this process needs to be manually reversed to produce an import assembly that doesn't throw exceptions. Consider the following COM method expressed in IDL:

```
interface ITest : IDispatch {
  [id(0x00000001), helpstring("Always returns E_FAIL")]
  HRESULT Thrower([out, retval] single* pRetVal);
};
```

The imported method signature will be in the following form:

```
.method public hidebysig newslot virtual abstract instance float32 Thrower()
  runtime managed internalcall
```

This declaration needs to be modified to the following to avoid an exception being raised in the case of failure HRESULTs (modifications in italics):

```
.method public hidebysig newslot virtual abstract instance int32 Thrower
  ([out] float32& retVal) runtime managed preservesig internalcall
```

The method's return value has been set to Int32, which is the underlying type of a HRESULT, the COM [out, retval] parameter has been returned to the method's parameter list and annotated with the managed [out] attribute, and the preservesig method modifier has been added. The MSDN Library provides a more detailed tutorial on techniques for round-tripping an Interop assembly through MSIL at http://msdn.microsoft.com/library/default.asp?url=/library/en-us/cpguide/html/cpconeditinginteropassembly.asp.

Modifying generated Interop assemblies is not a particularly intuitive or robust process. IL is not the preferred development language for many developers, and IL is not as type-strict as many high-level languages, which increases the chances of subtle bugs being introduced. As an alternative, it is possible to provide a definition of the COM interface in any .NET language, use the Tlbimp-generated assembly to create an object, and cast the object to the defined interface. The runtime will call the QueryInterface method of the COM object, and as the GUID identifier of the interface will be correct, the call will succeed. The C# definition of the interface method shown in IL is presented in the following snippet:

```
using System.Runtime.InteropServices;
[
// IID_ITest
Guid("3A0282C6-3D37-4BF0-8590-E0AF712FFAC1"),
InterfaceType(ComInterfaceType.InterfaceIsDual)
]
interface ITest {
 [PreserveSig] int Thrower([out] ref float32 retVal);
}
```

For COM interfaces that contain a large number of methods, manually defining the interface in a high-level language can be a tedious exercise. The interface methods must be in exactly the same order in which they appear in the COM type library definition, as this is used to construct the virtual function table (vtable) that COM uses to invoke methods. High-level language definition will generally be the best option for transforming a small number of methods, whereas MSIL round-tripping will be the best option if a large number of methods need to be transformed.

Benchmark tests on the two Interop definitions for the Thrower method show the version that does not throw exceptions is 3.5 times quicker than the exception-throwing version if a failure HRESULT is returned (see Test 13.09).

Managed C++

Unlike most other compilers that target the CLR, the C++ compiler can emit both managed and unmanaged code. Managed and unmanaged methods can be included in the same source file, making calls between managed and unmanaged code extremely easy, as shown here:

```
#pragma managed
void ManagedFunction(){
 int res = UnmanagedFunction();
}

#pragma unmanaged
int UnmanagedFunction(){
 return 1;
}
```

Mixing of managed and unmanaged code in Managed C++ is accomplished by a subset of P/Invoke informally known as IJW (which stands for It Just Works). IJW is cheaper than P/Invoke, and there is no stack walk to check for security permissions in the calling methods due to the automatic generation of

SuppressUnmanagedCodeSecurityAttribute decorations on unmanaged methods; however, the transition between managed and unmanaged code still imparts a performance hit, with a transition taking in the order of 10 to 50 machine instructions, depending on the parameters that need to marshalled across the call boundary.

The use of Managed C++ also makes including blittable parameters, which are cheaper to pass to unmanaged code as they require no marshalling, much simpler. Managed C++ can use the original header files that define unmanaged methods, and these files generally contain the definition of data structures that form the parameters to these methods, which allows parameters that are physically identical on the managed and unmanaged side to be employed.

The IJW technology makes porting existing C++ code to the CLR extremely easy, and allows for a method-by-method port. Dropping into native code for methods with high-performance demands can also be achieved very easily. From a performance perspective, the problem with IJW is that there is a tendency for a high number of transitions between unmanaged and managed calls to occur, and these transitions can be caused by both application code (an unmanaged function calls a managed function, or vice versa) and the compiler. Consider the following code block:

```
#include "stdafx.h"
#include <tchar.h>
#include <time.h>
#using <mscorlib.dll>
using namespace System;

class Base{
public:
  virtual int SecondsSinceUTCMidnight(){
    System::DateTime dt =  System::DateTime::UtcNow;
    return (dt.Hour * 3600 + dt.Minute * 60 + dt.Second);
  }
};

class Derived : public Base{
public:
#pragma unmanaged
  virtual int SecondsSinceUTCMidnight(){
    time_t now;
    time(&now);
    return now % (24*60*60);
  }
#pragma managed
};
```

```
int _tmain(void){
  Base* d = new Derived();
  Console::WriteLine(d->SecondsSinceUTCMidnight());

  Base* b = new Base();
  Console::WriteLine(b->SecondsSinceUTCMidnight());

  Console::ReadLine();

  return 0;
}
```

Base and Derived are both unmanaged types, with Base containing the virtual managed method SecondsSinceMidnight, and Derived overriding this function with an unmanaged method. The _tmain method creates a new Derived object, and accesses it indirectly through a pointer to the Base type. As both Base and Derived are not managed types, the runtime has no knowledge of their layout, and must make a transition to unmanaged code to determine which function to actually call. In the preceding example, the function that should be called is unmanaged, and this call will be executed, after which a transition back to the managed _tmain function will occur. The transition to unmanaged code will occur even if the function being called indirectly is a managed function, which means that every indirect call can result in a full transition to and from managed code.

This performance problem can be solved in two ways: Make everything managed using the Managed C++ extensions __gc and __value and avoiding #pragma unmanaged directives, or make everything unmanaged by removing the /clr compiler switch. By using the Managed C++ Extensions, standard CLR types can be generated, and the runtime can determine the correct function to call without making a transition to unmanaged code. Removing the /clr switch allows the file to compile with the standard unmanaged behavior of classic C++.

Monitoring Interop

Like many areas of functionality contained within the Framework, Windows's System Monitor is the optimum starting point when investigating performance problems. A dedicated Interop performance object is installed with the Framework, but the number of counters exposed by the performance object is quite limited, and disappointingly does not include a counter that tracks the number of transitions made or the number of security stack walks triggered by a transition. Of the three counters currently implemented, the # of marshalling counter is the only counter related to execution speed, with # of CCWs and # of Stubs only relevant to working set analysis. The # of marshalling counter can be used to identify sections of an application that use Interop calls with a significant portion of nonblittable parameters (blittable parameters, by definition, do not require marshalling); but as the performance of marshalling varies significantly depending on the level of conversion required, simply identifying the count of marshalling is not a strong indicator of performance.

Using unmanaged interception tools to monitor Interop call frequency is a feasible option for P/Invoke and COM Interop calls. A tool like API Spy (`http://madmat.hypermart.net/apis32.htm`) can intercept calls made to P/Invoke functions to monitor the frequency at which the calls are being made. For COM monitoring, the Universal Delegator presented by Keith Brown in the January and February 1999 editions of the "Microsoft Systems Journal" (`http://www.microsoft.com/msj/0199/intercept/intercept.aspx`) allows COM calls to be intercepted and monitored for performance tracking.

Conclusion

Three dominant factors determine interoperability performance—security, marshalling, and transition frequency. Security is an easy issue to deal with— it is there by default for COM Interop and P/Invoke calls, but can be moved from runtime to link time with `SuppressUnmanagedCodeSecurityAttribute`. Moving the check to link time should only be done in extraordinary circumstances, and only after a thorough security audit to analyze the impact of the lack of runtime checks. Haphazard application of `SuppressUnmanagedCodeSecurityAttribute` can undermine the Code Access Security model by allowing untrusted code to access functionality through unmanaged code that it would otherwise be prevented from accessing.

Automatic marshalling of data types is convenient and robust, and will be preferable in most situations. Significant optimizations are available by using stack allocation and performance hints present in parameter relations and documentation. For most applications, the use of automatic marshalling during development, followed by manual tuning during the optimization phase if required, will be the best option. Character sets are one exception to this rule, and the character set of any unmanaged function called should align to the internal character set of the host platform, which can be achieved by setting the `DllImportAttribute.CharSet` field to `Auto`.

For P/Invoke and COM Interop, a transition to unmanaged code is easy to identify, and the only concern is to avoid an unmanaged API that requires an excessive number of method calls to complete a single task. If an API like this must be employed, it is possible to use an unmanaged wrapper written in unmanaged C++ to reduce the number of transitions. For Managed C++, the situation is different, and transition frequency can become a real problem. By keeping a reasonable degree of separation between the unmanaged and managed sections of a C++ application, the number of transitions can be minimized.

CHAPTER 14

The Common Language Runtime

THIS CHAPTER CONTAINS SMALLER topics related to the CLR and Framework Library that do not fit neatly into any other chapter, and are each too small to justify a chapter of their own. The topics are largely self-contained, and can be consumed in isolation.

Process Initialization

This section focuses on the steps that a .NET application goes through when it is launched. While the material may appear dry and removed from high-level performance issues, these actions form a basis upon which the CLR executes code and are important to understand when considering higher-level performance issues.

Code that targets the CLR is usually housed in an executable image residing on disk, with the instructions stored in the form of Microsoft Intermediate Language (MSIL) instructions. This is not a requirement, though, and the Reflection.Emit types in the Framework Library support runtime generation of CLR-targeting assemblies. For the more common disk-based scenario, the file will be in the standard Portable Executable (PE) format; this allows the mature operating system image-loading infrastructure, which has been optimized over the life of the Windows operating system, to be leveraged.

The PE file header contains various header data, and part of this header data is a data directory that indicates the location of various standard structures that are common to executable images. There are currently 16 standard sections defined, and these sections contain data on items like file exports, imports, and embedded resources. The fifteenth standard section is the CLR header, and a nonzero size for this section is the definitive test of whether a particular executable targets the CLR.

Information contained in the CLR header is similar in nature to the data contained in the PE file header; but where the data directory listings are Win32 specific, the CLR header entries contain settings relevant to the CLR. A full list of the settings is contained in the IMAGE_COR20_HEADER structure, which is defined in the CorHdr.h file that ships with the Framework SDK.

The PE headers will contain the native entry point of the image, which will usually include bootstrap code that loads the CLR using functions exported from mscoree.dll, and hands process control over to the CLR. Once the CLR has been initialized, JIT compilation is carried out if necessary, referenced assemblies are loaded as required, and execution control is passed to the CLR entry point. The managed entry point is defined in the runtime header, and for executable images, this defines the first managed method that will be executed once loading is complete.

Locating Referenced Assemblies

The manifest of an assembly contains information on assemblies on which it is dependent for successful execution. As code is JIT compiled, references to types contained within these dependent assemblies will be found, and if the referenced assembly is not already loaded, the CLR loader will be employed to locate and load the newly referenced assembly. This behavior is in contrast to the Win32 loader, whose default behavior is to load all dependent DLLs when an application first starts. The delayed loading behavior of the CLR means that references to rarely used assemblies do not impart a significant performance cost until types from within the assembly are actually used.

The manifest of an assembly records the version of its dependent assemblies. For strongly named assemblies, application, publisher, and machine configuration files can all redirect the runtime to load a different version from the one nominated. Once the actual version of the assembly required has been determined, the loader needs to locate the actual file that houses the assembly. The first location searched is the Global Assembly Cache (GAC), followed by codeBase elements in configuration files that can specify a URL where the file is located, and finally directories relative to application root are probed. The application root is the directory where the configuration file of an application is located. For executables such as Windows Forms and console applications, this is the directory that the main executable file is located in, and for ASP.NET applications, the application root is the root of the virtual directory. For assemblies without a strong name, the version information is not used, and the GAC is not checked, as assemblies without a strong name cannot be placed in the GAC.

In addition to the application root directory, the configuration file (using the privatePath attribute of the probing element) and managed code (using AppDomain.AppendPrivatePath) can specify subdirectories of the root that will be searched in an attempt to locate the assembly. A private path is typically used to direct the loader towards a bin directory that contains all of an application's dependent assemblies.

The performance characteristics of the loading process are reasonably obvious—the more folders that need to be searched to locate an assembly, the slower it will be. Performance is not a critical factor when deciding on the location of assemblies in a deployed application, but overly intricate schemes involving assembly loads from a large number of locations are best avoided.

Loading Behavior

Loading images from disk or a remote server is an inherently expensive exercise to complete, and increases the working set of the process. Most loading events are unavoidable, and are simply caused by the need for functionality not available in the currently loaded modules. Commonsense steps like packaging similar functionality in the same assembly, keeping assemblies below the multimegabyte size, and not serving assemblies from a remote server that is congested or accessible over a low-bandwidth network should deliver reasonable behavior for loading. The steps that follow will not drastically reduce the effect of loading, and are targeted more at preventing load performance from becoming excessively slow.

Relocations

The base address of an executable image indicates the beginning of the address range in which the image would prefer to be loaded. Unmanaged code uses offsets from this preferred address to reference data and records this usage in the relocations section of the PE file. The Win32 loader will attempt to load every image in its preferred address range, but if another module is already occupying addresses in this range, the loader must load the new module in a different address range. To allow the program to function properly, the image must be copied into memory, and every entry in the relocations table must be transformed to reflect the new address range. This can be a significant performance cost when an application is starting up.

Managed code does not suffer from the problems of preferred address ranges and relocations, as MSIL uses symbolic names rather than addresses to refer to data entities. However, managed assemblies are packaged in PE files and contain a small native stub that can execute when the image is loaded. This stub simply calls out to mscoree.dll, and from then on, only managed code within the module is executed. The native code contains a single relocation entry, and versions of Windows from XP onwards have a PE file loader that is CLR aware, negating the requirement for the unmanaged stub.

When a managed module is pre-JIT compiled with the Native Image Generator (Ngen.exe) tool, the preferred base address and size of the original address space is used to calculate a new preferred base address for the native module. This prevents the managed and native module colliding, but if two managed modules have the same preferred base address, it is likely that their native modules will be located within the same address ranges. The native modules produced by the Native Image Generator have a standard relocation section typical of any unmanaged module, and attempting to load two pre-JITed modules at the same address space will produce the same performance hit as occurs with any other module containing native instructions.

To avoid the cost of preferred address collision, each managed library assembly should modify its base address so that it will not conflict with other modules. Executables, which are usually loaded first, do not need to modify their base addresses, as they will be loaded in their preferred address range in most cases. The recommended scheme for choosing a base address is to use the first letter of the module's name to derive the address. Table 14-1 presents a scheme for DLL base address determination that is included with the documentation for the Platform SDK tool Rebase, which can be used to change the base address of a DLL post-compilation.

Table 14-1. Recommended Base Address Relocation Scheme

FIRST LETTER	BASE ADDRESS
A–B	0x60000000
D–F	0x61000000
G–I	0x62000000
J–L	0x63000000
M–O	0x64000000
P–R	0x65000000
S–U	0x66000000
V–X	0x67000000
Y–Z	0x68000000

The base address of an assembly can be set on the Project Pages dialog box in Visual Studio. For C#, the setting is on the Advanced page of the Configuration Properties section, as shown in Figure 14-1. For VB .NET, the setting is on the Optimizations page of the Configuration Properties section, as shown in Figure 14-2.

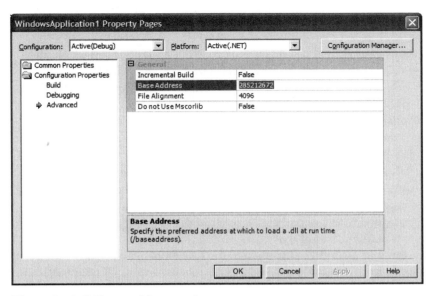

Figure 14-1. C# base address setting

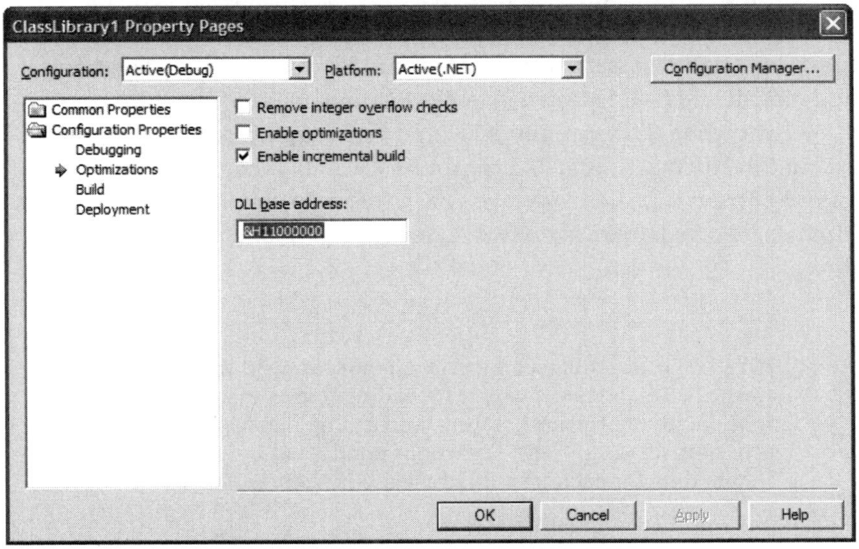

Figure 14-2. Visual Basic .NET base address setting

Strongly Named Assemblies

Strongly named assemblies contain a signature element embedded within the CLR header that is produced by signing a hash of the PE file with the software publisher's private key. This signature can be verified by decrypting it with the publisher's public key, which is contained in the assemblies manifest, and comparing it against a freshly calculated hash of the PE file. This ensures that the file has not been modified since it was signed. This check is done at installation time for assemblies installed in the GAC, and at load time for other assemblies.

The public and private key pair used for strong naming can be generated with the Strong Name Tool (Sn.exe), and are not derived from a digital certificate. A .NET assembly available for download from the Internet may have a strong name and be signed with a digital certificate, but the application of either security measure is independent of the other.

The reason that assemblies installed in the GAC only need the tamper check at installation time is that folders in the GAC are secured using Windows ACLs, which prevents non-Administrators from modifying them. Strongly named assemblies that are stored in other directories on the file system do not have this protection, and are therefore vulnerable to tampering.

The load-time check of strongly named assemblies located outside the GAC raises some performance concerns. To test the impact of the check, a large (1.2MB), strongly named assembly is created, and load speed for installations inside and outside the GAC is tested. Average load speed is 55.5 ms from inside the GAC, 93.3 ms when the assembly is located in the application base directory (a 68 percent time increase), and 82.2 ms for an assembly that is a codeBase binding (a 48 percent time increase over GAC). Given the small difference in the overall timings involved, there is no real performance advantage to GAC installation.

 NOTE The assembly load tests were not run with the Benchmark Harness. The once-off nature of loading makes the tests infeasible for Benchmark Harness testing, and a simple console application is used instead. A "warm-up" run is conducted before collecting timing data for each test to reduce the influence of disk caching on the results.

Multiple Module Assemblies

Assemblies can be spread over a number of separate physical DLLs. The DLLs that make up an assembly are known as *modules,* which is, confusingly, the same term used to describe a Win32 executable image loaded into memory.

Modules generally use the `.netmodule` extension, but this is purely a convention, and the actual file is a fully contained Win32 DLL.

For large assemblies that contain code and data elements that are rarely used, splitting the assembly into frequently and rarely used types may make sense. Modules are not loaded by the CLR until a type contained within that particular module is referenced, which means that an assembly can be partially loaded into memory. For deployment scenarios where application elements are being downloaded on demand from a remote server, splitting an application into separate modules will reduce download delays.

Multimodule assemblies can be created only through the command-line compilers and Assembly Linker (Al.exe) at present, and for Visual Studio .NET development, multimodule assemblies will rarely be worth the hassle. If an assembly is likely to be large, and composed of types that are loosely related and vary markedly in frequency of use, it may be worthwhile splitting the assembly into two distinct assemblies rather than resorting to multimodule assemblies.

Splitting an assembly into frequently and occasionally used types can be difficult if the types in the assembly have strong interdependent relationships. If a type that needs to be moved into the occasionally used assembly contains a reference to a type in the commonly used assembly, and the reverse relationship also exists, a circular relationship between the two assemblies exists, which can make compilation difficult and at times impossible. To solve this problem, a third assembly that defines common interfaces can be created, and the types in the two main assemblies can reference the interface assembly at compile time. The following snippet shows the before-and-after type relationships:

```
'strong relationship between frequently and occasionally used types
Class FrequentlyUsed
  Private _ou As OccasionallyUsed 'typically set to Nothing
  Public Sub OnlyCalledOccasionally()
    _ou = New OccasionallyUsed
    'use _ou
  End Sub
End Class

Class OccasionallyUsed
  Private _fu As FrequentlyUsed
  Public Property FreqUsed() As FrequentlyUsed
    Get
      Return _fu
    End Get
    Set(ByVal Value As FrequentlyUsed)
      _fu = Value
    End Set
  End Property
```

```
          End Class

          '******************
          '******************
          'weaken relationship

          '******************
          'in interface assembly
          Interface IFrequentlyUsed
          End Interface

          Interface IOccasionallyUsed
            Property FreqUsed() As IFrequentlyUsed
          End Interface

          '******************
          'in frequently used assembly
          Class FrequentlyUsedSplit
            Implements IFrequentlyUsed
            Private _ou As IOccasionallyUsed 'typically set to Nothing
            Public Sub OnlyCalledOccasionally()
              'assembly containing OccasionallyUsedSplit neeeded here
              _ou = New OccasionallyUsedSplit
                  'use _ou
            End Sub
          End Class

          '******************
          'in occasionally used assembly
          Class OccasionallyUsedSplit
            Implements IOccasionallyUsed
            Private _fu As IFrequentlyUsed
            Public Property FreqUsed() As IFrequentlyUsed Implements _
              IOccasionallyUsed.FreqUsed
              Get
                Return _fu
              End Get
              Set(ByVal Value As IFrequentlyUsed)
                _fu = Value
              End Set
            End Property
          End Class
```

Loader Optimizations

Application domains are units of execution that form the basis of memory isolation for managed code. A single Win32 process can house a number of CLR application domains, which means that the CLR must enforce certain safeguards to ensure data in one application domain is not accessible to other application domains. The primary defense against cross-application domain memory access is verifiable code, which is verifiable in the sense that it does not access any memory locations that it should not have access to. Nonverifiable code has the potential to access random memory addresses within a process, and requires the SkipVerification permission to execute.

Isolating application domains in the same process also requires static variable changes to be contained to the particular application domain in which the changes are made. There are two ways that this can be accomplished: by loading assemblies in a domain-neutral manner and keeping a collection of writable static variables for each application domain, or by loading an assembly specific to a particular application domain. The decision is a classic trade-off between memory and speed, and the loading technique that delivers the best overall performance is dependent on whether it is likely that a process will host multiple application domains. For ASP.NET applications, in which multiple application domains are likely to be hosted within the ASP.NET worker process, domain-neutral loading is preferred. Windows Forms applications, in which multiple application domains are unlikely, favor single domain assembly loads, but this can be explicitly specified with application of the LoaderOptimizationAttribute on the application's entry point, as shown in the following snippet:

```
[LoaderOptimization(LoaderOptimization.MultiDomain)]
static void Main() {
  Application.Run(new Form1());
}
```

For a custom runtime host, the assembly loading optimization is nominated using the flags parameter of CorBindToRuntimeEx.

Domain-neutral loading makes access to static variables considerably slower—about three times as slow for the test case of incrementing a 32-bit integer (see Test 14.01), but it is important to put this slowdown in perspective. Accessing static variables is very fast, and even at one third of the speed, access is still very quick. For static variables that are being written to throughout a program's execution, thread synchronization is usually required, and once the cost of the synchronization using a Monitor lock is included, the performance decrease caused by accessing static member variables in assemblies that have been loaded domain neutrally is less than 10 percent (see Test 14.01).

The vast majority of programs will never need to worry about the assembly loader optimizations described in this section, as the default settings chosen by the runtime host will generally offer the best trade-off between speed and memory usage. When designing an unmanaged executable that hosts the CLR, an analysis of application domain assembly loading needs to be performed. For a CLR host that has the characteristics of a client-side application, a single application domain per process will be the typical scenario, and in this case domain-neutral loading on assemblies should be avoided. For server-side applications, multiple application domains per process provide scalability and fault isolation characteristics that are critical, and domain-neutral loads should generally be favored.

Unloading Assemblies

Once an assembly is loaded into an application domain, it cannot be unloaded. For most applications, this limitation is not overly important, as the assemblies used will be fairly constant over the lifetime of an application. However, for a certain class of applications, particularly those that load assemblies dynamically to provide scripting or plug-in behavior, the inability to unload assemblies can cause excessive memory consumption in long-running processes. The CLR supports the ability to unload assemblies through the dynamic loading of assemblies into secondary application domains, which can be shut down when the assemblies they contain are no longer needed. Unloading an application domain results in assemblies that have been loaded dynamically into that application domain being unloaded as well. The code that follows demonstrates this technique:

```
class App {
 static void Main(string[] args) {
  AppDomain appDomain = AppDomain.CreateDomain("WorkerDomain");
  Type remoteWorkerType = typeof(RemoteAssemblyWorker);
  RemoteAssemblyWorker remoteWorker = (RemoteAssemblyWorker)
   (appDomain.CreateInstance(remoteWorkerType.Assembly.FullName,
    remoteWorkerType.FullName).Unwrap());
  remoteWorker.DoStuff();
  AppDomain.Unload(appDomain);
 }
}

public class RemoteAssemblyWorker: MarshalByRefObject {
 public void DoStuff(){
  Assembly dynamicallyLoadedAssembly = Assembly.Load("ClassLibrary1");
  dynamicallyLoadedAssembly.CreateInstance("ClassLibrary1.Class1");
  Console.WriteLine("In worker domain.");
 }
}
```

In the code sample, a new application domain is created, a MarshalByRefObject-derived object is created in the remote application domain, and a proxy to the remote object is retrieved by using the Unwrap method of the ObjectHandle returned by AppDomain.CreateInstance. This proxy can then be used to call methods in the remote application domain, and in the preceding code, the DoStuff method is called to dynamically load an assembly and create an object in the assembly. Once the program is finished using the dynamically loaded assemblies, the secondary application domain can be unloaded, which will remove the dynamically loaded assemblies from memory.

Just-In-Time (JIT) Compilation

The traditional job of a compiler is to transform high-level code into machine instructions that are directly executable by the processor. Compilers that target the CLR do not produce machine code, but instead produce a set of Microsoft Intermediate Language (MSIL) instructions. When a .NET application begins, a small native stub in the executable, or the image loader on Windows XP and above, calls the runtime shim (mscoree.dll), which begins the process of loading the CLR. As part of this process, the MSIL instructions at the managed entry point for the assembly are JIT compiled to machine instructions by mscorjit.dll, and any types referenced by the managed entry point function are compiled as well. As a program executes, types located in assemblies that are not loaded are referenced, and this causes a new cycle of loading and JIT compilation. Depending upon how the assembly is loaded, the JIT compiled instructions are discarded when the process exits (for application domain–neutral assemblies), or when the application domain is unloaded (for application domain–specific assemblies).

The recompilation of an assembly every time it is loaded has some interesting performance implications. On the negative side, time is wasted completing the same JIT compilation every time the assembly is loaded. The JIT compiler has a much tighter time budget than a "development-time" compiler, which can take essentially as long as it wants in optimizing the higher-level code, given the typical high-end nature of development machines and the infrequency of a Release compilation process.

The performance losses can theoretically be eclipsed by performance gains that the JIT compiler can produce by responding to the environment in which the machine instructions will actually be run. The JIT compiler can produce instructions that take advantage of the full instruction set of the target processor, whereas a traditional machine code–producing compiler has to take a somewhat lowest-common-denominator approach when producing machine instructions. Performance gains due to hardware optimizations are important, but in the relatively homogenous hardware world of Windows, the likely gains are not overwhelming for general-purpose applications. The JIT compiler that ships with version 1 of the Framework does not produce some of the more obscure machine instructions available, so the possible performance gains in this area of JIT compilation will not occur until the next major release of the .NET Framework at the earliest.

The real performance advantage of JIT compilation comes from allowing the compiler to observe how the code is being used, and based on this profiling, recompile methods on the critical path to run faster through inlining, loop unwinding, and other optimizations. The current JIT compiler does not perform heavy optimizations based on its environment, but this situation is likely to change as the .NET platform matures.

For long-running applications like server processes, JIT compilation is not a big deal, but for end-user applications that are launched and terminated frequently, the performance cost can be perceived as too high. To address this problem, the .NET runtime ships with a tool to pregenerate native images called the Native Image Generator. The current release of Ngen does not take advantage of the relaxed time restrictions that once-off compilation offers to produce a more heavily optimized version, and simply uses the same JIT compiler that would normally be used when launching an application.

To get a feel for the benefits of Ngen usage, the Scribble sample application that ships with the MSDN Library, which is modestly sized at around 1500 lines of code, is used to test the performance improvement that Native Image Generator on a Windows Forms application could offer. Two versions of the application, which differ only in their version number and Ngen state, are timed from application launch to the time the first line of managed code is executed. The launch speed of the two versions is very similar, with no more than a 10 percent difference observed on different hardware configurations (see Test 14.02), but the fastest version actually varies depending upon the machine the tests were executed on.

Producing a cached native image is not a performance panacea, and can cause some performance problems. Because native generation is done on a per-assembly basis, cross-assembly optimizations are not possible. In addition, the native image produced by Ngen can only be used when loaded as application domain specific, and if the runtime host has specified that application domains are loaded domain neutrally, the runtime will only load the original assembly.

If all the assemblies that are loaded into an application are native, the JIT compiler DLL (mscorjit.dll) is not loaded, which saves around 300KB of memory. This drop in memory usage is typically offset by the runtime's need to load both the MSIL and native version of assemblies; this can cause a significant jump in the working set for large assemblies that contain code that is not used, and hence never JIT compiled to native code in memory if Ngen is not used.

Method and Property Inlining

Microsoft Intermediate Language (MSIL) does not offer the ability to annotate a method as requiring inlining, and this limitation prevents any higher-level language from implementing any inlining functionality. The JIT compiler is free to inline methods to improve performance, and will do this in situations where inlining makes sense and is feasible. MSIL allows a method to specify the implementation attribute `noinlining` if inlining is inappropriate for the method, and high-level languages can implement a `noinlining` method by applying `MethodImplAttribute` with the `MethodImplOptions.NoInlining` flag specified in the constructor.

There are very few times when preventing inlining would make sense, but one possible application would be a custom security scheme that uses the `System.Diagnostics.StackFrame` type to examine the call stack and make some security decision based on the types and methods present in the stack. Suppressing inlining also delivers a more accurate exception stack trace when an exception occurs, but this comes at the expense of execution speed and is not a recommended practice.

The CLR does not currently have an equivalent to the Java Hotspot technology, which monitors an application's execution for a certain number of runs, and then uses inlining to boost performance on critical code paths. Future versions of the CLR may implement similar performance enhancement technologies, and a current Microsoft research project (`http://research.microsoft.com/act/`) is working on a .NET compiler that boosts performance through "dynamic compilation and incremental whole-program optimization."

Custom Attributes

Custom attributes provide the ability to annotate source code with metadata that can be retrieved and acted upon at runtime. Custom attributes do not impose any performance burden on the types and methods that they annotate until they are actually accessed (see Test 14.03). Some attributes provided within the System namespace, such as `DllImport`, are recognized by compilers, and the compiler will have special-case logic to actually generate instructions based on the attribute's properties. The performance impact of these attributes is totally dependent on the instructions generated by the compiler in response to the attribute's presence. Other attributes within the `System` namespace, such as `Obsolete`, are similar to custom attributes in that they have no direct effect on code execution.

For situations where type metadata needs to be frequently accessed at runtime, the performance cost of querying for custom attributes can be prohibitive. An alternative to custom attributes is to use an interface with no methods to designate a type as possessing a certain quality. Marker interfaces, as they are known, are about 30 times quicker to query for than custom attributes (see Test 14.04), which cause a significant performance improvement in tight loops. Marker interfaces do not offer the full functionality of custom interfaces—they can only be applied to types, and they cannot have parameters applied to them. The Framework makes very little use of marker interfaces—INamingContainer in the System.Web.UI namespace, which is used to manage unique identifiers for child controls, is one of the few examples that exist. Unless profiling indicates custom attribute access causes a significant performance hit, it is best to avoid marker interfaces where possible.

Managing the CLR

For the most part, the CLR is self-tuning, and the level of control that managed code has over the CLR is quite limited. However, at times tuning of various CLR parameters can deliver performance boosts. This tuning should only be done when profiling and performance monitoring indicate that the CLR is a bottleneck for the application, and the problem cannot be rectified with modifications to application code.

The full set of publicly released functions and interfaces for modifying CLR behavior is defined in IDL files that ship with the Framework SDK. The interfaces fall into the broad categories shown in Table 14-2.

Table 14-2. Unmanaged CLR Interfaces

CATEGORY	INTERFACES
Debugging	ICorDebugValue, ICorDebugGenericValue, ICorDebugReferenceValue, ICorDebugHeapValue, ICorDebugObjectValue, ICorDebugStringValue, ICorDebugArrayValue, ICorDebugEnum, ICorDebugObjectEnum, ICorDebugProcessEnum, ICorDebugBreakpointEnum, ICorDebugStepperEnum, ICorDebugModuleEnum, ICorDebugThreadEnum, ICorDebugChainEnum, ICorDebugFrameEnum, ICorDebugValueEnum, ICorDebugAppDomainEnum, ICorDebugAssemblyEnum, ICorDebugErrorInfoEnum, ICorDebugEditAndContinueSnapshot, ICorDebugEditAndContinueErrorInfo, IDebuggerThreadControl, IdebuggerInfo
Profiling	ICorProfilerCallback, ICorProfilerInfo, IMethodMalloc

Table 14-2. Unmanaged CLR Interfaces (Continued)

CATEGORY	INTERFACES
Publication	`ICorPublish, ICorPublishProcess, ICorPublishAppDomain, ICorPublishProcessEnum, ICorPublishAppDomainEnum`
Notification	`ICORSvcDbgInfo, ICORSvcDbgNotify`
Debugging symbols	`ISymUnmanagedDocument, ISymUnmanagedDocumentWriter, ISymUnmanagedMethod, ISymUnmanagedNamespace, ISymUnmanagedReader, ISymUnmanagedScope, ISymUnmanagedVariable, ISymUnmanagedWriter, ISymUnmanagedBinder`
Garbage collection	`IGCHost`
Verification	`IValidator, ILoader, IVEHandler`
General CRL control	`IObjectHandle, IAppDomainBinding, IGCThreadControl, IGCHostControl, ICorThreadpool, ICorConfiguration, ICorRuntimeHost, IApartmentCallback, IManagedObject, ICatalogServices`

Providing a detailed description of each of these interfaces could easily fill an entire book, but it is worth highlighting a few of the interfaces that allow interesting results to be achieved. The profiling interfaces, `ICorProfilerInfo` in particular, can be employed to modify the contents of a .NET method at runtime. This technique can be used to develop an *aspect-oriented framework,* which has the potential to improve performance by injecting highly optimized aspects into methods. See "Rewrite MSIL Code on the Fly with the .NET Framework Profiling API" (`http://msdn.microsoft.com/msdnmag/issues/03/09/NETProfilingAPI/default.aspx`) and "Aspect-Oriented Programming Enables Better Code Encapsulation and Reuse" (`http://msdn.microsoft.com/msdnmag/issues/02/03/aop/default.aspx`) for a fuller discussion of these ideas.

The `ICorThreadpool` interface can be used to set the size of the CLR thread pool, and this technique is discussed in Chapter 10. This chapter also discusses the use of `IGCThreadControl` to receive notification when the CLR is about to be suspended, which can be used to simulate a real-time environment. Setting a maximum ceiling for process memory usage using the `IGCHostControl` interface is covered in Chapter 7.

Using these interfaces in managed code does not support the full range of options that hosting the runtime through unmanaged code provides. A number of the parameters of the CLR can only be set when the CLR is initializing, which means that by the time the first line of managed code is run, the parameters are fixed. A number of the interfaces defined in the Framework SDK IDL files are not included in the mscoree type library, which means that the interfaces need to be manually added to managed code, which is more cumbersome than using the header file definition provided with the SDK in unmanaged code.

To interact with the unmanaged side of the CLR, either a reference to a Common Language Runtime Execution Engine Library (mscoree.tlb) Interop assembly or the manual definition of the relevant interfaces and classes from the IDL files is required. The CorRuntimeHost COM class exposes the most functionality for interacting with the CLR, and a programmatic reference to this class can be created in managed code by simply instantiating a new object of this type. The object created will by a reference to the runtime active in the current application domain, and can be used to call methods on a number of unmanaged interfaces. The code that follows demonstrates the use of the IGCHost interface to force a collection of generation 0 of the managed heap:

```
//using mscoree; at top of file
ICorRuntimeHost host = new CorRuntimeHostClass();
IGCHost gcHost = (IGCHost)host;
gcHost.Collect(0);
```

A significant portion of the functionality available through the hosting APIs is only accessible before the CLR is launched. Examples of this functionality include the nomination of the CLR flavor (workstation or server) that will be used, and the provision of an IGCHostControl-implementing object that can be used to cap managed heap size. For details on implementing a custom runtime host to access this functionality, see "Microsoft .NET: Implement a Custom Common Language Runtime Host for Your Managed App" by Steven Pratschner (*MSDN Magazine*, March 2001).

It is again worth emphasizing that the CLR is essentially self-tuning, and modifying CLR parameters is more likely to hurt performance if not done with great care and tested thoroughly under production loads.

Checked Arithmetic Code

The CLR has the ability to check arithmetic operations for overflow of integral variables. Overflow occurs when an attempt is made to assign a value to a variable of a particular type, and the value falls outside the range that the type can accommodate. Integer types have a MinValue and MaxValue static property that indicates the range of values that the data type can hold, and attempts to assign values outside these ranges will cause an overflow. The operations that can cause overflows are addition, subtraction, multiplication, and type conversion. In unchecked operations, an overflow will result in looping or truncation, which can cause unpredictability in numerical operations. Truncation occurs during a conversion operation, and simply involves disregarding the most significant bytes that do not fit within the target type. Looping occurs during addition and subtraction operations, and involves a value moving from the top of the MaxValue range to the bottom of the MinValue range or vice-versa. The following code demonstrates both truncation and looping:

```
int i = Int32.MaxValue;
int j = i + 1;
bool b1 = (j == Int32.MinValue); //true - j has looped

short s = (short)i;
bool b2 = (s == -1);  //true - s is the first 16 bits if i (0xffff),
                      // which is -1 for a short
```

All MSIL instructions that can cause an overflow have two versions: an unchecked version (add, conv, mul, and sub) and a corresponding checked version (add.ovf, conv.ovf, mul.ovf, and sub.ovf). The actual compilation of these instructions into x86 assembly instructions is dependent on the numeric type that the MSIL instructions are operating on. For operations on integers that have a size of 32 bits or above, overflow checking can be carried out with specific x86 instructions (JO and JNO), whereas for smaller integers the checks must be carried out with a series of assembly instructions that compare the result of the operation with the bounds of the type, which makes the checks slower.

The checked version of the MSIL instructions only applies to integral types, and this means that a checked version of division is not needed, as division of integral types cannot cause an increase in absolute value.

A simple benchmark that involves adding two integers together inside and outside checked blocks of code shows that for 32-bit integers, the cost of performing checked operation results in a 75 percent increase in execution time. For 64-bit integers, execution time is increased by 38 percent by the use of checked code blocks. As expected, the time increase for checked Int16 addition was the most pronounced, with a 148 percent increase in execution time observed for the checked case (see Test 14.05).

VB .NET allows the overflow check setting to be nominated on a compilation-wide basis, which means that a module is the smallest distribution unit for the application of checked or unchecked switch. The "Remove Integer Overflow Checks" setting on the Optimizations page of the Configuration Properties section in Visual Studio (visible in Figure 14-2) supports the production of an assembly with no overflow checks.

C# supports checked and unchecked contexts within the same source file, which allows the application of overflow checking to be applied at a very granular level, as shown in the following snippet. The C# compiler also supports a per-compilation setting to be nominated, with no overflow checking being the default.

```
int i = 0;
checked{++i;}
unchecked{++i;}
```

Decimal Type

The Framework Library provides a Decimal type for high-precision numerical operations. Unlike other numerical types like Int32 and Double, which are compiled into equivalent MSIL types, Decimal has no MSIL support, and is actually composed of three Int32 types that stores the decimal number and a Int32 flag that stores the sign bit and exponent of the decimal number. Numerical operations on Decimal types involve related operations on all the constituent Int32 member variables, and this, combined with the large size of Decimal compared to other numerical types, makes Decimal significantly slower for numerical operations.

A test case where a stack-allocated Decimal is allocated, has multiplication, addition, division, and subtraction applied to it, and is then assigned to a Decimal member variable of a reference type, is compared to the same operations conducted on a Double type (see Test 14.06). Decimal is 18.5 times slower than Double for the test case nominated.

Debug and Release Builds

Most developers realize that a release build of an application is generally quicker than the debug build, but the exact reason for the performance improvement is often not appreciated. This section offers an overview of the differences between the two builds, and although there are no real performance tips (other than a debug build should not be shipped as a general release, and performance tests should not be run against a debug build), some of the confusion that surrounds the two build configurations will hopefully be clarified.

The first point of note is that the ability to use the debugger to step through lines of code is not affected by the build configuration—both debug and release builds can be debugged in the Visual Studio debugger. To step through code in the debugger, a map of the source code statements to the generated MSIL instructions needs to be produced when the high-level language is compiled, and a map of the MSIL instructions to x86 instructions needs to be produced at JIT compile time. The default configuration for most Visual Studio project types is to emit a high-level language–to-MSIL map for debug builds only, but this can be easily modified within the project's configuration pages (on the Configuration Properties | Build page in C# and VB .NET). The code-to-MSIL mapping is stored in a program database file, which has the same name as the executable and has a PDB file extension. The program database file also contains information about the location and name of the source files that were used when the project was compiled.

The production of a MSIL-to–native offset map by the JIT compiler is controlled by the `DebuggableAttribute.IsJITTrackingEnabled` setting, which is contained in the assembly's manifest. When this property is set to true, the JIT compiler maintains an in-memory offset map, regardless of whether the assembly is JIT compiled in a process with a debugger attached. The MSIL-to–native offset map causes a noticeable increase in an application's working set; for a simple C# console application with a single `Console.ReadLine` call, `IsJITTrackingEnabled` results in memory consumption increasing from 4392KB to 4540KB. This size increase is not influenced by the presence of the PDB file, and for assemblies that will ship to customers, `JITTracking` should be turned off.

The most profound difference between debug and release builds comes from the `DebuggableAttribute.IsJITOptimizerDisabled` property. When this property is false (JIT optimization is enabled), the JIT compiler performs optimizations traditionally associated with optimizing compilers, such as method inlining, removal of unused variables, and reordering of calculations. The performance gain is hard to quantify and affects some areas more than others. For example, inlining can speed up property accessors by 50 percent or more by removing intermediate access methods, but for data access calls that have network bandwidth and SQL Server as the limiting factors, JIT optimizations will have no real effect. Performance gains of around 5 percent would be a reasonable estimation for the release build, but actual gains may vary considerably.

In version 1.0 of the Framework, the production of debug information can result in JIT optimizations being disabled. A workaround for this bug is to create an INI file with the same name as the original assembly (e.g., AppName.ini), and place the following text in the INI file:

```
[.NET Framework Debugging Control]
AllowOptimize=1
```

This problem does not exist in version 1.1 of the .NET Framework.

Managed Application Memory Usage

The memory usage of managed applications, particularly Windows Forms applications that are targeted for deployment to end users, has caused concern for a number of developers moving to managed code for the first time. The memory usage reported by the Windows Task Manager for a newly launched C# Windows

Forms application (using version 1.1 of the .NET Framework on Windows XP Professional) that contains no code or controls added to the application-wizard generated skeleton is 6920KB. This is considerably higher than the 2948KB reported for an equivalent unmanaged C++ application that uses MFC.

The first thing to note is that there is not much you can do to reduce this memory usage. Precompiling the application to native code alleviates the need to load mscorjit.dll into memory, which drops reported memory usage to 6492KB, which is still a lot higher than the unmanaged application's memory usage. The key point to note, however, is that most of the memory reported by Task Manager will be shared across other processes that launch the CLR.

The Virtual Address Dump (VADUMP) utility, which ships with the Platform SDK, can be used to produce detailed information about the memory usage of a process. Using this tool, the ratio of shared and shareable data to private data can be investigated. Analyzing the private memory usage of a process gives a more accurate picture of the impact of the application on total machine memory consumption, as the operating system can use the same physical memory in multiple processes if it is shared or shareable.

Of the 6920KB that the .NET application uses in total, 2356KB are private (34 percent), 336KB are shareable (5 percent), and 4228KB are shared (61 percent). The amount of private data within the process is only about a third of the total, but is still about the same level as the total memory in the unmanaged application.

Drilling into the details of the private data of the managed application, which is the real performance issue, only 1084KB are made up of dynamic data (memory heaps and associate data), with 1104KB used by loaded modules (DLLs), and 168KB used by the system. The dynamic (heap) data is 16 percent of the application's total memory usage, and the CLR managed heap, which is often blamed for the high memory use of .NET applications, only makes up about half of this total, or approximately 8 percent of the application's total memory at startup.

Microsoft has identified memory consumption as an area where improvements could be made, and is looking at making optimizations of future versions of the runtime.

Reflection

Reflection, which is the ability to program against the metadata of software elements at runtime, is a tremendously powerful technology that has many real-world applications. Reflection has an obvious performance impact compared to the early binding that occurs with normal code, where method signatures, types names, and other metadata are validated at compile time. The use of reflection should be minimized, and in performance-critical code sections avoided altogether. There are other techniques that can be used to complement or eliminate reflection, such as casting to an interface to avoid late-bound invocation and class factories to avoid calls to CreateInstance. The following sample shows the use of an interface to avoid reflection during method invocation for a component plug-in scenario:

```
Imports System.Reflection

Interface IPlugIn
  Sub PerformPlugInAction()
End Interface

Module PlugInUser
  'use reflection to create plug-in, but cast to known interface to
  ' avoid reflection hit for invocation

  Public Sub UsePlugIn()
    Dim assemblyName As String = "MyAssembly"
    Dim typeName As String = "MyType"
    Dim plugInAssembly As System.Reflection.Assembly = _
      System.Reflection.Assembly.Load(assemblyName)
    Dim o As Object = plugInAssembly.CreateInstance(typeName)
    Dim plugInInterfaceRef As IPlugIn = CType(o, IPlugIn)
    plugInInterfaceRef.PerformPlugInAction()
  End Sub
End Module
```

To put the performance costs of reflection into some context, the impact of using reflection for object creation and method invocation is tested. For invocation, the test case of calculating the hash code of an object (Object.GetHashCode) is used. Using Type.InvokeMember to make the call is 58 times slower than making the call directly through the object (see Test 14.07). For object creation, Assembly.CreateInstance is compared to operator new for types inside and outside of the test assembly. CreateInstance is 240 times more expensive than the new operator when the cost of creating an assembly reference is included, and still 225 times more expensive when the cost of creating the assembly reference is removed, and a call to Assembly.CreateInstance is the only line of code executed within the test loop (see Test 14.08). For types located outside the test assembly, the new operator is 112 percent more expensive than a new operator within the current assembly, but a call to Assembly.CreateInstance is 370 times more expensive (see Test 14.08). These results indicate that reflection is quite expensive in terms of performance, and can cause a dramatic slowdown if used inappropriately.

Conclusion

The CLR is a managed environment, and by its nature leads to a loss of control over a number of facets of code execution. This is a positive feature for developer productivity, as developers can focus on implementing business functionality without needing to worry about programming tasks like explicitly loading DLLs and remembering to free allocated memory. A managed environment can also result in better performance, as the environment in which code executes can be dynamically tuned based on various system parameters.

At times, a programmer will want to take manual control over the CLR, and there are a number of ways of manually tuning the execution environment. In addition to the unmanaged hosting interfaces, a number of Framework Library types, Framework tools, and MSIL instructions are available that can be used to fine-tune execution. The appropriate use of this functionality can significantly improve performance, particularly during the optimization phase of development, where profiling and load testing can present opportunities to apply special-purpose optimizations.

CHAPTER 15

Solving Performance Problems

THE FOCUS OF THE MATERIAL covered in previous chapters relates to performance characteristics of specific areas of the CLR and Framework Libraries. When searching for a solution to a performance issue that manifests itself simply as general "slowness," information on performance specifics is not the ideal aid. This chapter aims to provide information that will allow the developer or tester to identify the specific area of functionality that is causing performance issues, and to equip the reader with a toolkit for diagnosing problems and finding solutions for performance-related issues on the .NET platform.

Identifying and using the correct tool to diagnose performance issues is a critical step in any optimization exercise. No tool is universally applicable to all performance issues that can occur within a .NET application, and the use of an inappropriate tool can result in the failure to accurately identify the underlying cause of a performance bug.

The appropriate tools for a developer to keep in a toolkit is a personal decision, and the optimum tools for one developer will be useless in the hands of another developer. The critical step in building a toolkit is to acquire tools appropriate to solving the various performance problems that can occur, and being able to employ those tools effectively when required. The tools described in this chapter are effective in diagnosing performance problems, and can be adopted as-is, or used as a starting point for building a personalized toolkit.

Task Manager

The first line of defence against poorly performing code is Windows Task Manager. Having Task Manager open and hidden so that the CPU usage icon is visible in the Windows System Tray will allow excessive spikes in CPU usage to be visible during testing. Working set bloat is not usually as obvious, but excessive disk paging will give an audible warning of performance problems on many machines due to constant hard disk activity, and a quick glance at Task Manager can determine whether a problem exists. In addition to the basic measurements of CPU and memory usage, Task Manager can provide other vital performance clues. By doing testing and development on a multiprocessor machine, code with poor scalability characteristics can be detected by observing the CPU usage readings on the individual processors. If one CPU is sitting near 100 percent usage, and the rest of the CPUs are close to idle, a significant processing bottleneck exists, and some redesign may be required. Figure 15-1 shows Task Manager on a dual-processor machine, with a good distribution of load between the two CPUs. If the CPU graph shows a consistent underutilization of some processors on a multiprocessor machine, this is generally a sign of a scalability problem, and it is worth investigating the code that is producing this behavior to look for potential bottlenecks. Code that acquires and maintains a thread lock on data structures used across many threads for lengthy periods will lead to all the processing being isolated to the CPU that is executing the code that owns the lock, and redesigning to minimize locking is required.

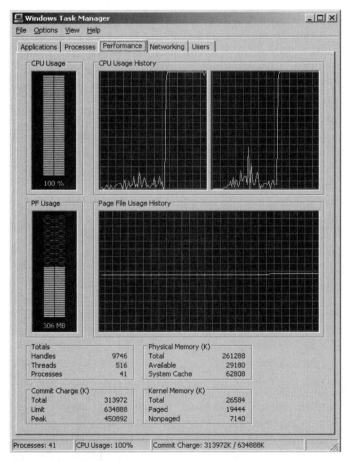

Figure 15-1. Task Manager

Task Manager supports the display of a wealth of information about the resources in use by a process. By selecting the menu item View | Selected Columns on the Processes tab, various data about a process can be displayed, and anticipated problem areas like excessive memory usage or IO can be monitored in an easy and noninvasive manner. Figure 15-2 shows the list of available columns in Windows XP. One column of particular interest is Virtual Memory Size, which displays the amount of private memory committed to a process, and does not include the memory contribution of mapped DLL memory and other sharable memory pages that are included in the Memory Usage column. Virtual Memory Size is a better indicator of the memory pressure that a process is exerting, and therefore is worth adding to the Task Manager display.

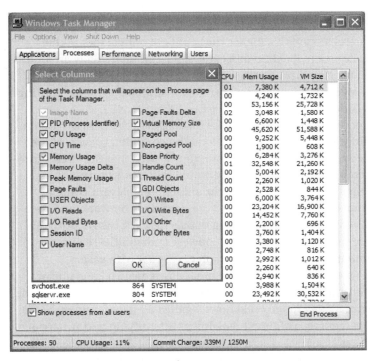

Figure 15-2. Task Manager columns

It can initially be difficult to gain a feel for some of the data displayed, but by looking at the usage patterns exhibited by other similar products, flagging problem areas will become easier. For example, if during the development of a desktop application with word processing capabilities it becomes apparent that the peak virtual memory size is an order of magnitude higher than in WordPad, a problem probably exists. Caution needs to be taken when comparing managed and unmanaged applications, but excessive resource usage needs to be investigated regardless of the application type.

A full description of each of the columns that can be selected for display is available in the Windows 2000 Server Resources Kit Books Online collection. The Books Online collection is available as part of the MSDN Library at
`http://www.microsoft.com/windows2000/techinfo/reskit/en-us/core/`
`fneb_mon_oyjs.asp.`

Code Profiler

In a simplistic sense, all code moves data from one format into another. For the result of any code to be tangible, a bunch of bytes that originate for an HTTP request, a mouse click, or a file residing on disk are transformed into a different bunch of bytes, such as an HTTP response, a new bitmap to display on the screen, or a new series of bytes on disk. Somewhere in performing this transformation, a performance problem can occur, and the transformation is slower than expected.

Identifying where and under what conditions this slowness occurs is a task that code profilers excel at, and this makes the profiler a critical tool in the developer's toolkit. A quick inspection of a code block can often allow an obvious performance bug to be identified, but for nonobvious code slowdowns, the human brain is a woefully inadequate tool for diagnosing the problem. Starting with the high-level code written in a language like C# or VB .NET, the brain would first have to convert this to MSIL, and then x86, load the relevant dependent Framework Libraries libraries, and also load the compiled version of the millions of lines of code that make up the operating system that the CLR is running on. Having accomplished this, the brain would then have to run through hundreds of thousands of x86 instructions, simulating the relevant context switches and inserting appropriate delays for the hard disk, network, and user interactions along the way, and record timing details for each instruction executed. The human brain, despite its amazing powers and abilities, cannot achieve this monumental task, whereas a profiler can do it with ease.

A good profiler will display a percentage breakdown against each line of source code executed and allow the child methods of any particular line of code to be drilled into, with a percentage breakdown against all these child methods as well. With these percentages of time breakdowns, identifying performance problems is a trivial task.

No version of Visual Studio .NET ships with a commercial-quality profiler, but every version from the Framework SDK up ships with a sample profiler in the [Visual Studio Install Path]\SDK\v1.1\Tool Developers Guide\Samples\profiler directory. Although the sample demonstrates the interesting details of how a profiler works, most developers will prefer a more complete commercial offering. The free Compuware DevPartner Profiler Community Edition is an excellent entry-level profiler that is sufficient for profiling any nondistributed .NET application, and its integration with Visual Studio .NET makes the product very easy and convenient to use. For distributed applications, the Community Edition is inadequate, and an enterprise offering that allows code on the client and server machines to be profiled simultaneously and the results collated into a digestible form is required. Compuware, AutomatedQA, and Rational all have products capable of distributed profiling, and trial or demo versions are available for download from the vendors' Web sites.

Many developers have a fear or reluctance to use code profilers, and it is not uncommon to see long and bitter arguments break out in workplaces or on newsgroups about the cause of performance problems without either party ever testing their theory with a profiler run. Installing and running a profiler is about as complex as debugging code inside the Visual Studio IDE, and is a trivially simple task for anyone with basic computer literacy skills.

A typical profile run involves activating the profiler, which can be done through a command button or menu command, executing the program under typical stress loads, and, after program execution, inspecting the generated performance statistics. Commercial profilers generally have excellent documentation on interpreting test results, and in most cases, identifying the lines of code that take the longest to execute will allow the problem to be identified immediately.

When using any form of processing, it is important to realize that the data collecting activities that occur will slow the profiled application down considerably, and the speed of a software system running under a debugger should not be taken as representative. The timing data collected is relative only, and is best used to determine why a particular section of an application runs slower in comparison to other sections.

Figure 15-3 shows the output from the Compuware DevPartner Profiler Community Edition for a sample run of a C# application that contains a deliberate performance bug that boxes and unboxes a value type unnecessarily.

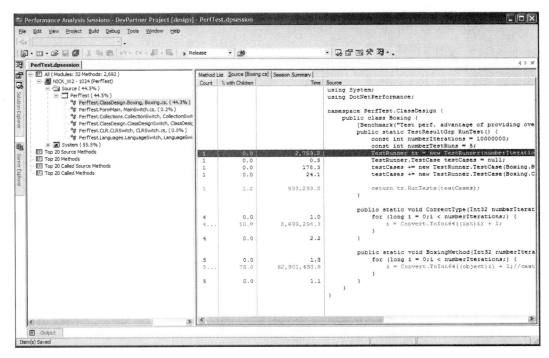

Figure 15-3. Compuware DevPartner Profiler Community Edition

System Monitor MMC Snap-In (PerfMon)

The System Monitor MMC snap-in (PerfMon) is one of the most powerful tools in diagnosing performance bottlenecks, particularly problems that occur in distributed or deployed systems. Three characteristics make System Monitor an excellent tool for problem diagnosis: the wealth of information it can display on a wide range of system entities, the ability to add performance counters from any machine with network visibility (permissions permitting), and the fact that System Monitor is preinstalled on NT-based operating systems. Convincing network administrators to install debuggers and profilers on production machines is (quite rightly) a difficult task, given the security and system stability problems that may be introduced, but as long as a machine is visible on a network and the relevant security permissions have been correctly configured, the System Monitor counters and objects relevant to that machine will be accessible.

A sample System Monitor session is shown in Figure 15-4. The + addition button can be used to add more counters, and the characteristics of the existing counters can be accessed by right-clicking the grid display at bottom-right and selecting Properties from the menu that appears. Figure 15-4 shows an example graph with three performance counters selected for display.

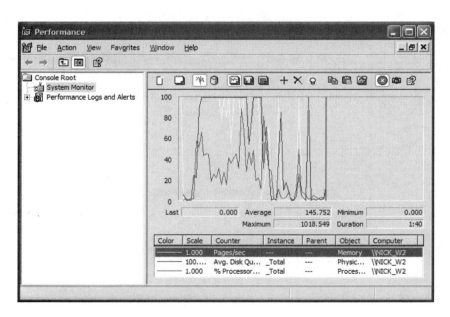

Figure 15-4. Sample System Monitor graph

The number of performance objects, and the number of counters that each of these objects expose, can make getting started with System Monitor difficult. System Monitor can be employed in two distinct patterns: shotgun and theory-driven. In shotgun mode, counters are added to get a general idea of what may be happening, and the counters and objects that are selected for display are essentially guesses. This mode might or might not work in determining where the performance problem is located, and the likelihood of success is dependent on how good the guesses are.

Theory-driven System Monitor usage is accomplished by proposing a reasonable theory regarding the cause of the performance problem, locating performance counters that can confirm or repudiate this theory, and observing these performance counters under a representative load. If the theory is confirmed, the performance problem has been identified; but if the theory turns out to be inaccurate, a new theory is developed, and the process starts again. In the process of disproving one theory, System Monitor results may give hints that can result in a new theory, but if this isn't the case, a new theory needs to be developed from scratch. Developing a theory usually isn't too difficult—a system will be slower at some point compared to others, and by having some knowledge of the system's internal workings, reasonable guesses at the cause of the problem can be made. If the system is lacking in accurate documentation, the technologies in use are not known, and all reasonable theories are disproved; in such cases, taking a shotgun approach or further research is warranted.

When choosing performance counters and analyzing the data that they publish, it is important to understand the exact meaning that each counter is displaying. Every counter is accompanied by an explanation that varies in depth from a couple words to a couple hundred words. Read the explanation carefully, as there may be important exclusions or limitations regarding the data displayed. It is particularly important to determine whether a reading is an average value, or simply the last observed value. For counters that change rapidly, a last-observed-value counter could result in an important event being missed, and multiple runs are necessary before it can be determined with reasonable accuracy if a theory is accurate. If the explanation of a counter is superficial, hassle the product vendor to get a better explanation. The .NET performance objects have excellent performance counter explanations—the .NET CLR Interop object has a performance counter called "# of stubs," which is explained as follows: "This counter displays the current number of stubs created by the CLR. Stubs are responsible for marshalling arguments and return values from managed to unmanaged code and vice versa during a COM Interop call or PInvoke call." In contrast, the SMTP Server object "Bad Messages (No Recipients)" counter is explained like this: "The number of messages sent to badmail because they had no recipients." The explanation could possibly elaborate on where bad mail is physically routed, whether the counter is a cumulative or instantaneous reading, and whether there are any related counters.

The performance counters that ship with the .NET Runtime are described at `http://msdn.microsoft.com/library/en-us/cpgenref/html/gngrfperformancecounters.asp`. The operating system performance counters are documented in the Server Resources Kits, which ship as part of the CD/DVD MSDN Library or are available online in the TechNet library (http://www.microsoft.com/technet). For Windows Enterprise Server performance counters, the Books Online documentation that ships with the Windows Enterprise Server is the definitive reference.

Writing Custom System Monitor Counters

To allow System Monitor to display a clear picture of the performance characteristics of a system, the right counters need to be available and selected for display. The previous section covered techniques to help in the selection of the correct counters for display, but if the right counter is not available, the effectiveness of System Monitor performance tuning is severely diminished. It is therefore critical for both developers and architects to be aware of performance counters as an excellent means of system instrumentation and to add counters at appropriate locations in a program.

The obvious candidate for additional System Monitor objects is custom server and system-level software in which the new objects will be very similar to the objects exposed by the operating system and the Windows Enterprise Servers. In this case, the performance objects will represent the components of the software that have external visibility, and may include such things as processing queues and interface devices. Adding counters for logical and business-level events, though less obvious, is equally as useful. It is important to remember that System Monitor counters are often viewed on systems without source code and debuggers installed, and that low-level counters, like those that describe network, disk, and SQL Server activity, can be hard to map back to high-level application activities like shipping orders processed or digital assets prepared for publication. Adding these high-level counter objects can make it easy to map the cause of excessive activity in low-level counters to high-level application activities and identify the offending component or method. Without this information, relating known low-level problems back to the source code can become a tedious task, especially if the system contains black-box components that may be the cause of the problem.

The documentation in the MSDN library that explains developing and deploying custom performance counters is more than adequate. As with profiling, developing custom performance counters can seem like a difficult task at first, but is actually quite simple. Readers are encouraged to complete the MSDN Walkthrough "Changing and Retrieving Performance Counter Values" (http://msdn.microsoft.com/library/en-us/vbcon/html/vbwlkEnumeratingPerformanceCountersOnServerStepByStep.asp) to appreciate how simple the Visual Studio .NET Server Explorer makes performance monitor creation and interaction.

Memory Profilers

Programming in a managed environment means giving up control of a number of activities, particularly those related to memory management. Under most conditions, automatic memory management is a great thing—the developer does not need to remember when to release memory, and the garbage collector keeps the working set of the application at a reasonable level. When the working set gets too high, or OutOfMemoryExceptions start occurring, it is important to know how to work with and inspect a process's memory usage and diagnose any problems that may be occurring.

Diagnosing memory problems involves two basic steps: working out if the excessive memory usage is in managed or unmanaged code, and then using techniques specific to each code grouping to determine the cause of the problem. The first step of the problem involves doing a dump of the memory address ranges that are used by a process, determining which address ranges are excessively large, and then identifying whether the offending address range belongs to managed code or unmanaged code.

An excellent entry-level tool for memory investigation is the Virtual Address Dump (VADUMP) utility, which ships as part of the Windows Platform SDK tools, and is available as a free download from the Microsoft site. This tool allows a thorough exploration of all the memory address ranges in use by a process, and identifies memory pages that are shared, private, and shareable. By using the -o command line switch, information on all the heaps currently in use by a process will be displayed, and the heaps that are taking up the most memory can be identified.

The .NET Allocation Profiler tool, available as a free download in compiled and source form from the Users Area of the GotDotNet Web site, makes identifying the managed heap a simple task. Simply start the application using the Allocation Profiler, click the Show Heap Now button, and choose View | Objects By Address from the menu. A graphical representation of the managed heaps is shown, with color-coded type information and the address ranges at the left-hand side of the graph. These address ranges will correspond to a heap range displayed by the Virtual Address Dump utility. If the information from Allocation Profiler indicates that the excessive memory usage occurs outside the managed heap, and no unmanaged code interoperability is used by the project, traditional Win32 leak trackers need to be employed to identify the problem. These trackers have been available for a long time, and most developer tool companies have an offering. If interoperability with unmanaged code is used, memory leaks caused by managed code failing to free unmanaged memory is the likely culprit, and all unmanaged memory allocations need to be checked to ensure that a corresponding memory deletion call is made.

For excessive managed heap size, Allocation Profiler has a number of features that can help with tracking the problem down. The Allocation Graph, which is shown in Figure 15-5, is displayed by default when the profiled application exits or has a snapshot taken and shows allocation size and percentage of total for each method called. The size of the connector lines is proportional to the size of the memory allocated in the child methods that have been traced, so by following the thickest line, the problem method can be quickly identified. The View menu allows other representations of the managed heap to be selected for display, which can help track down allocation problems that are hard to diagnose with the Allocation Graph alone. Like all tools, a developer or tester's proficiency increases with more use, and it is worthwhile running these tools on a well-behaving application during the development phase to get a feel for the memory usage, allocation, and garbage collection that occurs with the CLR.

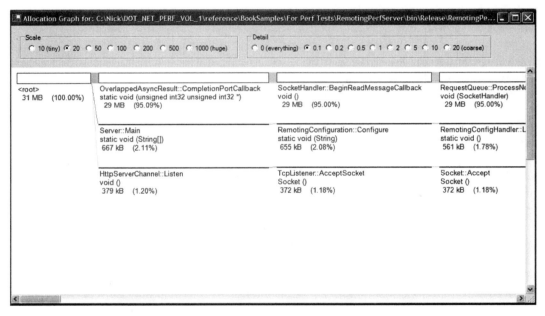

Figure 15-5. Allocation Profiler

Below the Source Code

It is critical that developers take ownership of problems that appear to be caused by software layers below the application's source code. It is rare that a fully patched operating system will experience memory leaks or performance problems that are totally outside the influence of the developer, and much more likely that an API or class library has not been used in the correct way. A wealth of information and tools are freely available to analyze what is happening between application source code and the hardware, and a small amount of effort in this area can make problem diagnosis very easy.

The first step in monitoring what is happening beneath the application code level is to install the operating system and CLR debug symbols. These symbols are freely available for download from the Microsoft Symbol Server, which cannot be accessed directly because it requires the symsrv DLL to download the files. This tool comes with the freely available DDK debugging toolkit, and can be integrated with Visual Studio .NET by following the instructions in Microsoft Knowledge Base Article 319037. With the symsrv DLL properly configured, every time a module is loaded during debugging the Microsoft Symbol Server is checked for debug symbols for that file. If the symbols are available, they are downloaded into a local cache that is used in preference to the Symbol Server in future debugging sessions.

With the CLR and OS debug symbols installed, the call stack is transformed from a collection of DLL names and hexadecimal offsets into the call stack that would be present if all of the source code for the OS and CLR was installed and compiled to emit debug info. The actual lines of source code are still missing, but a great wealth of information like variable names and private method names becomes available. Hard-to-diagnose performance problems can be solved very quickly with the symbols installed. To offer a real-life example, a performance problem in a GUI-intensive .NET application was recently presented on the `microsoft.public.dotnet.framework.clr` newsgroup. The application performed well on Windows 2000 machines, but had dreadful performance on NT 4.0 and Windows 98 desktops. After some discussion, the application author installed the OS and CLR debug symbols, and the cause of the problem become clear relatively quickly. A routine called `NonNT5WaitRoutine`, which was called internally by the Framework, was the root cause of the problem. Although the debug symbols didn't offer a solution to the problem, they at least gave the developer enough information to understand why the problem only occurs on machines with older operating systems installed.

Third-Party Tools

The focus up to this point has been tools that can be freely downloaded and tools that come with Visual Studio .NET. There are, however, numerous third-party products commercially available that can simplify and extend a number of the techniques described in this chapter. Rational and Compuware both have strong performance analysis and tuning offerings, and the enterprise products from both vendors have applications that support the integration of performance tuning into the software development life cycle.

There are also many small vendors that have great performance-tuning tools available. The AQtime .NET profiler (see `http://www.automatedqa.com` for details) offers all the basic features of the freely available Compuware DevPartner Profiler Community Edition but also has additional functionality that may make it worth purchasing for some users. The Dispose tracker that ships with AQtime

.NET keeps track of IDisposable-implementing objects that have been allocated, and if the Dispose method of these objects is not called, this is highlighted to the tester at the end of a test run.

One of the best tools for dealing with memory problems is the .NET Memory Profiler from SciTech Software AB (http://www.scitech.se). Rather than switching between tools as described earlier in the chapter, the .NET Memory Profiler allows a unified view of managed and unmanaged memory usage and leaks. The tool also supports easy comparison between two memory snapshots, which is very useful in identifying leaks or excessive memory users. The tools ships for a very modest price tag, and the current version is $65.00.

Code Rules

Identifying problems after they occur is sometimes necessary, but preventing the problem in the first place is certainly preferable. Tools that support enforcement of code rules can prevent certain performance bugs from entering production code. The Visual Basic .NET On Error Resume Next functionality that exists to allow source-code compatibility with VB 6, but which imparts a large perfor- mance hit when used in VB .NET, can easily be detected and flagged as a problem with a code-rule engine that supports regular expressions. Code rules can be used by organizations to feed hard-won experience in diagnosing and solving performance bugs back into the development cycle to prevent problems reoccurring.

Microsoft Product Support Services (PSS)

Microsoft Product Support Services (PSS) are a great tool to employ when attempting to solve difficult or obscure performance issues, and experienced developers should not shy away from using their services. Many developers hold the incorrect belief that PSS is only effective in helping novice users find a mini- mized taskbar or the "any" key, but this notion is totally incorrect; the deeper tiers of PSS have good access to the product teams that actually developed the software. MSDN subscriptions in many regions contain a certain number of free PSS support incidents, and even for regions where no free PSS support incidents are available with a MSDN subscription or Visual Studio purchase, the cost asso- ciated with a support incident is trivial in the scope of a software project.

Working through the various regional groups and internal tiers of PSS can take time, especially for obscure problems, and it can take many days before the escalation process brings the issue to the attention of parties within Microsoft that can effectively deal with the problem. It can also take some persuading to push an issue through the various tiers, but with a little persistence, problems will be escalated effectively.

Producing the simplest reproduction of a problem is a critical step when preparing a problem for inspection by parties external to a project, and PSS is no different. Not only does this allow the external party to effectively solve the problem, but it can also bring about insights that allow the problem to be solved with any external help. At worst, producing a simple reproduction will act as a sanity check that the problem really does exist and is not readily solvable with the tools presented previously.

Enterprise Tools

For large distributed software systems, a different suite of tools is needed to analyze performance problems. The tools in the previous sections can be effectively used to analyze the various applications that form a distributed system, but end-to-end testing suites are required to generate load and capture performance statistics of the system acting as a combined entity.

The price tag of enterprise tools can be significantly higher than the cost of tools that can only work with a single application, but the cost of a distributed system will also be much higher, and the proportional cost of the tools compared to the system that they can analyze is not significantly greater. Although it is tempting to use single-application tools and manually merge the results to gain a system-wide view, this process can be error prone and time consuming, and will often result in a greater cost to the client than the use of an enterprise tool that is better suited to the job.

Distributed Profilers

Profilers that can simultaneously profile software across machine boundaries and collate the results into a manageable form are a must for enterprise-level performance tuning. Distributed profilers can have significant price tags attached, but the time and embarrassment saved by fixing a poorly performing product or project is well worth the cost. When choosing a profiler for use during development, it is worth ensuring that the profiler can be upgraded to an enterprise version if needed, so that developers and testers on the project will have experience and confidence with the particular profiler.

Visual Studio Analyzer

Visual Studio Analyzer is a distributed performance-monitoring tool included in the Enterprise Edition of Visual Studio .NET. Visual Studio Analyzer is split into server components that generate events and client components that collect and collate the event data. Like System Monitor, Analyzer comes with predefined event sources like SQL Server events and supports the addition of custom application-defined events. The tool is heavily geared towards Windows DNA–based applications, and support for .NET events needs to be manually added. Code samples that ship with the Visual Studio Analyzer SDK offer some CLR bridging through COM Interop, but the level of support for .NET is very limited. Analyzer is essentially a Visual Studio 6 utility that is still shipping due to its usefulness in analyzing performance in non-.NET development. The need to install the server components on machines before data can be collected makes Analyzer a nonoption for debugging problems in a deployed system, and the ease of working with System Monitor in the .NET Framework makes Analyzer redundant.

Load Generation Tools

Application Center Test (ACT) is a tool that ships with the higher-end editions of Visual Studio .NET, and allows stress testing of system functionality exposed through the HTTP protocol like ASP.NET and SOAP. ACT allows test cases to be scripted so that a known and repeatable load can be exerted on a server, which is crucial for achieving measurable performance improvements. There is no comparable tool for testing Windows-based applications that ship with Visual Studio .NET, but a number of third-party tools are available on the market for this task. Mercury Interactive is a widely used and established vendor in this market, and the tools it produces, such as WinRunner, can be used to build test runs across a variety of client and server technologies.

Performance Tuning and Optimizing ASP.NET Applications by Jeffrey Hasan and Kenneth Tu (Apress, 2003) provides a comprehensive guide for the use of ACT to performance tune distributed systems and is an invaluable resource for the performance tuning of ASP.NET applications.

Conclusion

Choosing the correct performance analysis tool is critical for accurately diagnosing and fixing performance problems. Code profilers are the workhorse of the performance tuning toolkit, but will not be the appropriate tool for all performance problems. By augmenting the use of profilers with other offerings like System Monitor, memory profilers, and load generation tools, performance analysis becomes significantly easier. For deployed applications, System Monitor will often be the only tool available to diagnose performance problems, and this makes having the appropriate performance counters available for display critically important. Designers and implementers of enterprise systems should ensure that their software publishes sufficient performance counters to allow monitoring in a production environment.

Benchmark Test Harness for .NET

WHEN MIGRATING TO A new platform like .NET, many questions regarding performance arise. Presented with a choice between multiple ways of accomplishing the same task, performance can often be the deciding factor when figuring out which technique to use. Determining which technique is the quickest may seem simple, but can rapidly deteriorate into complexity. This appendix presents a performance test harness that allows for consistent and robust execution of performance test cases; the results of benchmark test harness were used to conduct the tests that are presented in this book. Chapter 2 presents a discussion of techniques and practices that assist in developing an accurate benchmark, whereas the focus of this appendix is a description of the implementation of the harness.

Comparing Performance

Analyzing the comparative performance of two or more software technologies involves two critical steps. The first step is describing a representative test case for each technology, and the second step is accurately timing the test cases. Describing a representative test case is the domain of software engineering judgment and experience, but there are a number of guidelines that can help:

- Each test case should accomplish the same or similar end result. If the performance of the stream-based XML parsing in the Framework Library is being compared to the traditional DOM-based XML parsing, the XML test document and result processing for each test should be as similar as possible.

- The supporting infrastructure for the test case should be the same as it is in production cases. For example, consider a piece of code that needs to pull data from SQL Server and cache the data in custom business objects. The System.Data.DataReader type should be the quickest option, but System.Data.DataSet has some added functionality that may be useful if the performance delta is small. When testing the relative performance, it is important that the configuration of SQL Server and the load that the server is experiencing is the same as the production case. It may turn out that running the stored procedure to collect that data and transporting it over the network takes 95 percent of the time, and the choice between DataReader and DataSet is insignificant in performance terms.

- The test case should be profiled to ensure that supporting code is not taking up a significant amount of the time. If a test is aimed at determining the performance cost of a virtual function compared to a nonvirtual function, ensure that the code inside the functions is not overly expensive.

- The test case should be conducted enough times to make the cost of setting up the test harness and calling the test method insignificant. A profiler can assist in making this determination.

- The test case should not be so insignificant that the JIT compiler can discard it. Inspection of the x86 assembly code generated by the JIT compiler for a release build of an assembly will allow a determination of the inlining and discarding that has occurred.

Once representative test cases have been chosen, conducting the tests seems like a simple step. The code that follows shows the simplest implementation possible:

```
DateTime startTechniqueA = DateTime.Now;
TestNamespace.TechniqueATest();  //run test
DateTime endTechniqueA = DateTime.Now;

DateTime startTechniqueB = DateTime.Now;
TestNamespace.TechniqueBTest();  //run test
DateTime endTechniqueB = DateTime.Now;

TimeSpan timeTakenA = endTechniqueA - startTechniqueA;
TimeSpan timeTakenB = endTechniqueB - startTechniqueB;

Console.WriteLine("Test A: " + timeTakenA. ToString());
Console.WriteLine("Test B: " + timeTakenB. ToString());
```

There are a few problems with this code:

- If the test case executes a method that has not been called previously, JIT compilation of the method will occur. This will distort the results in favor of the method without the JIT compiler hit.

- The ordering of the tests may distort the results in some cases. For example, if data is being retrieved from SQL Server, the second test can run quicker due to caching by SQL Server.

- Some code is required to process the results of the tests into a form easily comprehensible. The code for result processing is not test specific, and should be factored out.

- Some tests will require setup and teardown functions to execute either side of the test, and the time taken for these functions should not be included in the test results. Mixing setup code with the timing functionality code obscures the intent of a function, and increases the chance of error.

- The results of some tests should be thrown out. Criteria for throwing a test result out are test specific, but will typically involve the occurrence of a significant event that takes processor time away from the executing test.

- Some tests should be executed on a priority thread to minimize the interference from other threads executing on the same processor. The code to set up a secondary test thread should be factored out into a reusable test harness.

- Some tests take a long time to execute, and visual feedback of the test progress is desirable.

- The `DateTime` class is not an accurate timer of operations that complete in under a second, and a timer with higher accuracy is preferable.

- It is possible for one test to run for a different number of loops than other tests if the loop-termination literal is embedded in the test method. In the process of testing, it is common to change the loop-termination literal a number of times until the tests run for a reasonable time period. Failing to have a formal method for using the same loop-termination literal in all tests can lead to incorrect results.

- A future version of the CLR may include a progressively optimizing JIT compiler, which implies the tests should be run a number of times to simulate the execution of critical path code in a real program.

This list highlights the need for a test harness that can alleviate these issues, which is presented in the following sections.

Implementing the Benchmark Test Harness

A number of issues need to be considered in the design of a harness for generating timing data on benchmark runs. Setting up and running test cases should not be overly onerous or difficult, and different categories of test runs need to be supported. Producing accurate results is the most important design goal, however, and failure to achieve this goal will render the test harness useless. Choosing the correct technologies to use is as important as bug-free harness code, and this section covers the motivation for the current implementation of the harness.

Function Invocation

The first step in the harness design is deciding how the test case will be created and executed, where a *test case* is defined as a method that contains the code necessary to exercise a technology or technique in a representative manner. Creating test cases should be simple, and the overhead of calling these functions should be minimal so as not to distort the test results. The common language runtime (CLR) exposes a number of techniques for implementing the function invocation section of the harness. These include

- *Interfaces:* Each test could be contained in a class that implements a test interface. The interface would expose a `RunTest` method, and the harness could iterate over a number of objects, calling the `RunTest` method on each.

- *Reflection:* A series of object references could be passed to the harness, and a standard method, say `Test`, could be bound to and invoked on each object.

- *Delegates:* A test method delegate could be defined, and methods that contain test cases could be added to the delegate invocation list.

When using reflection, it is not possible to ensure that an object registering for performance testing exposes a `Test` method at compile time. Following the widely accepted programming principle that it is better to use compile-time enforcement over runtime error detection and the performance impact of late-bound method invocation, the use of reflection was rejected.

The use of interfaces would require a separate type for each test method, which could become cumbersome. In contrast, delegates support the chaining together of a number of methods in a single invocation list, and allow for the use of numerous methods for the same type, as shown in the following snippet.

Given these qualities, delegates where chosen as the function invocation mechanism.

```
public delegate void DoSomething();

//returns two delegate methods using the same return value
public DoSomething ReturnDelegateList(){
  DoSomething ds = null;
  ds += new DoSomething(FirstDelegateMethod);
  ds += new DoSomething(SecondDelegateMethod);
  return ds;
}

//another method in the same type that returns a single delegate
public DoSomething ReturnSingleDelegate(){
  return new DoSomething(FirstDelegateMethod);
}

public void FirstDelegateMethod(){
  return;
}

public void SecondDelegateMethod(){
  return;
}
```

The cost of making the delegate call will be included in the overall timing for a test method call, and must be very small. The cost of making a function call is generally proportional to the amount of indirection that the runtime must go through to locate the pointer to the underlying function. The level of indirection for "direct" calling technologies like static, instance, and virtual functions can be determined by the number of x86 MOV instructions needed to execute the call. An inspection of the x86 instructions that the JIT compiler produces to call a delegate indicates that only three MOV instructions are needed to locate the function pointer for the delegate method, which is less than the four MOV instructions required to call a virtual method through an interface. Having only three MOV instructions indicates very little indirection is required to call a delegate method.

Function Ordering

The order in which the test cases are called and the practices of only executing test functions for a single run were identified as problem areas earlier. The harness needs to accommodate calling the test methods more than once and in a random order. The System.Delegate.GetInvocationList returns a Delegate array, making calling the test functions multiple times and in a random order simple. Generating a random sequence for test method call ordering is easy with the aid of the System.Random type, and is illustrated in the GetRandomSequence method in the test harness:

```
//reference to a delegate list that is populated by the users of the harness
TestCase testCaseDel;

//get a list of individual delegates in random order
Delegate[] testCases = testCaseDel.GetInvocationList();
Int32 numberTestCases = testCases.GetLength(0);
Int32 totalNumberRuns = numberTestCases*_numberRuns;
Int32[] runNumberOrder = GetRandomSequence(numberTestCases,
  totalNumberRuns);

//run tests
for (Int32 i = 0; i < totalNumberRuns; ++i){
  Int32 testCaseToRun = runNumberOrder[i];
  TestCase tc = (TestCase)testCases[testCaseToRun];
  //start timer
  tc(_numberIterations); //actual test case invocation
  //stop timer and record results
}

//helper method to get test number execution in random sequence.
protected virtual Int32[] GetRandomSequence(Int32 numberTestCases,
  Int32 totalNumberRuns){

  //al stores a list of each test number in sequnce. A random number that
  //is bounded by the length of al is generated, and this test number is
  //removed from al and added to the return sequence.

  ArrayList al = new ArrayList(totalNumberRuns);
  Int32[] retSequence = new Int32[totalNumberRuns];
  for (int i = 0; i < totalNumberRuns; ++i){
    al.Add(i);
  }
  Random rand = new Random();
  for (int j = totalNumberRuns - 1; j != -1; --j){
    Int32 index = rand.Next(0, j+1);
    retSequence[totalNumberRuns-j-1] = (int)al[index] / _numberRuns;
    al.RemoveAt(index);
```

```
    }
    return retSequence;
}
```

Setup, Cleanup, and Test Result Rejection

Some test functions will need setup and cleanup code to be executed as part of
the test, but the time taken to execute these functions should not be included in
the test results. To achieve this, a delegate function is needed to allow cleanup
functions to be defined for the test harness. An instance of the delegate may
force a garbage collection or delete a series of files from a folder. The harness
will check for the presence of pre- and post-cleanup methods, and call these
if present.

The same technique can be used to register a delegate method that the
harness can employ to determine if a particular test run is valid. A method that
conforms to this delegate can be grouped with a collection of benchmark test
cases and passed into the harness. After each test, the harness will call the test
validity checking delegate method if present, and based on the results of this
method, the test run may be rejected and rerun. A test harness property determines the maximum number of retries the test harness will attempt before
simply accepting a result.

Eric Gunnerson's boxing tests presented on MSDN (http://
msdn.microsoft.com/library/default.asp?url=/library/enus/dncscol/html/
csharp03152001.asp) provides a good example of a test suite where setup functionality is required. In Eric's test, the contents of a large text file are read using
a stream, and a hash table is used to perform a count on the unique words
contained in the file. The results presented showed that extracting the file from
disk took about 70 percent of the test time, and the time taken for test initialization code execution had to be manually discarded to understand the test results.
The example application included in the book download samples (available at
http://www.apress.com) shows the tests rewritten using the test harness with the
file I/O and stream initialization code separate from the real boxing tests.

Delegate Design

The test harness must expose delegates that define the return value and parameters that the test, cleanup, and validity functions must take. For cleanup
functions, no generic return types or parameters are required, and the following
delegate declaration is used:

```
public delegate void TestCleanup();
```

It may initially appear that defining a delegate like this imposes a lot of state-related restrictions on implementing functions, and that a delegate that takes an `object[]` parameter list would be better. This is not the case, and by using instance rather than static methods as delegates, state information can be used within the delegate function in a clean and object-oriented manner, as shown in the following snippet:

```
public class DelegateUse {
  public delegate void DoSomething();

  public DelegateUse(int state){
    _someStateParam = state;
  }

  public void DelegateUsingState(){
    DoSomething ds = new DoSomething(DelegateMethod);
    ds();
  }

  public void DelegateMethod(){
    Console.WriteLine(_someStateParam);
  }
}
```

The delegate that defines a test case is slightly different. Most test cases involve iterating over a particular technique for a certain number of times. The number of iterations should be constant across all tests to ensure an accurate comparison is being made, and to make certain that this is the case, the iteration count is made a parameter of the test case delegate. The delegate used to define a test case is

```
public delegate void TestCase(Int32 numberIterations);
```

Defining a group of test cases for execution by the harness is now a simple matter of authoring test methods that have the same function prototype as the delegate, and passing them to the harness for execution:

```
public class ExampleTest {
    [Benchmark("Compares Technique 1 with Technique 2")]
    public TestResultGrp RunTest() {
        const int numberIterations = 50000000;
        const int numberTestRuns = 5;
        TestRunner tr = new TestRunner(numberIterations, numberTestRuns);
        TestRunner.TestCase testCases = null;
```

```
        testCases += new TestRunner.TestCase(Technique1);
        testCases += new TestRunner.TestCase(Technique2);

        return tr.RunTests(testCases);
    }

    public void Technique1(Int32 numberIterations){
        for (int i = 0;i < numberIterations;++i) {
            //actual code for Technique1 here
        }
    }

    public void Technique2(Int32 numberIterations){
        for (int i = 0;i < numberIterations;++i) {
            // Technique2
    }
    }
}
```

For tests that require pre- and post-cleanup functionality or the ability to discard the results of some tests, a TestGroup type is defined to group together the delegates for the test case. If all the TestGroup delegates are not required, the test harness provides a NoOp method of the required signature. If a garbage collection should occur before a test case executes, but no action is required after the test case execution, the NoOp method can be used as the TestGroup post-cleanup method. The following snippet shows the ExampleTest type rewritten to force a garbage collection before each test case run:

```
public class ExampleTest {
    public static void ForceGC(){
        GC.Collect();
    }

    [Benchmark("Compares Technique 1 with Technique 2")]
    public TestResultGrp RunTest() {
        const int numberIterations = 50000000;
        const int numberTestRuns = 5;
        TestRunner tr = new TestRunner(numberIterations, numberTestRuns);

        TestGroup tgTechnique1 = new TestGroup(
            //test case
            new TestRunner.TestCase(Technique1),
            //force a GC before test
            new TestRunner.TestCleanup(ForceGC),
```

```
        //no action after test
        new TestRunner.TestCleanup(TestRunner.NoOp),
        //default validity test
        new TestRunner.TestValidity(TestRunner.TestOK));
    tr.AddTestGroup(tgTechnique1);

    TestGroup tgTechnique2 = new TestGroup(
        new TestRunner.TestCase(Technique2),
        new TestRunner.TestCleanup(ForceGC),
        new TestRunner.TestCleanup(TestRunner.NoOp),
        new TestRunner.TestValidity(TestRunner.TestOK));
    tr.AddTestGroup(tgTechnique2);

    return tr.RunTests(null);
}

public void Technique1(Int32 numberIterations){
    for (int i = 0;i < numberIterations;++i) {
        //actual code for Technique1 here
    }
}

public void Technique2(Int32 numberIterations){
    for (int i = 0;i < numberIterations;++i) {
        // Technique2
    }
}
}
```

Test Execution

The test harness has now been defined to the point where it is known that a delegate of test cases will be available, and some of these test cases will have supporting delegates. The test case delegates need to be executed, and the time taken for each run must be monitored and recorded. The list of qualities that a robust and reliable test harness should possess imposes three restrictions on the test case execution: the ability to run on a high-priority thread must be supported; the test cases should be executed a number of times to negate the effects of JIT compilation, module loading, and other once-off performance hits; and the user should be given feedback about the progress of the test execution.

These criteria necessitate that the test cases should be executed on a secondary thread, and all tests should be executed a number of times.

The .NET Framework makes multithreading a simple exercise. The System.Threading.ThreadStart delegate allows for the nomination of the function to execute when a thread starts, and the thread priority is a public property of the System.Threading.Thread type. The test harness uses a default thread priority of ThreadPriority.Highest, and an overloaded method allows the thread priority to be specified for a test run.

The tests are timed using the high-resolution QueryPerformanceCounter function exported by kernel32.dll. A wrapper type that allows the high-resolution timing capability of QueryPerformanceCounter to be used without repetition of the arithmetic necessary to derive real-world time data has been developed by Shawn Van Ness (http://www.arithex.com/hirestimer.cs.html), and this type is used in the benchmark harness.

A running test case supports interaction with the user by displaying a dialog-based progress bar that provides an indication of the test case's progress. An event is raised after the execution of each test case, and the completion percentage of the tests is available through an event delegate parameter.

The user can cancel a running test case via a Cancel button on the Progress dialog box. System.Threading provides a mechanism to terminate threads in a clean and safe manner by exposing a Thread.Abort method, which throws a ThreadAbortException inside the thread, allowing any nonmemory resources to be freed prior to the thread exiting.

Executing the test cases can now produce a rectangular array of System.TimeSpan values that represents all the test results.

Result Analysis and Presentation

A stand-alone array of System.TimeSpan values that represent test results, viewed through a message box or debugger window, is not the most easily digestible form of information. Some basic statistical analysis would be beneficial. To support this analysis, a TestResult type is defined to store the results. The type contains fields for TestName (extracted from the test delegate via reflection); a string array indicating any errors that occurred during test execution; the raw results; minimum, maximum, mean, and median statistics; and the median normalized to the lowest medium of all test results. Median, which is defined as the middle value in a sorted range, is used in preference to the mean to prevent the results being distorted by outliers that may be due to external events interfering with a particular test run. The TestResult type and test result processing function support extensibility through inheritance.

Three methods of result presentation were implemented for the test harness: XML file output, chart output, and message box display. XML output is implemented using the XmlTextWriter type, which makes the creation of well-formed XML files extremely easy, and is much easier to use than the DOM-based approach offered by XmlDocument.

Chart output was accomplished using the MSCHART ActiveX control that shipped with Visual Studio 6. No .NET charting component has been released when the test harness was written, and the ActiveX control interoperability technology in the .NET Framework is quite stable and reliable. The chart output allows two types of interchangeable chart presentation: a 3D bar chart and a 2D bar chart. The 3D bar chart displays the derived test result data for all tests, and allows for quick identification of test result outliers. The 2D bar chart shows only the normalized medium of the test cases, and is what is typically used for the ultimate analysis of the different test cases (see Figure A-1).

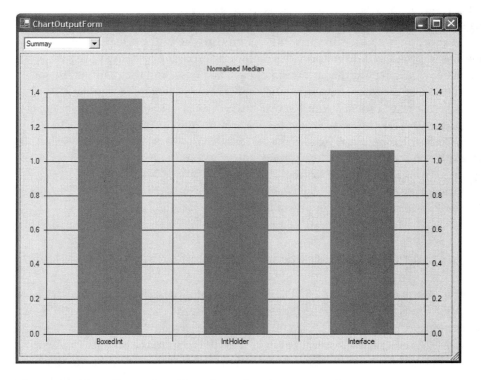

Figure A-1. Two-dimensional bar chart showing test results

Message box output is supported as a quick and easy form to view all the test result data, and the ability to capture the text of a message box using Control-C in Windows 2000 and above makes the message box output a good option when the results of the tests need to be easily included in a text document. Figure A-2 shows the text box output for the same results shown graphically in Figure A-1.

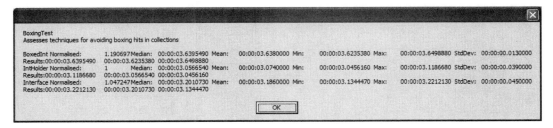

Figure A-2. Message box output of the test results

Test Harness Architectural Summary

The final system architecture is shown in Figure A-3. A clean separation of test execution, progress display, and result presentation has been achieved, and extensibility of the test harness is possible in a number of ways. The following list details extensibility points, and makes reference to types and methods shown in Figure A-3:

- `Output.DisplayResults` has an overloaded version that allows a new object derived from `ResultOutput.Output` to be passed in. A hypothetical `DatabaseOutput` type could be passed into this method, allowing test results to be persisted to a database.

- The `TestResult` type can be derived from to add additional statistical parameters.

- `TestRunner` can be derived from to provide an extended implementation of `PostProcessResults` if advanced statistical analysis is required.

- A new listener can be registered for `PercentageDoneEventHandler` to allow an alternative test progress display mechanism to be used. The default Windows Forms–based progress dialog box can be turned off using an overloaded version of `TestRunner.RunTests`.

- Authoring and running new test cases is simple.

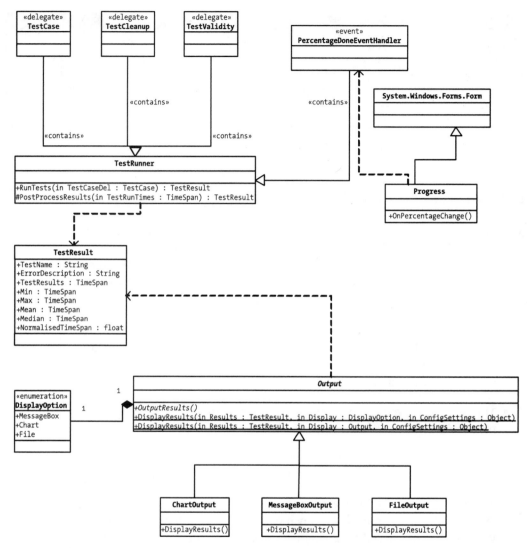

Figure A-3. UML static structure representation of harness architecture

Conclusion

The .NET Framework provides a new level of ease in developing software solutions. An extensible performance-testing harness was developed using the .NET Framework that allows the comparative and absolute execution speed of various routines to be tested and reported in a robust and consistent manner. The performance-testing harness is fully extensible and will support test execution for a wide variety of scenarios.

Index

Symbols

forums.apress.com

FOR PROFESSIONALS BY PROFESSIONALS™

JOIN THE APRESS FORUMS AND BE PART OF OUR COMMUNITY. You'll find discussions that cover topics of interest to IT professionals, programmers, and enthusiasts just like you. If you post a query to one of our forums, you can expect that some of the best minds in the business—especially Apress authors, who all write with *The Expert's Voice*™—will chime in to help you. Why not aim to become one of our most valuable participants (MVPs) and win cool stuff? Here's a sampling of what you'll find:

DATABASES
Data drives everything.

Share information, exchange ideas, and discuss any database programming or administration issues.

INTERNET TECHNOLOGIES AND NETWORKING
Try living without plumbing (and eventually IPv6).

Talk about networking topics including protocols, design, administration, wireless, wired, storage, backup, certifications, trends, and new technologies.

JAVA
We've come a long way from the old Oak tree.

Hang out and discuss Java in whatever flavor you choose: J2SE, J2EE, J2ME, Jakarta, and so on.

MAC OS X
All about the Zen of OS X.

OS X is both the present and the future for Mac apps. Make suggestions, offer up ideas, or boast about your new hardware.

OPEN SOURCE
Source code is good; understanding (open) source is better.

Discuss open source technologies and related topics such as PHP, MySQL, Linux, Perl, Apache, Python, and more.

PROGRAMMING/BUSINESS
Unfortunately, it is.

Talk about the Apress line of books that cover software methodology, best practices, and how programmers interact with the "suits."

WEB DEVELOPMENT/DESIGN
Ugly doesn't cut it anymore, and CGI is absurd.

Help is in sight for your site. Find design solutions for your projects and get ideas for building an interactive Web site.

SECURITY
Lots of bad guys out there—the good guys need help.

Discuss computer and network security issues here. Just don't let anyone else know the answers!

TECHNOLOGY IN ACTION
Cool things. Fun things.

It's after hours. It's time to play. Whether you're into LEGO® MINDSTORMS™ or turning an old PC into a DVR, this is where technology turns into fun.

WINDOWS
No defenestration here.

Ask questions about all aspects of Windows programming, get help on Microsoft technologies covered in Apress books, or provide feedback on any Apress Windows book.

HOW TO PARTICIPATE:
Go to the Apress Forums site at **http://forums.apress.com/**.
Click the New User link.